# Urban Appetites

 **HISTORICAL STUDIES OF URBAN AMERICA**

*Edited by Timothy J. Gilfoyle, James R. Grossman, and Becky M. Nicolaides*

*Also in the series:*

# Urban Appetites

## Food and Culture in Nineteenth-Century New York

CINDY R. LOBEL

The University of Chicago Press
Chicago and London

Portions of chapter 4 were previously published in *Winterthur Portfolio* as "'Out to Eat': The Emergence and Evolution of the Restaurant in Nineteenth-Century New York City," 44, nos. 2/3 (Summer–Autumn 2010).

A small portion of chapter 5 was previously published in "The Sideboard Takes Center Stage: The Evolution of the Dining Room in the Nineteenth Century," *Common-Place* 7, no. 1 (October 2006), at http://www.common-place.org.

Portions of the introduction and chapter 6 were previously published in *NY Foodstory: The Journal of the Culinary Historians of New York* as "Eating the Big Apple: Foodways and Metropolitan Growth in 19th-Century New York City," 1 (Fall 2012).

The University of Chicago Press, Chicago 60637
The University of Chicago Press, Ltd., London
© 2014 by The University of Chicago
All rights reserved. Published 2014.
Paperback edition 2015
Printed in the United States of America

24 23 22 21 20 19 18 17 16 15    2 3 4 5 6

ISBN-13: 978-0-226-12875-7 (cloth)
ISBN-13: 978-0-226-32267-4 (paper)
ISBN-13: 978-0-226-12889-4 (e-book)
10.7208/chicago/9780226128894.001.0001

Library of Congress Cataloging-in-Publication Data

Lobel, Cindy R., author.
    Urban appetites : food and culture in nineteenth-century New York / Cindy R. Lobel.
        pages cm — (Historical studies of urban America)
        Includes bibliographical references and index.
        ISBN 978-0-226-12875-7 (cloth : alk. paper) — ISBN 978-0-226-12889-4 (e-book) 1. Food consumption—Social aspects—New York (State)—New York—History—19th century. 2. Food supply—Social aspects—New York (State)—New York—History—19th century. 3. Food habits—Social aspects—New York (State)—New York—History—19th century. I. Title. II. Series: Historical studies of urban America.
    HD9008.N5L63 2014
    306.4—dc23                                                    2013035122

♾ This paper meets the requirements of ANSI/NISO Z39.48–1992 (Permanence of Paper).

CONTENTS

# ACKNOWLEDGMENTS

This book was very long in the making. My father liked to remind me that the longer it took to complete, the more history would occur. So too the more debts incurred. I don't imagine that I can adequately thank everyone who helped me along the way. But what follows is a stab.

First thanks are due to Carol Berkin. Her patience and unflagging support of this project and of me are but the tip of the iceberg of her generosity and influence on me and my scholarship. Thanks also to Thomas Kessner, Lou Masur, David Nasaw, Barbara Welter, and Ann Fabian, who supported this project at various stages and served as models of scholarly brilliance and integrity.

Fellow historians Kathy Feeley, Delia Mellis, Terence Kissack, Erica Ball, Peter Vellon, and David D. Doyle have helped to keep me sane and grounded as well as offering sage advice about matters academic and otherwise. In this group is also Megan Elias, to whom special thanks are owed. She read and commented on every word of this manuscript (and many other words as well) and is a rigorous critic, relentless cheerleader, and dedicated foodie. I also thank my former colleagues from Big Onion Walking tours, including Seth Kamil, its director, who more than anyone provided me with the opportunity to really understand the city as physical space. Annie Polland, Jennifer Fronc, and Jeffrey Trask not only slogged through the streets of Lower Manhattan and the Lower East Side with me (and dozens of eighth graders) but also helped me hone the ideas and concepts that take shape in this book and bolstered me through the rigors of the publishing process. I cannot blame Angelo Angelis, Phil Pappas, and Carol Berkin, the members of my Sunday morning writing group, for any mistakes in this book, but I can certainly thank them for much of what is good about it. And for the signposting.

At Lehman College, I am blessed with amazing and supportive colleagues—Evelyn Ackerman, Tim Alborn, Marty Burke, Dina LeGall, Marie Marianetti, Jose Luis Renique, Andy Robertson, Robyn Spencer, Duane Tananbaum, Robert Valentine, Chuck Wooldridge, and Amanda Wunder. Along with my students, these scholars remind me every day of the joys of a career in academia. In terms of this project, Tim Alborn read the entire manuscript and offered his typically incisive and constructive critiques. Marty Burke, Andy Robertson, Duane Tananbaum, Dina LeGall, and Evelyn Ackerman offered me help in navigating the publishing process. Also at Lehman, thanks to my Writing Across the Curriculum colleagues, Tyler Schmidt, Elaine Avidon, Marcie Wolfe, and Jessica Yood, who have helped shape my writing as well as my teaching. I held a one-year position at Barnard College where I was lucky to meet Owen Gutfreund, who has been an extraordinary mentor to me as to many other urban historians.

This book benefited as well from comments that I received at conferences and invited talks throughout the years. Thanks to Andrew Sandoval-Strausz, Barbara Penner, Richard Gassan, Kacy Grier, Amy Earls, David Jaffee, Psyche Forson-Williams, William Grimes, John Mariani, Suzanne Wasserman, Jonathan Deutsch, Annie Hauck-Lawson, Andrew Haley, Audrey Russek, and Adam Zalma. And thanks to the ever supportive and lovely culinary historians Cathy Kauffmann, Joy Santlofer, and Linda Pellaccio.

Outside of the academy, my good friends—Stephanie AuWerter Stafford, Jennifer Todor Grimes, Alexa Malungu Mbowa, and the rest of the George School 10, as well as Alex Sherwin and David Mizner—have helped nourish my nonacademic appetites and remind me of the importance of friends of very long and regular standing. I appreciate both Sridhar Pappu's love of New York history and his abiding interest in this project.

I am grateful for the financial support offered by PSC-CUNY, which awarded me two grants for researching and writing, as well as the Faculty Fellowships Publication Program, its members (Peter Vellon, Kathy Lopez, Lotte Silber, Jodi Roure, Victoria Nunez), and faculty mentor Virginia Sanchez-Korrol for their valuable feedback on two chapters of the book.

And I'm thrilled that I finally get to thank the American Antiquarian Society, my scholarly home away from home, where I was blessed to spend a full year on a fellowship. There, I met Manisha Sinha and Nina Dayton, who took me under their wing. I am still inspired by their brilliance and generosity. Generosity is the name of the game at the AAS, and I benefited from it in spades, especially from John Hench, Caroline Sloat, Joanne Chaisson, Marie Lamoreaux, Jackie Penny, Tom Knoles, Elizabeth Pope, Laura Wasowicz, and Paul Erickson. The AAS also introduced me to my fellow girls of summer, Laura Schiavo and Kate Haulman, and to my fellow Brooklyn foodie Amy Brill.

At the University of Chicago Press, I had the benefit of two acquisitions editors—Robert Devens and Tim Mennel—and one amazing editorial assistant, Russell Damian, who filled big shoes without a single misstep. I am also grateful to the three anonymous reviewers. Along with Robert, Russ, and Tim, their pointed and incisive critiques helped me imagine the manuscript into an actual book. Special thanks to Timothy Gilfoyle, whom I've always admired as a scholar and now appreciate as a mentor. His support of this project has been unflagging, and he has gone above and beyond what anyone could expect of a series editor, holding my hand through some rough patches and using his editor's pen incisively and compassionately to make this a far better book than it was when he received it.

Ben Benjamin created the beautiful maps in this book and put up with a *lot* of changes, edits, and working out of the process with me. Jennifer Rappaport, copy editor extraordinaire, stepped in at the end and applied a fine-toothed comb to my prose. Earlier versions of some of the text appeared in the *Winterthur Portfolio* and the newsletter of the Culinary Historians of New York.

And last but certainly not least, to my amazing family: my sisters, Jodi Lobel, Susan Lobel, and Debbie Lobel (who came to conferences, read chapters, and cheered me on unflaggingly); and my brothers-in-law, the talented Paul Godwin (who took my author photo) and Denton Clark (who read and offered feedback and deserves his forthcoming signed copy). To my in-laws, the Kafkas, for their unflagging support. And to Rona Bartholomew, who helps take care of my home life so my work life runs more smoothly.

My husband Peter Kafka has created space and time for me to work on this book and has pushed me along with a combination of humor, wine, and a heavy dose of (sometimes tough) love. He has made me a better writer by example, even if I use ten words to every one of his. The best contribution he has made to my life and my work is our two sons, Benjamin and Jonah. They were barely a glimmer in my eye when this project began and now they are old enough to ask, "Are you finished with your book, Mommy?" I am grateful to them every minute of every day for making me laugh and reminding me of what is important, even when it's just fulfilling their own urban appetites for Cheerios and ice cream cones.

This book would not exist were it not for the constant love and support—emotional and financial—of my wonderful parents, Arthur Lobel and Kaaren Lobel. It is for this reason and many others that it is dedicated to them.

INTRODUCTION

"New York City is the food capital of the world," trumpets the food policy page of New York City's government website.[1] A hundred and fifty years ago, commentators were similarly impressed by New York's food offerings. In 1869, New York journalist Junius Henri Browne proclaimed: "To a stranger, New York must seem to be perpetually engaged in eating," leading him to wonder: "Is the appetite of the metropolis ever appeased?"[2] This image of New York as a center of gastronomy is a long-held truism. It has become so naturalized that it is easy to suppose that it has always been this way, as if New York were born with a *Zagat* guide and a greengrocery on every corner. But that would be akin to believing that New York has always been a concrete-covered metropolis, inhabited by millions of people. In fact, these two iterations of New York occurred together in the nineteenth century. New York became a food city when it became a metropolis. *Urban Appetites: Food and Culture in Nineteenth-Century New York* explores this dual transformation.

Over the course of the nineteenth century, the city itself and its food system underwent remarkable change. In 1800, New York was a seaport town with a mere sixty thousand residents. Its population was diverse in origins but mainly native born, and the city was a walking city with industry, residences, and commercial concerns located on the same blocks, sometimes even in the same structures. While they did not socialize together and inequities were significant, individuals of different social classes interacted on the streets and in public spaces, including the public markets which were popularly viewed as democratic realms where all New Yorkers gathered together. At this point, New Yorkers' food came from nearby farms, waters, and forests. Farmers, fishermen, and hunters brought their goods to the city's six public markets, which were part of a highly regulated system, overseen by the municipal government. Little food processing existed with the notable exceptions of sugar, wheat, and other cereals. Public, commercial dining was a rare occurrence, reserved mainly for visitors to the city. New Yorkers ate their meals at home.

By the end of the nineteenth century, the picture was completely different. In 1890, the magazine *The Christian Union* described "the work of supplying New York['s]" food needs as "an elaborate industry" involving "an army of men with millions of capital." These included the dairymen and truck farmers of Long Island, New Jersey, and Westchester; the ranchers of the West; the granary owners of upstate New York; and the proprietors of orchards and fruit fields in the southern states, the Caribbean, and the Mediterranean. Within Gotham, various middlemen—wholesalers, commission merchants, country brokers, small retailers, operators of market stands, hucksters, peddlers, and grocers—distributed these goods to shops, restaurants, and households throughout the city. And on the consumer side, New Yorkers could dine in thousands of restaurants "vary[ing] in character," as the *Christian Union* explained, "from Delmonico's to the curbstone coffee-stand."[3]

In sum, by the 1890s, Gotham boasted more restaurants and a greater diversity of them, had a greater abundance and variety of food options in its markets and food shops, and processed more food from more parts of the world than any other place in the United States. The city also had a more divided population, a more corrupt government, and more inequities in access to foodstuffs and standards of living. These developments evolved simultaneously; in many ways they still describe New York City today. The most cosmopolitan, diverse, and sophisticated city in the nation by the late nineteenth century, New York also served as an index to the potentials, contrasts, and inequities of the United States as the city developed into a world power and the seat of industrial capitalism.

This book traces these transformations, showing how geography, culture, economics, and politics interacted to bring about change in New Yorkers' foodways and patterns of daily life.

This study covers the nineteenth century, the period of the greatest growth in New York's history. The book begins in 1790, when the city emerged from the American Revolution, an event that also paved the way for important regional, industrial, and technological changes. The endpoint is 1890 when new forms of industrialization and nationalization transformed the food supply yet again and the changes in New York became national in scope. During these years, New Yorkers saw a shift in the main source of their food supply, from public markets to private food shops. They witnessed the emergence and development of a restaurant sector that would become inseparable from the consumer culture with which Gotham was increasingly becoming identified. The dining room emerged as a requisite space in the middle-class home, and the food spaces of the domestic realm became important loci of consumer culture. And the city's food culture grew increasingly international both in derivation and reach. The chapters of this book explore these transformations, demonstrating the very explicit links between urban growth and changing foodways and the linked forces that brought about these changes.

*Urban Appetites* visits the dairies, public markets, and private food shops of the city; taking a seat in the dining rooms and kitchens of Gotham's middle-class homes and tenements; and delving into the basement restaurants that served spaghetti, shark's fin soup, and Hungarian goulash to immigrant diners seeking a taste of home. The book examines the hierarchy of New York restaurants from the lowly cake-and-coffee shop to the heights of Delmonico's, and explores the horizontally and vertically integrated commission firms that gathered, distributed, and processed teas, jellies, oils, and other provisions to American homes. Along the way the strong links among food, economics, culture, and society emerge, shaping and illuminating both the appetite and the metropolis and the connections between the two.

The constellation of new food procurement and eating patterns makes up New York's "food culture." This category includes various areas of the food system—supply, distribution, consumption, regulation. Food culture also incorporates expected behaviors around food and eating: the setting in which the food is eaten and the meanings applied to the setting; as well as the use and role of food in articulating status and reinforcing distinctions of class, race, and gender. The food culture of nineteenth-century Gotham was distinct from the foodways that characterized the colonial food procurement system, in which most food traveled a direct route from farm to market to table. In this earlier system far fewer middlemen or agents were involved, no restaurant culture existed, and no home-dining-space culture dominated.

New York's nineteenth-century food culture was both national and international, extending far beyond New York in terms of connections and influence. New York's hinterlands reached well above the northern tip of Manhattan Island, across the Atlantic, all the way to the West Coast and beyond. New York gathered and distributed food—from oysters to spices to tropical fruits—from all around the world. The city's food processing and manufacturing plants dotted the metropolitan region. New York's furniture and housewares manufactories and wholesalers shipped household goods far and wide. Manhattan's restaurateurs and cuisines hailed from the four corners of the globe. And Gotham's gastronomic influence and renown was felt across the United States as New York oysters were shucked in New Orleans oyster houses, restaurants opened on the New York model in towns and cities around the country, Midwestern householders tried to replicate recipes that they had tried in New York restaurants, and decorating and furnishing advice and goods arrived in American homes in catalogs, magazines, and crates bearing a New York postmark.

Looking at the simultaneous rise of New York as metropolis and food capital opens a unique window into the intersection of the cultural, social, political, and economic transformations of the nineteenth century. For example, the rise of restaurants and behaviors practiced in them addresses far more than the act of eating in public. Public dining highlights gender mores and conventions as well as the articulation of social class based on behavior and income rather than occupation. Studying restaurant culture also touches on new areas of entrepreneurship and social integration for native-born and immigrant New Yorkers. Likewise, looking at the changing regulatory structure of the city's food market system expands our view of nineteenth-century urban politics. The shift from public food markets to private food shops highlights the transition from the patrician government of the early national period to the laissez-faire machine politics of the mid- and late nineteenth century. And the increasing symbolic importance and attention to the middle-class dining room highlights the strong connections between the public and private spheres, complicating our understanding of how domesticity and commerce interacted in the Victorian era.

New York's role as a food city is well known. Yet scholarly studies of its development into one are scarce. Studies of the city's growth into a metropolis have explored a variety of areas from economics to politics to culture but have paid little attention to food and eating.[4] Meanwhile, scholars who have explored the interplay between food and social, cultural, economic, and political developments have done so on a national level, not a local one, and few of them have looked at the particularly urban characteristics of these transitions. They thus have missed important precedents to the story they tell, locating the rise of restaurant culture or the industrialization of the food supply at the turn of the twentieth century.[5] This study shows that these developments occurred earlier in New York City, which served as a vanguard of national change.

Likewise, most of the impressive literature on American consumer culture focuses either on the eighteenth-century consumer revolution or on the turn-of-the-twentieth-century rise of mass consumption and slights the important developments of the early and mid-nineteenth century.[6] The earlier works overstate the complexity of eighteenth-century consumer culture. The later studies date the beginnings of American consumer culture at too late a point. Those that do address the mid-nineteenth century tend to focus more on department stores and other loci of consumerism and entertainment rather than looking at restaurants and food markets as part of this process.[7]

But while covering new ground, this book draws on the significant scholarship in food history, urban history, and cultural history of the last several decades. The book tries to emulate the best food histories, those that look at food and foodways not as antiquarian artifacts but as a locus of and lens into economic processes, political culture, cultural change, and power relationships in general.[8] Likewise for cultural history. This study presents culture not in a descriptive way but as a dynamic process. It highlights the way cultural behaviors and attitudes—dining out, for example, or shopping for food in an interior rather than an exterior setting, or designing one's home as a space both of comfort and display—reflect and shape economic relationships, changing social mores, and the structures of power. As an urban history, this book explores the intersection of urban development and urban culture, including the relationship between urban politics and foodways; between food patterns and economic structures; and the rise of the metropolis writ large both as an economic and political entity and a cultural one or, more accurately, one that incorporates many subcultures.

Finally, this study uses food to illuminate nineteenth-century New York's public culture in formation. The restaurants, food shops, and food-connected commercial centers of the nineteenth-century city were part of an evolving public culture that was simultaneously inclusive and exclusive. Virtually all New Yorkers participated in the new food culture of the city. Restaurants emerged to serve almost everyone on the social spectrum. Likewise, everyone felt the effects of the shift from public markets to private food shops, of the growing industrialization of food, and the increasing distance between producer and consumer. And yet, these new institutions—restaurants, groceries, middle-class dining rooms—also served to segment New Yorkers, through expense, proximity, and behavior, along economic, racial, and gender lines. This simultaneous inclusion and segmentation itself characterized the public culture of urbanizing New York City, and food spaces and foodways played a central role in shaping it.[9]

New Yorkers' food patterns also became consumer patterns over the course of the nineteenth century. Food did not *become* a commercial item in this period; from the seventeenth century forward, most New Yorkers obtained the bulk of their food from the market rather than growing it themselves. And consumerism had characterized urban life in the eighteenth century as large numbers of colonial New Yorkers (and Americans in general) participated in the Atlantic market by buying and drinking tea, using Wedgwood and other ceramics, and purchasing household furnishings. But the consumerism of the nineteenth century was qualitatively different from that of the eighteenth. The early industrialization of food, government deregulation of markets, and growing distance between producer and consumer made food transactions more impersonal and required more discernment and care on the part of the consumer to ensure a quality product at a fair price. And restaurant dining made eating a form of entertainment and an object of conspicuous consumption as well as sustenance. The relationship of status to food consumerism became far more pronounced for New Yorkers during this time.

Indeed, New York's food culture incorporated conspicuous consumption in a variety of ways.[10] As the city grew and became more stratified by class, where one lived increasingly became linked to economic status. When the municipal government began to deregulate the public markets in 1843, much of the city's retail food provisioning fell to local retail shops located in the city's neighborhoods. The wealthier the neighborhood, the finer the food shops. Status also became associated with *how* one shopped as the nineteenth century progressed. In the eighteenth century, all New Yorkers made their food purchases outdoors at the public markets (or in the semi-outdoor market structures). But as the markets were deregulated and shifted mainly to a wholesale function, grocery stores opened throughout the city. In wealthier neighborhoods, these shops were well appointed and clean and worked very hard to distinguish themselves from the unsanitary tenement groceries where most poorer New Yorkers procured their daily necessities.

Space thus became more important in spelling out the status of the food shop. Proprietors paid more attention to cleanliness, arrangement of goods, and attractive decors. Furthermore, purchasing food on carts in the open air came to be associated largely with the poor; wealthy people made their purchases inside. This distinction related not just to food but to all manner of consumer goods from housewares to clothing. Peddlers' baskets and pushcarts came to be associated exclusively with working-class and poorer neighborhoods, a shift from the eighteenth century when all New Yorkers had bought from these itinerant vendors.

Environment was important in delineating status in the public and private dining rooms of the city as well. In restaurants, decor and behaviors played a crucial role in determining a restaurant's respectability. Here, class and gender interacted to create codes of conduct and rituals, which regulated interactions among strangers. These codes created safe spaces, especially for middle-class women concerned about their reputations. The same process occurred in other semipublic areas in the industrializing city and beyond, including department stores, hotels, steamships, and railroad cars.[11] The codes of polite society included manners and behaviors around the table and within the walls of the restaurant. But the physical environment of the restaurant was important. Restaurant designers used lavish furnishings and opulent interiors in order to replicate the domestic parlor and thus create female-friendly niches in the public sphere of the commercial city. As New York's restaurant sector grew more complex, first-class restaurants also served as stages to articulate power and status. To see and be seen at Delmonico's was a mark of prestige in the metropolis. Hence, the new food culture involved an important element of conspicuous consumption beyond the food itself.

These rituals and practices were carried over into the private home as well. As the dining room became a more requisite space in middle-class New York homes, public consumer culture was put to service in creating an idealized domestic setting. A host of consumer items—dining furniture, flatware sets, silver service, cookstoves, refrigerators, and household gadgets—became necessary to keeping up a middle-class home in the nineteenth century. Household advisers and homemakers put commerce at the service of domesticity. Historians have often presented these two in opposition, but in fact, commerce and domesticity worked together to create the ideal middle-class dining room during a time of important ideological formation.[12]

New York was the center of manufacturing for household furnishings and housewares, and its manufacturers, advertisers, and retailers helped to shape the contours of the ideal dining room. They relied on a host of consumer products to best support the homemaker's task of creating a comfortable and nurturing space for her family. They also urged middle-class homemakers to see certain rooms of their homes, particularly the parlor and dining room, as an extension of the public sphere and to model behaviors for their children around the dining table that they would display in the public, commercial, and mercantile spaces of the city. Table manners served to mark individuals as middle-class, both within the home and outside of it, adding another element of conspicuous consumption—and its counterpart, conspicuous leisure—to New York's food culture.

The growth and articulation of New York's food culture related to other forms of consumer culture in the nineteenth century. Restaurants, theaters, public lectures, dime museums, amusement parks, and daguerreotype studios all formed part of a larger entertainment sector that emerged in New York in the antebellum period and expanded in subsequent years. In terms of consumer culture, private food shops and fancy grocers emerged at the same time that department stores and high-end dry goods vendors changed shopping and the relationship of the consumer to the goods he or she purchased.[13] In the early nineteenth century, Lower Broadway and the Bowery became central shopping and entertainment districts—the former for middle- and upper-class New Yorkers and the latter for the working classes. In both cases, consumer venues that served food were located alongside other kinds of shops including dry goods, clothing, and department stores.[14]

Ladies' Mile, which moved from the city hall area around Chambers Street up to Astor Place, eventually creeping up Sixth Avenue toward Herald Square, included all manner of shops that sold housewares, clothing, and sundry other items. It also included restaurants that catered to the ladies' trade, purposefully situated to take advantage of the interconnections in New York's consumer culture. For example, Taylor's Restaurant, the foremost ladies' restaurant in the mid-nineteenth century, was located across the street from A. T. Stewart's Marble Palace, the first department store in New York City. Eventually, the department stores incorporated restaurants, as Macy's did in 1879, explicitly recognizing the interdependence of the various consumer sites in the city.

By the second half of the nineteenth century, New York was not only a food city and a metropolis but also the most cosmopolitan city in the world, incorporating the most diverse population and a business sector with tentacles that reached around the globe. New York's public culture incorporated this cosmopolitanism but did so in a paradoxical way. On the one hand, immigrant food shops and restaurants offered entrepreneurial opportunities to foreign-born New Yorkers. These businesses also served important functions in Gotham's ethnic communities. In addition to offering a taste of home, restaurants, cafes, and groceries served as impromptu banks, post offices, and social centers in Kleindeutschland, Little Italy, Chinatown, the Jewish Lower East Side, and other immigrant enclaves. At the same time, New York's cosmopolitan food culture reflected New York's role as an empire of gastronomy, replete with the social Darwinism, exoticism, and assumptions of racial hierarchy that attend concepts of empire.[15] Native-born New Yorkers celebrated the range of foods and cuisines available in the restaurants and food shops of Manhattan. But they simultaneously approached foreign cuisines with some skepticism and a good deal of derision. In important ways, native-born New Yorkers' experimentation with ethnic cuisines, especially Chinese food, served to confirm their own cultural superiority. In this way, cosmopolitan cuisine served a similar role to other forms of popular culture in the nineteenth century from minstrelsy to the midway exhibits of the world's fairs that showcased the "exotic" peoples of the non-Western world.

Studying these various and linked developments is important not only for what it tells us about the past but what it reveals about the present. Food-related buzzwords of today—sustainability, organic, locavore—would have had little meaning to New Yorkers of the nineteenth century. But the concepts would ring familiar. At the nineteenth century's beginning, their food supply system was face-to-face and personal. And at the century's end, it was far less so. Food came from farther afield, the gap between producer and consumer was ever widening, and food production and distribution had begun to undergo industrial processes.

Unquestionably the food culture of nineteenth-century New York was qualitatively different from today. But similarities exist between the two eras, and the developments of the nineteenth century fostered roots of the food landscape that we eventually inherited. Many of the developments that this book addresses will look surprisingly familiar to modern readers. The strong connections that we see in the early twenty-first century between geography, income, and food quality—characterized most dramatically in "food deserts," or a lack of fresh, healthy foods in poor neighborhoods and regions—parallel similar issues in nineteenth-century New York. The increasing distance between producer and consumer of foodstuffs is not, as popular belief assumes, a late twentieth-century development related to agribusiness but instead a concern shared by our great-great-grandparents. So too the rise of industrial processes in food manufacturing and distribution. And the frequent scandals of tainted and adulterated food and demands that the government take action to address them, as well as the complicity of the government in bringing them about, can be seen in nineteenth-century New York. Likewise, the simultaneous attraction and revulsion toward new foods and ethnic cuisines and the provincial smugness of "foodies" in trying the latest new thing. One might easily assume that these developments are new to the late twentieth and early twenty-first century. But in fact, these changes are rooted in the nineteenth century with the rapid urbanization of New York City and the profound shifts to its food system that accompanied it. *Urban Appetites* takes us back to that moment, reopening a window on New York in the process of becoming a metropolis, a commercial powerhouse, and the food capital of the world.

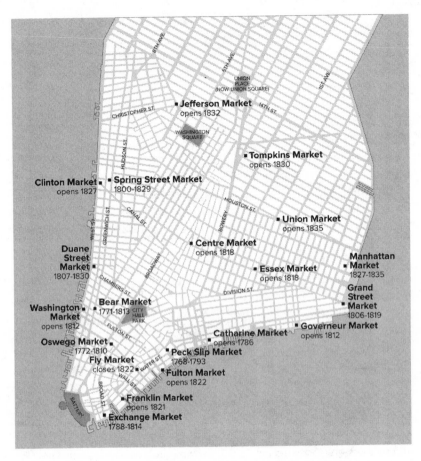

*New York City's Public Markets, 1786–1830* (Map by Ben Benjamin)

# ONE

# "Convenient to the New York Market": Feeding New York City in the Early National Period, 1786–1830

John Pintard was a New York foodie 150 years before the concept existed. Like today's epicures, Pintard enjoyed locally sourced ingredients from vendors whom he interacted with personally, sometimes daily. His varied diet included such delights as duck, oysters, crab, chocolate, and tropical fruits like pineapples and oranges. At home, Pintard cooked beef à la mode, roast sirloin, and broiled quail.[1] He participated in supper clubs where he and his fellow members engaged in conversations about political and literary topics over steaks and fine wines. And he followed the markets closely, reporting on when new foods arrived in the city—such as the first peas in the spring, or unusual fruits from far-off climes.

But Pintard's time was not our own. The former secretary of the Mutual Assurance Company and the New York Chamber of Commerce was born in an era before refrigeration, canals, railroads, and steam power. Real estate development, overfishing, hunting, and environmental pollution had not yet depleted the rivers, forests, and farms of New York City's near hinterlands. Like other New Yorkers of means, Pintard purchased a wide variety of food items in the city's markets. But he also contended with scarcity and seasonality and developed personal relationships with food vendors to avoid swindles, scams, and poor-quality food.

Pintard regularly recorded his interest in food as well as his marketing and dining adventures—mainly in his letters to his daughter Eliza in New Orleans. Pintard's letters thus provide a window into the landscape of food provisioning in early national New York City, showing the preindustrial patterns of procurement and regulation of the food supply. The public markets provided the great bulk of Pintard's and other New Yorkers' food requirements, carrying all fresh produce, meats, and fish. Private grocers supplemented these offerings with spices, beverages, and preserved and packaged foodstuffs. Dairy products were found in the markets or delivered to grocers and private homes. And New Yorkers obtained their daily bread from the city's artisan bakers, who sold it from their bakeries or through retail grocers.

Pintard's diet and marketing habits were circumscribed by the limits of an era before refrigeration and reliable transportation. He visited the markets an average of four times per week in the 1810s and 1820s and daily in the bountiful summer months.[2] These frequent and regular visits to the market were necessary because the offerings changed if not daily, certainly with the seasons. Pintard also acknowledged the seasonal nature of New York's preindustrial market system by remarking on the arrival of young butter or the first spring vegetables in the public markets.[3]

Pintard recorded face-to-face transactions with regular vendors, including "Stickler the grocer" and Mrs. King, "our green grocer," who brought her two young sons to Pintard's Broome Street home to watch the 1831 Fourth of July parade.[4] These descriptions reflected the high level of personal interaction with food producers both within and outside of the market. Indeed, even the foodstuffs that Pintard received from farther afield originated with vendors who were only one or two degrees removed from him. Stickler the grocer, for example, contracted with "one of the best dairies in Orange Co[unty]" to provide Pintard's milk and butter.[5]

Inherited from the seventeenth century, New York's market system changed dramatically in the antebellum years. But in the early national period, as in the colonial era, all food came from farms, forests, and waters located a few miles from the city. A patrician city government oversaw and regulated the city's public markets, which existed to provide a centralized space for local producers to sell their harvests and catches to Manhattanites. Purchasers and vendors thus enjoyed direct contact with one another and experienced daily the visible hand of the city's Common Council. In many ways, the early national period represents a transitional moment for New York's markets, between the market economy and practices of the eighteenth century and the laissez-faire, free market era of the antebellum years. While New York was the largest and most sophisticated city in the new nation by 1820, preindustrial rhythms characterized marketing and food choices, as they had for two centuries. But change was afoot and some of it had already begun to take hold.

The transitional nature of the period can be seen in the character of the food supply, the nature of the city's markets, and the city government's stance toward them. New Yorkers' foodways still adhered to preindustrial patterns. Yet the farms around New York were already growing more commercial and the food supply beginning to move toward industrialization. A loose moral economy still governed citizens' expectations and the government's position toward its markets. But market vendors clashed frequently with each other and the city government over regulation. Thus, the early national food supply reflected almost two centuries of food provisioning and marketing and, at the same time, forecasted the massive changes to the food system that would occur in the nineteenth century.

When John Pintard made a note in his letters, such as: "on Sat$^y$ I bought 24 large ears of Indian Corn . . . a peck of Sky beans, small Lima beans . . . eight Musk melons" and a "powerful water melon," he did not reflect on where these foods were produced or how they got to the Fly Market, where he likely purchased them.[6] But an entire network of food producers, sellers, and purchasers undergirded the market system of early national New York. We can reconstruct this network in some measure, following fresh food from farm, forest, and waters to the tables of New York's public and private markets. Hardly an ad hoc affair, the provisioning of New Yorkers even in the early national period involved significant coordination, cultivation, and regulation.

The food began on the farms. The most prolific and successful commercial farms in the early United States were those that served the markets of New York City. Residents of a commercial seaport from the very beginning, New Yorkers relied on outsiders to provide food while they busied themselves with financial and industrial concerns. The healthy market for farm-produced foodstuffs in New York City encouraged extensive agriculture on Long and Staten Islands, New Jersey, Westchester County, and Connecticut by the early eighteenth century. Even lands that were nominally fertile capitalized on their proximity to New York City to realize the commercial potential of market farming. For example, the rocky soil of Staten Island was never as productive as some of the more distant surrounding lands. But the island *was*, as advertisements for its farms noted, "convenient to the New York market," and so its farmers took advantage of science and technology to bring their fields into cultivation. Likewise, the soil of some parts of Long Island was, as French visitor Médéric Louis Elie Moreau de St. Méry remarked, "poor, sandy, stoney, and shallow." But the land proved valuable nonetheless, Moreau de St. Méry explained, "because the nearness of New York assures a market for all farm products."[7]

By the middle of the eighteenth century, some areas around New York were devoted almost entirely to agricultural production for the city's markets. For example, New Yorker William Smith described Harlem as "a small flat cultivated for the city markets." And the town of Newtown, in Queens, was covered with farms producing fruits, vegetables, and meats for the markets of Manhattan. Meanwhile, cattlemen in New Jersey, Westchester and Dutchess Counties, and as far away as New England set up ranches for raising livestock for the New York market. These commercial farms were the most fertile in the eighteenth-century colonies (far more so than frontier farms, for example) because farmers cultivated the soil for productivity.[8]

Nonurban Americans in the New York region thus enjoyed strong and long-standing connections to the city and its food system. Agricultural specialization and market farming shaped the relationship of these folks to their own land and production. Instead of producing the diversity of crops that the rich lands would allow, they specialized for the market. Rather than growing a variety of crops for their own use, they turned their lands to commercial production and relied on the public markets of New York for many of their own daily necessities, agricultural and manufactured. The city's symbiotic relationship with its hinterlands extended to fertilizers as well. Manure was mined from the streets of the city and shipped to the farmlands of New Jersey, Westchester County, and Western Long Island for use as fertilizer. In 1811, the City of New York earned almost $5,000 (compared to $6,600 in market fees) for selling its street manure to local farmers. Long Island farmers also imported manure from New Haven, New London, and Hartford, Connecticut, and sought fertilizer from other sources, including potash factories to the north of the city and fish bones from the Long Island Sound.[9]

Most of the farms that supplied Manhattan's markets were located on surrounding islands—especially Staten and Long Islands—as well as in Westchester County, New Jersey, and Connecticut. Manhattan Island did host some agricultural production—a 1780 survey found over 130 farms from the Bowery to Harlem, ranging in size from one acre to 300.[10] But these farms provided a small percentage of the produce that stocked the city's markets. Most came from off island. Real estate advertisements for early national farms extolled the lushness of the land and the strong links to the markets of New York City. For example, an ad for a Newtown, Long Island, farm located seven miles from New York City boasted of 140 acres of "excellent land," including "two grafted orchards of the best fruit . . . and a choice piece of meadow land of clover and timothy," as well as "an excellent well and running springs throughout the farm."[11] And a Bergen County, New Jersey, farm advertised for sale in 1801 featured "good arable land and meadow," as well as "a saw mill, a good farm-house and barn, apple and peach orchards, and great quantities of strawberries, in the season, for N.Y. market."[12]

These descriptions also point to the relationship between New York City and its hinterlands. "From Long Island," French visitor M. Moreau de St. Méry explained, "New York gets cattle, chickens, pigs, sheep, game, a great quantity of fruit, many vegetables, an abundance of grain, and particularly Indian corn, eggs, fish, and oysters."[13] Notices for farms around New York also frequently mentioned their convenience to the city's public markets, suggesting their market orientation. For example, a "small compact farm" in Brooklyn boasted a "remarkably healthy and pleasant" setting, suited to "any person who would pay attention, and cultivate necessaries for the supply of the New-York market."[14] And an 1803 ad for a 140-acre Mt. Pleasant, Westchester, farm noted that "three market boats go weekly to New-York" from this location.[15]

Given the fecundity of local lands, New Yorkers enjoyed a bounty of fresh foods the year round, varying of course according to the season: apples, potatoes, turnips, and other root vegetables in the cooler months, and peas, asparagus, corn, berries, melon, and other summer fruits and vegetables when the weather turned warmer. New Jersey and the counties north of Manhattan, especially Orange, Dutchess, and Westchester Counties also were known for their dairies. Part of the Bear Market (eventually Washington Market) on Manhattan's lower west side, was known as the "Buttermilk Market" long after it ceased to be mainly a depot for dairy vendors. Jersey farmers of Dutch descent arrived in the city on a daily basis with their stocks, especially butter, which they sold to New York householders from market stands.[16]

As for livestock, cattlemen contracted with drovers to bring their cattle from farms as close as New Jersey, Westchester, and Long Island and as far away as New England, whose ranchers pioneered large-scale cattle raising in the eighteenth-century colonies. Wherever they hailed from, drovers led their herds overland and via ferry to Manhattan and then to the stockyards on the Lower East Side. After making their livestock purchases, butchers led them to any of various slaughterhouses located around the city. Thanks to the decentralized slaughterhouse system of early national New York, butchers had dozens, even hundreds, of abattoirs from which to choose. They had to slaughter, butcher, and transport their livestock quickly to market; in the pre-refrigeration era, twelve hours was the outer limit for holding on to dressed meat, less in the warmer months. Pigs, chickens and other livestock arrived in New York with the same farmers who brought vegetables, fruits, and dairy products to the public markets. Additionally, the hogs that famously wandered the streets of the city might also be found for sale at tables under the market-house roofs. More exotic, wild offerings like wild turkeys, ducks, geese, and game also graced the market stalls, provided to the poulterers, butchers, and country vendors by local hunters.[17]

Finally, fishermen from Long Island, New Jersey, and Staten Island piloted their boats or "fish-cars" to docks near the markets. There, they would unload their haul from local waters, including over fifty varieties of fish: shad, bluefish, blackfish, sea bass, flounder, as well as shellfish like clams, oysters, scallops, shrimp, and lobster. Like the nearby farms, local fisheries were commercially oriented. The Cortelyou family of Kings County established a lucrative shad fishery, which sold almost twenty-five thousand fish per year in the early 1790s. And Staten Island's oystermen had already made the island a central contributor to the lucrative oyster trade in New York City by the early nineteenth century, even before oyster cultivation began in earnest in the 1820s.[18]

Located on an island, New York received most of its food supply via water. So systems of transport and distribution emerged from an early point in the city's history. Ferries and markets went hand in hand—the earliest markets in New York sprang up near ferry landings such as Coenties Slip and other points of rural-urban contact. Like the markets themselves, the ferry system dated back to the seventeenth century when the Dutch authorities began to farm out annual licenses to individuals interested in operating boat service between Manhattan and its surrounding lands. In the eighteenth century, the Long Island ferry ran every weekday from a spot in Brooklyn near present-day Fulton Street, discharging at three different spots in Lower Manhattan—all located near public marketplaces. In subsequent years, the city established and leased additional ferries, connecting Lower Manhattan to Upper Manhattan, New Jersey, and Staten Island. The official ferries were not the only mode of transport for market goods. Some country people navigated their own small craft laden with market produce.[19]

By the early national period, six ferry services operated in New York harbor and the carriage of market produce comprised a large proportion of ferry business. Unlike the rowboat ferries of the seventeenth and eighteenth centuries, early nineteenth-century ferryboats were powered by horses who motored the wheels of the craft. Some individual ferries carried passengers but all ferry services included at least one boat for market provisions.[20] Indeed, the markets and ferries were so tied together that the East River ferries docked in Brooklyn overnight, ready to be loaded up with farm goods in the morning. Rather than going to the public markets for their own provisions,

Brooklyn residents regularly traveled at dawn to the ferries and purchased directly from the farmers loading their goods for passage over to Manhattan.[21]

The early national ferry system was well developed, yet somewhat primitive and undependable. In December 1795 "one man and seven fat oxen were drowned," when "one of the Brooklyn ferry-boats was overset in passing the East River," one New York newspaper reported. Even if the boat arrived safely on the shores of Manhattan, the journey could be unpleasant for the commuters and travelers who were packed into the ferries alongside market carts, cattle, chickens, and sheep.[22]

Nonetheless, water remained the most efficient system of transport into the nineteenth century. Colonial roads were primitive and overland transportation was prohibitively expensive. This situation continued into the early nineteenth century and influenced the geography of New York's food provisioners. In 1816, a United States Senate Committee Report noted that transporting a ton of goods from Europe to the United States cost the same as carrying the same load a mere thirty miles overland within the United States. Transporting fresh produce over long distances was impossible because the food spoiled before reaching its destination. This reality limited New York's hinterlands to nearby farms.[23]

Upon entering New York City, food traveled by boat, cart, and wagon to the public markets. These markets were part of a regulatory system that dated back to the seventeenth century. In the early nineteenth century, the major markets were the Fly Market and its 1822 replacement, Fulton Market, both on the east side of Manhattan, and Washington Market on the lower west side. Catharine Market was also an important food supplier on the east side. Several smaller neighborhood markets, including Centre, Grand Street, and Essex Markets, supplemented the larger concerns.

Individuals like John Pintard might do their major shopping at one of the big markets and shop for daily necessities at the smaller, more local marketplaces. By and large, farms from Long Island (including Brooklyn and Queens) stocked the markets on Manhattan's east side while farmers from Staten Island, New Jersey, and Westchester sent sloops across the Hudson River loaded with fresh fruit and vegetables, grains, beef, pork, and potatoes for Manhattan's west-side markets.[24]

The markets were official institutions with a host of vendors and a well-understood organizational structure. Vendors were divided into distinct groups. The licensed butchers were afforded a privileged space inside the central market houses. The fishmongers and farmers (referred to as "country people") sold goods by the day in the fish and country markets. Finally, marginal figures were not officially part of the market but were tolerated along its edges. The market houses followed a set layout, established in the eighteenth century. The center aisle held the butchers' stalls, recognizing these artisans' central position in the public markets. In the peak spring season, these stands were laden with cuts of beef, pork, mutton, and veal. Birds and game of various sorts hung overhead. Country vendors set up the produce they brought from their farms at tables and stalls around the edges of the structure. While the butchers' booths were leased on an annual basis, country vendors' produce stalls were rented by the day, on a first-come, first-served basis. Farmers and their agents jockeyed for position at the tables under the market house roof and the number of vendors generally exceeded the number of tables.

As the city grew, its markets expanded beyond simple structures. By the end of the eighteenth century, the Fly had three separate market houses—one for meats, one for country produce, and one for fish. Meanwhile, Washington Market, completed in 1812, took up a whole city block on the lower west side. The structure was built like an atrium, with the center open for the accommodation of produce vendors. In addition to this outdoor space, the two-story market structure housed fifty-five butchers' stands and a country market for produce vendors and fishermen near the back of the main building. The upper story was used as a watch-house.[25]

Fulton, the grandest of the early nineteenth-century public markets, was housed in "an elegant quadrangular structure, superior in accommodation perhaps to any thing of the kind, probably even in Europe," and filled with an "abundant display of every variety of Meats, Fish & Game, exceed[ing] any thing that I Have witnessed in this city," John Pintard noted at its opening in January 1822.[26] The new market contained eighty-eight butchers' stalls, thirty-four stands for fruit, vegetables, and poultry, four sausage stands, and sixteen stands outside of the market houses for country vendors. Fulton Market also housed sixteen cellars to accommodate grocers and coffee and cake sellers.[27] By 1822 (the year that Fulton Market opened), New York City boasted ten markets.[28]

While New York's markets offered an impressive variety and abundance of foodstuffs, they were quite different from our own. This foreignness underscores the preindustrial rhythms of market life. The early national markets were open every day except for Sunday, operating from dawn until 2:00 p.m. in summer and 3:00 p.m. in winter. Necessity dictated these hours. In the pre-refrigeration era, produce rotted quickly in the warmer months and perishable foods had to be purchased on a daily basis. The major market day was Saturday when the markets stayed open until 4:00 p.m. and had

This 1826 image of Fly Market shows the open-air character of the market structure and the uses of the space outside of the market by huckster women selling goods from baskets. *Fly Market from the cor. Front St. and Maiden Lane, N.Y., 1826.* Lithograph by George Hayward. (Emmet Collection, Miriam and Ira D. Wallach Division of Arts, Prints and Photographs, The New York Public Library, Astor, Lenox, and Tilden Foundations)

Washington Market in 1829, before its expansion into the city's central wholesale market. *Washington Market, N.Y.C., 1829.* Print by Samuel Hollyer. (Picture Collection, The New York Public Library, Astor, Lenox, and Tilden Foundations)

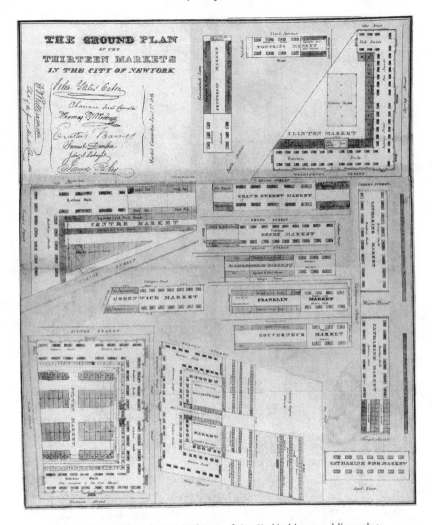

This 1833 map shows the interior layout of New York's thirteen public markets.
*The Ground Plan of the Thirteen Markets in the City of New York.*
(Maps Division, New-York Historical Society)

additional evening hours in recognition of the high volume of trade.[29] On Saturday evenings, the markets became social gathering spaces for the city's youths and laborers.

Because market produce was finite and perishable, the quality—and prices—declined over the course of the day. Those in search of choice pickings had to arrive at the market at dawn. John Pintard was among them, scheduling his market visits before the workday began both for efficiency purposes and to ensure that the markets' best offerings were still available.[30] Pintard could afford to do his marketing early, when the prices were highest. Those of lesser means would wait until later in the day in the hopes of taking advantage of bargain prices as vendors sought to clear their inventory before departing for the afternoon. Nineteenth-century market chronicler Thomas De Voe recalled the practice of class differentiation in the markets. "Customers made it a practice to go early to market to procure the choice pieces, and those who came late had to take such as was left," De Voe explained. This schedule ensured that "by ten o'clock the market was considered through, although many poor persons and others, who were looking for bargains, would come home after that hour or late on Saturday nights to pick up the remnants."[31]

The market schedule thus indicated class variations in access to quantity and quality. Not surprisingly, the later-day prices also reflected a poorer quality of foodstuffs. Poor New Yorkers purchased items similar to their wealthier counterparts, but the quality was almost always inferior. The poor also found bargain prices by purchasing secondhand market goods from hucksters and peddlers. These vendors bought market fruits and vegetables at the end of the market day and sold them on the streets outside of the market houses. Again, while the prices were right, the quality of these foodstuffs was generally inferior to that found in the morning markets. The class component of the marketing schedule complicates the common picture of the early national markets as a highly democratic space. Expressed in Theophilus Eaton's 1813 poem, many contemporaries and historians have viewed the public markets as a place "where no distinctions lie, all sects and colors mingle there."[32] According to these assessments, the public markets experienced a golden age in the early national period compared to their decline in the antebellum years. Yet disparities of class were ever present and influenced both the rhythms of individual marketing and the quality of food one enjoyed.

So too, the system of market licensing and regulation was governed by a rough moral economy that left considerable room for conflict. The system of licensing and regulation dated back to the Montgomerie Charter of 1731, which spelled out the "Rights and Privileges" of the city government. Along with areas of infrastructure like bridges, wharves, and the ferry system, the Common Council had jurisdiction over the public markets. In 1735, the council created a Markets Committee and codified its relationship to the markets—a regulatory stance in keeping with the paternalistic ethos of the eighteenth-century colonies. The basic structure and purpose of the public-market system was the same in the early national period as in the early eighteenth century—to ensure a healthy, regular, and reasonably priced food supply for New Yorkers, most of whom were engaged in artisanal or commercial trades rather than in growing and harvesting food.

While the Common Council oversaw and regulated the markets, these civic institutions were funded on a public-private model. Local residents petitioned the Common Council to establish a market in their neighborhood, and they purchased subscriptions to fund the construction of the market house. The Common Council had to approve these applications as well as the proposed site, which generally was on public land. In some cases, the subscribers successfully petitioned the city to kick in some funding when budgets fell short. But overall, the funding of the markets was a private responsibility, assumed by local residents on a subscription basis. Once the market was built, the Common Council's Market Committee oversaw its operation and the licensing of vendors, themselves private enterprises. As for maintenance of these markets, the Common Council paid for repairs and extensions out of the market's revenue, but in some cases, local residents also helped out, buying subscriptions to support market maintenance.[33]

Private involvement aside, regulating the markets was a government responsibility and few questioned the government's jurisdiction in this area. Ideally, early republican markets were governed by a moral economy whereby the municipal government was responsible for the health and well-being of its citizenry, including its pocketbook. Market policy sought to balance between the rights of individual vendors and the common good, which more often than not was of paramount concern. Market regulations fell into four broad areas: price control, public health, consumer protection against frauds and swindles, and oversight of vendors, especially the highly regulated butchers.[34]

To control prices, the Common Council set assizes—or price mandates—on important food staples, particularly bread, to prevent prices from spiking as a result of fluctuations in the price of wheat. A typical assize in 1786 required a loaf of wheat bread made from "fine Flour to weigh two Pounds & a Quarter" and to cost seven cents or four cents for a loaf of a pound and a quarter. The Common Council changed the assizes to account for rising flour prices but still maintained control over the ultimate cost of the bread. Thus, in the 1786 case, a month after the previous assize was set, the government responded to a bakers' petition about the rising price of flour and changed the assize to seven cents for a loaf weighing two pounds, two ounces.[35]

In addition to controlling prices, the Common Council sought to prevent shortages by outlawing fishing and hunting during spawning and mating seasons. Since city residents were so dependent on others for their daily necessities, the provisioning of the markets was important for public health. So the Common Council enacted legislation that prohibited unhealthy foods and practices like selling "unwholesome or stale victuals," "blown meat [meat infested with flies' eggs] or leprous swine," and "the Selling or Giving unripe fruit and Oysters within the City of New York." Other laws aimed to protect the public pocketbook by outlawing price gouging, cheating at the scales, or engrossing (hoarding market produce to artificially drive up prices).[36]

This regulatory system, however, was more paternalistic than altruistic. The city's regulatory stance stemmed from a need to keep order in the markets and the city at large. Even when it touched on social welfare work—for example, giving poor women the right to engage in huckstering as a means of earning a living—the goal of the Common Council was to maintain order, promote public health, and prevent strains on the public purse. Market licensing and regulation also served as an important source of municipal revenue. Market fees helped pay the salary of the mayor and market clerks and contributed to the city's treasury. And even with the checks on the market, plenty of competition and contention still characterized eighteenth-century market dealings. Evidence for this situation can be found in the numerous petitions and complaints to the Common Council about both the failure to enforce the market laws and the perceived overreaching of the council in the laws that they did enforce.[37]

The largest and most contentious area of market regulation involved the vendors, particularly the city's licensed butchers. In fact, at root, New York's market regulations emerged from a series of rules enacted in the seventeenth century to regulate the sale of fresh meat.[38] The city's butchers—unlike most farmers, for example—lived and worked within the city limits and thus were subject to municipal taxation, licensing, and regulation. Licensed butchers had to undergo an apprenticeship and pay taxes to the city in exchange for the ability to sell meats from designated stalls in the public markets. The city leased butchers' stalls out on an annual basis and collected "rent" on these stalls as a percentage of the revenue. The municipal government reserved the right both to grant butchers' stalls and to take them away if the butchers did not perform their job properly. For instance, in 1787, the Common Council revoked the licenses and stands of butchers Charles Dawson and William Everit in the Oswego and Fly Markets because the butchers had "totally neglected to attend their Business at their Stalls or Standings in the Market."[39]

Individual butchers thus were associated with particular markets and sold their meats only from their allotted stalls. One exception to this rule was the Fly Market, whose stalls were sold at auction in 1796, following an expansion of the market house. The Fly Market butchers treated these stalls as their own individual property, which they traded and passed on to their widows and heirs. Further, when the Fly Market closed in 1822, its butchers successfully sued the city for reimbursement of what they viewed as their confiscated property.[40]

The regulation of the butchers came with protections as well as responsibilities. The 1793 Market Laws stipulated that only licensed butchers could sell "Beef, Pork, Veal, Mutton or Lamb," in the public markets or city streets. Violators were subject to a ten-shilling penalty.[41]

Nonetheless, while market regulations were relatively straightforward, several loopholes made the actual practice a bit more complicated. First, country vendors, or those who sold "meats of small animals, raised and slaughtered on their own farms," could sell meat without a license. The law assumed that these farmers came to market only from time to time and that they were acting as middlemen.[42] Second, the city leased tables, called "shirk stands," to unlicensed small meat vendors in the lower markets, away from the central markets. These butchers—some of whom had served a full apprenticeship but failed to get one of the limited butchers' stalls—sold small cuts of meat while waiting for the opportunity to purchase one of the coveted butchers' stalls. They served a purely retail function, buying already-slaughtered cuts from the slaughterhouses to sell in their market stalls.[43]

Another important loophole was created as the city grew in the early nineteenth century. Newly developed parts of the city often lacked nearby markets. Consequently, the Common Council gave out provisional licenses to butchers to sell from private shops.[44] The government justified these provisional licenses because the butchers who claimed them were too far from the public markets to pose a competitive threat to licensed market butchers. But as more of the population moved uptown, this situation eventually contributed to the deregulation of the butchers and the shift to retail meat shops.

The conflicts around market regulation highlight both the ethos of the early republican market economy and challenges to it. In debates over market regulation, republican rhetoric touting the public interest and common good clashed with liberal ideals of free markets and antimonopoly. Many food-based artisans and workingmen's advocates resisted the long-standing market licensing system, arguing that it reduced competition and did more to line the city's coffers than protect the public good.

The case of bakers' assizes serves as an example. While the Common Council generally did not regulate prices, it did set the price of flour from the seventeenth century through the early 1800s. Bakers chafed against these assizes. Throughout the early nineteenth century, they demanded that the city overturn them, claiming they violated their rights to practice their trade freely. In 1801, the bakers organized a work stoppage to protest the price controls. In response, a group of New York merchants formed the co-operative New York Bread Company. The bakers reacted swiftly, lambasting what they called monopoly practices and insisting that the bread company's facilities were less sanitary than the bakeries of the guild bakers.[45] They thus defended the merits of protections and monopolies while at the same time protesting against them. The city did finally overturn the bakers' assizes in 1821. This move foreshadowed the deregulation of the markets in general and illuminates this period as a transitional one between the patrician market economy of the colonial years and the laissez-faire economy of the antebellum era.

Even the butchers—a protected class under the licensing system—cried out against monopoly when their interests were at stake. To be sure, most licensed butchers complained loudly and vociferously when the city failed to protect their exclusive monopoly over the sale of fresh meat.[46] But when these same butchers lost their stalls in failing markets or unsuccessfully sought stalls in newly opened ones, they attacked the city government's licensing practices which they claimed thwarted their ability to freely pursue their trade and livelihood.[47] In no sense did artisans as a whole, or butchers in particular, present a monolithic position on these matters. Some favored continued regulation and licensing of artisan trades. Others lumped government oversight and regulatory measures together with the evil monopolies that they blamed for constraining their trades and constricting their prospects.[48] Again, these reactions illustrate the complex grounding of food artisans' position in the shifting political rhetoric and economic theories of the day.

The arguments over regulation extended to the vendors who sold foods near the markets. Primary among these marginal figures were the hucksters—individuals who bought up market produce at the end of the day to resell on the streets or door-to-door. Huckstering was a last recourse for some of the poorest and most economically vulnerable New Yorkers. The trade was dominated by black and white poor women and children who had no other means of support. Some laboring women kept gardens near their homes and sold their own produce in the streets of New York. But most female hucksters resorted to buying market fruits and vegetables at cut rates or to scavenging for the goods that they vended. Working-class women and their children were familiar sights on the wharves, beaches, and streets of the city, foraging for roots and berries, fish and clams, and whatever other items might produce a bit of income and keep them from the poorhouse.[49]

Chroniclers of early nineteenth-century New York life frequently mention the ubiquitous female and child peddlers who filled the streets with their legendary cries, a staple of New York city lore. "Here's your beauties of Onions: here's your nice, large Onions!" was but one of the thirty-two "Cries of New-York" featured in an illustrated children's book of that name published in 1808. Among the other food items that were sold accompanied by a hawker's cry were strawberries, cherries, oranges, pineapples, potatoes, sweet potatoes, baked pears, rusk, buttermilk, radishes, muffins, gingerbread, oysters, milk, clams and of course, corn. This last item was attached to perhaps the most famous street cry of New York: "Here's your nice Hot Corn! Smoking hot! / O what beauties I have got! / Here's smoking Hot Corn, / With salt that is nigh, / Only two pence an ear,— / O pass me not by!"[50] The hot-corn girls—poor young women and girls who sold hot corn on the cob from a bucket or basket in the late summer months—were iconic figures in early nineteenth-century New York street culture.

In personal reminiscences of early nineteenth-century New York, hot-corn vendors and their counterparts were a quaint and colorful reminder of days gone by. Diarist George Templeton Strong recalled being "lulled to sleep" by the sound of the hot-corn cries.[51] But in fact, street peddling was among the most degraded occupations and a symbol of female poverty in the early national city. The desperation attendant to such work is perhaps most vividly expressed in a variation on the hot-corn cry: "You who have money, (alas! I have none,) Come buy my lilly white corn, and let me go home."[52]

The Common Council's stance toward hucksters reflected the particular market economy carried over from the colonial period in which huckstering served as a form of welfare work for so many of the city's female poor. But the council also weighed the interests of the hucksters against those of fee-paying market vendors and passed several laws regulating the peddlers. These regulations were encoded in the 1731 market laws, which stated that retailers and hucksters could not purchase market goods for resale until the afternoon. The same laws prohibited hawking or street peddling, stipulating that goods should be sold only "in Shops Warehouses or in Publick Mar-

The Hot Corn Seller

This watercolor of a hot-corn vendor by artist Nicolino Calyo was one of a series of images depicting New York street vendors in the 1840s. This vendor's race and gender mark her as a typical hot-corn seller. *Hot Corn Seller, New York Street Cries, 1840–1844.* Watercolor by Nicolino Calyo. (Museum of the City of New York / The Art Archive at Art Resource, New York)

ket on Market Days."[53] These rules ostensibly sought to protect householders from price gouging, assuming that the fewer the middlemen, the lower the opportunity for rising prices and fraud.[54] But it was the vendors, not the householders, who complained most vociferously about the hucksters, again highlighting the competing interests that came together in the market system of the early republic. Butchers and country sellers claimed that these marginal market types represented unfair competition since they did not have to pay market fees. Throughout the eighteenth and early nineteenth centuries, the Common Council strengthened the law against hucksters.[55]

But the city was quite lax about enforcing these laws, and the complaints registered by market proprietors attest to the persistence of the practice.

Whether seen as a nuisance, a colorful feature of city life, or a symbol of female dependency and financial desperation, female hucksters remained a fixture of early national New York street life and public-market culture. Few called for the abolition of their trade. The forestallers were another matter. A bone of contention from early on in the history of the public markets, these vendors purchased market produce outside of the markets and sold it for higher prices within the market structures. Meeting up with farmers arrived at market to sell their goods, the forestaller might offer three or four shillings for a pair of ducks and then resell them within the market house for four or five shillings. Or they met cattle drovers north of the city and bought up their stock, reselling it to the licensed butchers at much higher prices. Forestallers also sometimes hoarded market goods and produce, artificially driving up the cost and then benefiting from the heightened prices when they put the goods out on the market. In some cases, forestallers were essentially male hucksters who bought their goods from middlemen. In rare instances, these peddlers might make enough money to rent a stall inside the market or even open an independent store.[56]

Some forestallers were very tricky, posing as country vendors or their agents and taking up all of the country stands in official markets so that the bona fide vendors were forced onto the streets. There, the country vendors became victims to the forestallers twice over. Desperate to sell off their fresh produce before returning home, the farmers were open marks for forestallers' lowball offers. The government attempted to control the forestallers with laws and regulations that banned the sale of market goods outside of the markets, forbade the sale of fresh produce until the afternoon, and prohibited measures that would artificially drive up the prices of market goods.[57] While these efforts failed to eliminate the forestallers, they reflect the visible hand of the Common Council in regulating the city's food supply and attempting to protect the public pocketbook as well as the rights of individual licensed vendors to ply their trade. They also demonstrate that the markets were a contested space, characterized by competition and cutthroat practices even in their "golden age."

Likewise, the extent of the government's intervention into market affairs was restricted. For example, the visible hand met its limit when it came to fixing prices. In the eighteenth century, the Common Council had attempted to control prices through assizes but other than bread, these assizes gained little traction. The city's butchers and the country vendors resisted the new regulations and called for their repeal as soon as they were passed. In public petitions to the Common Council, market sellers complained about monopolies and trusts while defending their rights to determine the value of their own products.[58] The council softened its stance. And while it continued to regulate market prices through the Revolution, there were no additional assizes in the nineteenth century, a portent of the laissez-faire era that was to fundamentally transform the city's relationship to its markets in the antebellum period.

Early national market prices fluctuated significantly, again highlighting the preindustrial nature of the markets. Irregular weather patterns, epidemic diseases, and wars seriously affected the availability of foodstuffs, driving up the cost of daily necessities. During the 1793 yellow fever epidemic, for instance, market vendors stayed home rather than risk infection in the crowded city. The Common Council permitted butchers to sell meats from their homes for the duration of the epidemic. But country people simply stopped transacting business in the city. The prices of market goods soared. Similarly, during harsh New York winters, snow and ice prevented market boats from reaching the shores of Manhattan. A food shortage resulted, with an attendant rise in prices. Economic downturns during the 1790s, during and after the War of 1812 and in 1819 also led to exorbitant market costs. In the 1810s, meat commanded an inflated two shillings per pound, milk sold for a shilling per quart, and even lowly fat was available only at the astronomical price of eighteen pence per pound. Farmers and merchants also might drive up prices when greed (or business savvy) led to market scarcity. Some merchants, for example, chose to export their goods for better prices rather than sell them in the local markets. In other instances, vendors cornered the market, shutting out competition and thus raising the prices of their goods.[59]

Residents noted the fluctuations in market prices. In the difficult summer of 1816 for example, John Pintard complained of unprecedentedly high prices in the markets as well as for rent and fuel. Likewise in 1819, a year of financial panic, Pintard remarked on the high price of bread. And the following year, while prices for vegetables and fruits were receding, the cost of meat was rising: "Butchers meat is high, 10d. for the prime pieces. Poultry is excessively dear. . . . I paid five shillings for a very handsome pair w^h is exorbitant." In May 1818 and again in 1827, Pintard forecasted that the late frost would lead to a poor growing season.[60] Pintard proved prescient in 1818 as that year saw particularly high market prices. As one chronicler complained: "The exorbitant prices demanded for all description of provisions is a serious and alarming difficulty, that has long occupied the attention of all classes of citizens. Provisions are now sold at higher prices in this city than in any part of the world."[61]

Food prices still fluctuate today, of course, but are less affected by minor changes in weather, disease, and political developments because of far more reliable transportation, preservation, and storage facilities. The modern food supply also originates from a much larger geographical area. But before the transportation and technological revolutions of the nineteenth century, bad weather or a yellow fever epidemic could destroy much of the local food supply for an entire season.

Conversely, an especially good season could yield amazing abundance and variety in the markets. In fact, the number of species of wild game, fish, and fowl that New York's immediate hinterlands could potentially yield was higher in the early nineteenth century than it is today, following industrialization, development, and environmental degradation. As he did on scarcity, Pintard commented on abundance. In 1820, thanks to improving commercial conditions and a good growing season, Pintard proclaimed that "the substantial comforts of life are very reasonable," citing the prices he had paid at the market a few days prior: "24 large ears of Indian Corn, for one shilling, a peck of Sky beans, small Lima beans, for *ninepence*. Eight musk melons for one shilling! each as large as I have paid eighteen pence a piece three years ago. A powerful watermelon at least 10 pounds for eighteen pence, w$^h$ w$^d$ have been cheap formerly for half a dollar." And in 1826, he predicted that the heavy rains would yield a healthy vegetable crop.[62]

Visitors to New York in the eighteenth and early nineteenth centuries also noted the plenty and variety in the city's food markets. In his 1790s travelogue, Frenchman J. P. Brissot de Warville praised the abundance and high quality of New York's markets, concluding: "It is difficult to find so many good things in one place."[63] Brissot's compatriot Moreau de St. Méry concurred, describing fifty-two kinds of "animals, game, kid, bear, opposum, hare, rabbit, etc." He counted sixty-three varieties of fish, "as well as oysters, lobsters, sea and fresh-water crabs, crawfish, fresh- and salt-water prawns, other sorts of shellfish," and turtles, "in great quantities, and at extremely reasonable prices."[64] Cookbooks published at this time offered recipes for up to forty varieties of fruits and vegetables all of which, they claimed, could be found "in the public markets of our cities."[65]

Of course, even in normal years, the season determined market availability. Fruits and vegetables, which overflowed the market in the summer and fall months, were virtually nonexistent in the spring and winter, with the exception of root vegetables. The slim pickings that were available were of poor quality and extremely high in price. In general, winter offerings were scarce, consisting of butchers' meats, poultry and wild fowl, and shellfish, especially oysters. While beef was found in the markets year round, other kinds of meat entered the market seasonally. So veal arrived in the spring months, lamb in the summer, and pork in the fall and early winter. In the summer of 1795, a New York resident complained of the poor quality and scarcity of food in the Exchange Market: "Meats spoiled in the market-place uncommonly quick, and those which were brought home, apparently fresh and good in the morning, were often found unfit to be eaten when cooked and brought upon table. . . . Vegetables in general, and especially fruits, were usually poor, tough, and tasteless." But by and large, summer and fall were the most prodigious and crowded times for the public markets, their stalls overflowing with fruits, vegetables, meats, and fish. Shoppers also visited the markets more frequently during the warmer months since food spoiled more quickly, necessitating daily shopping.[66]

While central, the markets were not the only places in town to procure foodstuffs. Fresh food had to be sold within the markets, but preserved and imported items were found in the city's groceries. Grocers formed a relatively new occupational group in the eighteenth century. But by 1790, almost 180 grocers plied their trade in New York City, making them the most prominent food vendors outside of the markets. Some of these grocers were, in fact, merchants who retailed imported and local goods, in addition to carrying on a larger wholesale trade from their warehouses. Others were craftsmen who sold a variety of manufactured items in addition to their own handcrafted ones. And some were part of the burgeoning group of shopkeepers that expanded the ranks of New York's retailers over the course of the eighteenth century.[67]

Early national grocers advertised and sold an astonishing variety of goods. Yards of fabric, ironware and plateware, jewelry and mirrors, and myriad trinkets from combs to snuff boxes graced the ads and shelves of New York's merchants and grocers. In addition to these dry goods, merchants and grocers carried a variety of dried fruits, sweetmeats, and other luxury food items from Europe and the West Indies. In his 1790 advertisement in the *New York Morning Post*, grocer S. Hugget advertised an impressive array of imported foodstuffs, including capers, olives, anchovies, almonds, raisins, currants, Turkey figs, prunes, rice, "Scotch & Pearl Barley," "French and Italian Oyl," and "White and Brown Sugar Candy." Hugget also had on hand several spices—nutmeg, mace, cinnamon, allspice, and black and cayenne pepper as well as three kinds of tea, coffee, and chocolate.[68] Hugget's colleague Josias Ten Eyck offered for sale "Basket salt," cheese, mustard, "and every other article in the Grocery line" from his Wall Street store, and their fellow grocers Bruce & Morison advertised "400 bls pickled Herring," along with " a few quintals prime Codfish, & 11 tierces Salmon."[69]

More specialized food vendors also emerged during the eighteenth century and continued to ply their trade near the markets in the early national period. Confectioner Joseph Delacroix, for example, sold sugar candy and other delights from his William Street shop. In a 1794 advertisement, he listed the variety of goods he had for sale, including "sugar plumbs assorted, lemon candy, peperminth drops and lozengoes, cinnamon drops, burnt almonds, and caraway comfits," as well as "potatoes, biscuits of almonds, creame macarons . . . ice creams of different tastes, syrups of raspberry, vinegar, capilaire, orgeat, lemonade, gumauve, &c."[70]

In the early national period, the groceries and other food shops played a complementary rather than competitive role vis-à-vis the public markets. John Pintard, for example, supplemented his market jaunts with visits to local grocers who offered many goods that were not available within the market structure. His letters and account books show transactions with a pair of regular grocers—Joseph Stickler and Lewis Hartman—as well as the greengrocer Mrs. King.[71] The grocers provided Pintard with butter, spices, and food-related items such as crockery and cooking utensils. Wholesale grocers like Charles Dusenberry even supplied hucksters and peddlers who sold goods near the markets.[72]

But while the grocers were not part of the markets, they *were* a part of the market *world*, along with other extra-market vendors like hucksters, cake and coffee sellers, rag pickers, and peddlers. In fact, by the turn of the nineteenth century, the neighborhoods around the market houses became extensions of the market themselves. The Common Council gave approval to these practices by ignoring their own laws against setting up market carts outside of the market, and eventually chaining off the streets around the market houses to accommodate extra-market vendors. Food and nonfood retailers set up their shops in proximity to the public markets, and these areas turned into proto–shopping districts, precursors to the exclusively retail districts that emerged in New York in the nineteenth century.[73]

The areas around the large markets thus became hubs of commercial and social activity, centralized gathering places for various groups in New York society. The market houses themselves contained space for nonmarket purposes and accommodated municipal needs. For example, the second floor of Washington Market house accommodated a guard house. And in the cellars of the larger markets were found retail shops, cake shops, and eating houses.

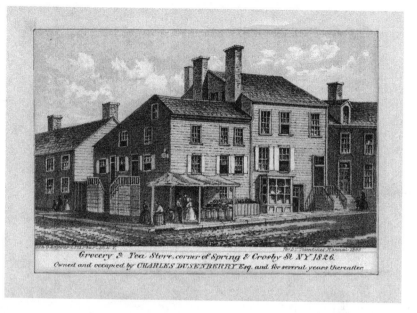

*Grocery & Tea Store, corner of Spring & Crosby St. N.Y. 1826.*
*Owned and occupied by CHARLES DUSENBERRY Esq. and for several years thereafter.*

This 1826 image depicts the exterior of Charles Dusenberry's grocery store,
on the corner of Spring and Crosby Streets. *Grocery & Tea Store Corner of Spring and
Crosby St. N.Y. 1826.* Lithograph by George Hayward.
(Emmet Collection, Miriam and Ira D. Wallach Division of Arts, Prints and Photographs,
The New York Public Library, Astor, Lenox, and Tilden Foundations)

Markets also served as social gathering spaces. The city's white laborers sought entertainment after-hours at the city's markets, especially during
late-night hours on Saturday when the markets reopened at 4:00 p.m. and
transacted business well into the night. One 1825 reporter called Catharine
Market "the great emporium for the mechanics and laborers on Saturday
evening."[74] Free and enslaved African Americans from Long Island and New
Jersey were also a familiar and oft-noted presence in the Bear and Catharine
Markets in the early nineteenth century. In a practice continued from the
eighteenth century, enslaved African Americans staged impromptu markets
on Sundays, selling foodstuffs and other items to each other and to the
general public. Some of the items for sale were grown on their masters'
farms—grains, meats, and produce, for example. Others they gathered from
the woods and shores of the waters surrounding the city—oysters, clams,
fish, berries, roots, and herbs. Once they had sold their merchandise, these
vendors would stay on and socialize with each other in the area surrounding the market houses.[75] These events, accompanied by music, games, and

gambling, served as important rituals of sociability and a cultural outlet for the city's African American population.

The most famous of these rites were the dance contests in which African American dancers competed for money or for food, especially the fish and eels for which Catharine Market was known. Competitors shuffled and spun along planks while their friends tapped out beats around the edges of the circle. The winners collected coins from market butchers, other vendors, and onlookers, many of whom came to the markets to watch these very spectacles.[76] The contests drew African American competitors from Long Island, New Jersey, and beyond as well as spectators of various backgrounds from all over the city. They serve as an excellent example of the market culture of the early national period. First, the market served as a backdrop to these informal gatherings, a space for sociability and intermingling for various types of New Yorkers. Second, the gatherings drew a cross section of New York society to them, as did the markets themselves.

The markets' role as gathering places and spaces of public entertainment demonstrates their important civic as well as nutritive function for early national New Yorkers. But the question remains: what were they actually eating? The answer to this question lay partly in social class, of course. The higher your means, the more varied and abundant your diet. Just as social class influenced one's market schedule, it determined one's dietary options.

For example, while he had lost his fortune, John Pintard remained a man of means and thus had access to the most varied diet available to New Yorkers of the turn of the nineteenth century. The bounty of the markets was truly his and was reflected in his accounts of his market visits and the foods he enjoyed. Thus, in addition to staples such as bread, butter, corn, and pork, Pintard's table was graced with poultry like geese, chickens, turkeys, and ducks; shellfish such as crab and oysters; and a plethora of fruits over the course of a year, from peaches, pineapples, and oranges to musk melons, watermelon, and *fruits de pays*. Pintard's account books and letters show that his family partook of a healthy amount of meat throughout the year, especially red meat. In the colder months, they also enjoyed oysters, poultry, and other fowl, and in the summer, several varieties of fish made their way onto the Pintards' table.[77]

While the variety of Pintard's table was class specific, the basic breakdown of his diet was typical of most early nineteenth-century New Yorkers. In fact, the early republic included some bright spots for the diets of ordinary New Yorkers. First, like their counterparts elsewhere in the colonies and the early republic, New Yorkers of all classes enjoyed a rising standard in terms of food supply throughout the period. Second, New Yorkers—even of relatively meager means—enjoyed a protein-rich diet, with plenty of meat. Indeed, the ability even of laboring New Yorkers to afford meat served as evidence of mobility in the eyes of European immigrants.[78]

Beef, which provided the bulk of the Pintards' protein needs, also was the predominant meat on the tables of New Yorkers in general. Contrary to common assumption, Americans in general ate more beef than pork in the colonial period and into the nineteenth century.[79] On average, early national New Yorkers consumed four to eleven pounds of beef per month and ten to sixteen pounds of red meat in general. This figure remained relatively steady throughout the year. Early national New Yorkers were big meat eaters overall, consuming on average ten to sixteen pounds of fresh red meat monthly.[80] In fact, thanks to economies of scale, which created a large market in New York for freshly slaughtered livestock, city dwellers were more likely than their country counterparts to enjoy fresh meat regardless of class orientation.[81] New York's rich waters also provided a varied bounty of fish, which most residents could enjoy.

New Yorkers supplemented their protein-heavy diet with grains, especially wheat and corn, dairy products such as butter and cheese, and seasonal fruits and vegetables. The spring and summer months were most abundant, and fresh fruits and vegetables were cheap enough to be affordable even to the city's laborers. For example, William Otter, a young laborer newly arrived in New York City from England in 1801, snuck off his ship to visit Fly Market for provisions. Otter was pleased and surprised to find peaches for a mere 12.5 cents per peck. The same fruit would have cost two cents per piece in London.[82] So too meat choices varied according to the season, as did prices. Again, the spring and summer months brought the greatest abundance of meat at the lowest prices and all but the poorest New Yorkers could include some animal protein in their meals.

While New Yorkers of varied means could eat similar *kinds* of food though, the preparations, frequency, and reliability of an individual's food choices were shaped by social class. First, those of means could afford to plan ahead and lay in suitable provisions for the colder months. Pintard was among them. His ready income allowed him the money to purchase "in bulk," the equipment to preserve foodstuffs, and the domestic space to store the pickled, canned, and nonperishable foods.[83] For example, in November 1816, Pintard bought a supply of turnips and potatoes and readied his butter for storage. A few years later, Pintard described making winter preparations, including storing "Fuel and winter roots" as well as "Butter, Apples, Flour & Meal." Pintard made pointed reference to the importance of planning in a preindustrial environment when he wrote: "To be provident in due season of the indispensable wants of life, relieves ones mind from the horrors of approaching winter without provision for its comfort."[84] Cookbooks of the time devoted entire chapters to preserving, drying, canning, and pickling foods for winter use. Susannah Carter's popular volume, *The Frugal Housewife, or Complete Woman Cook,* contained twenty-eight recipes for preserving and pickling, with names like "To Keep Green Peas till Christmas," and "To Keep French Beans All the Year."[85] But many New Yorkers did not have the means to lay in extensive provisions for the winter, or even to enjoy all that the markets had to offer during the prodigious spring and summer months.

Wealthy and middling New Yorkers also had access to more varied and interesting food preparations than did poorer individuals. The most common cooking methods were boiling and frying, techniques encouraged by the limits of the rudimentary stoves available in the eighteenth and early nineteenth centuries. Households of moderate means and above could add some dash to these dishes with herbs, salt, imported spices, and sugar—a luxury enjoyed by all but the very poor—purchased at local grocers' shops. The poorest New Yorkers probably ate their meager meals of bread and meat cold, rather than expend the money on fuel for cooking. Furthermore, many working-class households in the early republic lacked cookstoves, pumps, or storage space for fuel.[86] Nonetheless, the diet of poorer New Yorkers was actually more varied and healthful in the preindustrial era than it would become in the antebellum period.

As New York City emerged from the Revolutionary era, its food economy and public-market system adhered to preindustrial rhythms established in the seventeenth century. Food came to New York from local farms, forests, and waters located in northern Manhattan, New Jersey, Long Island, Staten Island, Connecticut, and Westchester County. Lacking reliable transportation or refrigeration, food producers needed to get their perishable goods to market quickly and sell them within a day, even a few hours in the summer months. Seasonality thus characterized the markets and the goods sold within them. Politics, health epidemics, and weather also shaped bouts of scarcity and abundance from one season to the next. Even with the preindustrial rhythms, however, local farms and fisheries embraced a commercial orientation. Producers kept the New York market in mind in the crops they grew and the techniques they used in order to optimize production.

The municipal government maintained strong oversight of New York's public markets. The Common Council was concerned with protecting public health and the public pocketbook, balancing the interests of individual purveyors with the public good. Producers and consumers engaged in face-to-face interactions in the markets. In most cases, food vendors were also producers, or aligned with them through family relations. Market vendors were organized along well-understood lines with the highly regulated butchers at the top of the hierarchy, fishermen, dairy men, and daily country vendors in the middle, and hucksters and other extra-market characters at the bottom end of the scale. A hierarchy characterized market purchasers as well. The daily market schedule was class defined, the wealthiest shoppers availing themselves of the choicest early morning pickings and the poorest New Yorkers waiting for cut-rate goods sold either within the markets or outside of them at the end of the day. These class determinations notwithstanding, however, the markets were governed by a rough moral economy and touched the lives of all New Yorkers, from the poorest to the wealthiest. Given regulations that required that meats and some produce could only be sold in the public markets, they were the only procurement option for these items for all New Yorkers, regardless of class. Thus, the markets, while marked by division, did in some ways live up to their reputation of sponsoring a common public culture for early national New Yorkers.

But change was afoot in the markets of New York, as it was in the city at large. As the technological transformations of the nineteenth century started to unfold, New York's food supply began to undergo a very significant shift. This transformation included greater regularity, cheaper prices, and more variety. But it also entailed less regulation, more corruption, and greater disparities in the food supply between those who had and those who had not.

*New York City's Public Markets 1865, and Select Private Food Shops.* This map shows the constriction of the public market system from 1830 (as shown in chapter 1). It also offers visual reference to Caroline Dustan's vendors, referenced in the chapter. (Map by Ben Benjamin)

# TWO

# "The Glory of a Plenteous Land": The Transformation of New York's Food Supply, 1825–1865

In 1825, James Fenimore Cooper's fictitious "traveling bachelor" predicted that New York City would become "the empire of gastronomy." As the bachelor explained: "It is difficult to name fish, fowl, or beast that is not . . . to be obtained in the markets of New-York." Manhattan's markets abounded with fruits from the islands, fowl from the West, and fish from the North. This happy situation arose from the "extraordinary combination of the effects of different climates, the union of heat and cold, and of commercial facilities, added to the rare bounties of Nature." When Paris eventually passed on its "culinary sceptre," the bachelor forecasted, "I know of no spot of the habitable world to which [it] is so likely to be transferred," as New York City.[1]

Cooper was prescient. New York may not have supplanted Paris, but it did become the culinary capital of the United States. As the commercial center of the young nation, Gotham was the central importer, exporter, and reexporter of foodstuffs in nineteenth-century America. Technological, industrial, and transportation improvements created a national market for consumer goods, and New York emerged as its vital hub. The city's food markets reaped the benefit of these developments. "On any morning of the five days out of the six of our weekly calendar," noted the *New York Mercury* in 1856, "Jefferson Market—in this emporium of the New World—represents a lap of luxury—the glory of a bountifully supplied and plenteous land." This "Cornucopia of the meats, the fruits, and the granaries of this fructiferous land," the *Mercury* continued, was irresistible to all except "a perfect monster Graham-misanthrope," a reference to Sylvester Graham, the well-known diet reformer and advocate of an abstemious diet.[2]

The cornucopia the *Mercury* described was made possible by decades of technological and industrial developments. Better transportation, household inventions, and improvements in food storage and preparation yielded a remarkable expansion of food options for ordinary New Yorkers. By boat, train, and horse cart, foods made their way into the markets of nineteenth-century New York City in unprecedented amounts and varieties. Thanks to the quickening and cheapening of carriage and processing, city residents had access to a range and quantity of foods unknown to earlier generations. The marketing of foodstuffs changed as well. As the city grew, the public-market system yielded to private food shops, street vendors, and neighborhood grocers. Once supplementary to the markets, these businesses became the main suppliers of New Yorkers' food. The public markets remained, but they came to serve mainly a wholesale population.

These developments entailed a marked change. Gone was the early republican system of local food supply, vaunted public markets, and municipal oversight. The direct contact between farmer and consumer ceded to distant food producers, middlemen, and the early industrialization of foodstuffs. The public markets became so crowded with produce and foodstuffs imported from near and far that they developed distribution bottlenecks and garnered constant calls for reform. Thus, along with the transportation and market revolutions of the early nineteenth century came a food revolution for New Yorkers. This revolution brought the foodways of mid-nineteenth-century Manhattanites much closer to our own.

The nineteenth-century transportation revolution ushered in a new culinary era for New Yorkers. Until the 1840s, the most significant transportation development was unquestionably the opening of the Erie Canal. Before the completion of the canal in 1825, the far hinterlands of New York sent agricultural goods east and southward at great price to the consumer. Transportation costs were so high that they more than trebled the market value of the individual products.[3] Canals on the other hand, offered extremely low-cost transportation over long hauls. Carrying a one-ton load from Buffalo to New York cost one hundred dollars in the pre-canal era. Using the canal, a shipper could expect to pay as little as seven dollars per ton along the same route. By 1860, the ton-mile average along the Erie Canal was over 95 percent lower than it had been fifty years before.[4]

Even in advance of the Erie Canal's opening, boosters, observers, and pundits predicted great times for New York's markets. The day the canal bill passed, John Pintard exclaimed to his daughter: "This is certainly a stupendous undertaking . . . the completion of which will render this City the Emporium of the Lakes & the Ocean." A few years later, as the canal construction continued, Pintard gushed: "What unbounded resources are before us, & what an immense city N York is destined to become."[5] In 1820, another canal booster predicted: "The fish-markets of the cities on the Hudson will be greatly improved by the canal. New species will be brought down in ice, in a perfect state of preservation, and the epicure of the South will be treated with new and untried dishes of the highest flavor."[6] Among the goods that this great emporium would receive and distribute were fish, wild game, grains, and fruits from the North and West.

New York City quickly felt the canal's impact. In 1826, a year after the waterway opened, a New York newspaper announced a shipment of "about five hundred weight of fresh salmon from lake Ontario . . . exhibited for sale in Fulton Market this morning . . . conveyed to this city via the Erie Canal."[7] Pleased to see his predictions of market abundance realized, Pintard marveled: "The consumption of this increasing city is immense & great supplies are sent from our western country by means of the Canal."[8]

Canals were but one thread in a web of early national transportation improvements. The local ferry system also continued to expand during the early nineteenth century, when steam began to rule the waters. Owned and operated by Robert Fulton and Robert R. Livingston, the first steam ferries in New York enjoyed a state-sanctioned monopoly to operate or license steamboats in the waters around Manhattan. As a result of this monopoly, steam ferry service was somewhat slow to begin in the area, even after the technology existed to operate the ferries. But in 1824, the Supreme Court (in *Gibbons v. Ogden*) overturned the Fulton-Livingston monopoly, opening the way for a proliferation of steam ferries in New York's waters. Ferry service expanded from a mere six boats to over seventy on the eve of the Civil War.[9] By then, the New Jersey lines began to be linked to and owned by railroad companies, and ferry service became the first (or last) leg in a journey to and from agricultural areas west of New Jersey to Manhattan.[10] Steam technology alleviated some of the dangers of the crossing, the time it took (a mere four to five minutes), and the price of transporting market wagons across the water, allowing more farm goods to enter New York from its hinterlands in New Jersey, Staten Island, Long Island, and upstate.[11]

While largely used as passenger vessels in the period before the Civil War, steamboats also played an important role in freight carriage, especially along the larger rivers. Steam-powered tugboats hauled freight-laden barges on rivers as well as the Atlantic coast. And steamships carried American goods across the Atlantic to Europe and the Caribbean and came back laden with manufactured products for American markets.

New York also joined in on the railroad boom, doubling the amount of track in the state during the 1850s, from about 1.4 million to just over 2.7 million miles. By 1860, railroads were the predominant mode of transport for agricultural goods from the West to New York City. Faster transportation along rail routes cheapened and quickened the carriage of goods to market. The Long Island Railroad, for example, enabled the farmers near it to ship to New York City "in a few hours produce that by boat had taken as many days." Trains carried two-thirds of the freight that traveled from west to east and back and did so five times faster than other modes of transportation. According to the 1860 census, New York State's railroads carried over two million tons of "vegetable food" and "products of animals," at a value of about $300 million.[12] The net result of these transportation developments was a 95 percent decline in overland transportation rates between 1815 and 1860. Freight charges along the Hudson River dropped accordingly as well.[13]

Locally, the Long Island and New Jersey Central Railroads combined with steam ferries to convey loads of goods to the New York market. Advertisements for these railroads began to boast of their appeal to market gardeners. For example, an 1841 advertisement announced to "Farmers, Marketmen, Gardeners, &c." that beginning on June 1, the Long Island Railroad would offer freight train service every Saturday from Hicksville and Hempstead to New York City, "in time to arrive in market by daylight with every description of freight: Vegetables, Grass, Fish, Clams, Meats and Market Truck generally." The ad also pointed to connections within the city, particularly a ferry boat that would meet the train at South Ferry and transport passengers and freight to Fulton Market.[14] These same networks linked the farms of Staten Island, New Jersey, and Westchester to the markets of New York City. Railroads brought not only fruits and vegetables from New Jersey and Long Island but also fish from northern rivers, even as far as Maine.[15]

Thanks to faster transportation options, the seasons—and sources of fresh foods—extended. Far-off farmers could move their fruits and vegetables to market more quickly. Produce which previously rotted on wagons, canal boats, and sailing ships was now delivered to New York unspoiled. The fruits of Georgia, Florida, and the Caribbean covered the tables along the sides of the market houses while turkeys from Vermont, geese from Ohio, duck from Virginia, and quail from the western states of Wisconsin, Illinois, Ohio, Indiana, Michigan, and Iowa adorned stalls along the center. Fresh poultry, game, and fish arrived in New York from Canada and the Ohio Valley in refrigerated railcars, essentially "ice boxes on wheels."[16]

New York City was both the recipient and driver of food-based changes. The city's needs affected the farms in its near and distant hinterlands, which expanded and adapted to the new possibilities the canal and railroads offered. With upstate and western lands taking over the cultivation of grain and cattle, local farmers ceased growing wheat and other grains for the New York market and turned their farms to gardens. Meanwhile, dairy and wheat production shifted farther north and west than before since upstate farms now could ship these goods at a fraction of the pre-canal price. The Genesee Valley in particular became the major supplier of wheat to New York City and beyond. And farms in that area yielded thousands of bushels of wheat per year. Rochester, at the heart of the valley and of wheat production in New York State, yielded over $1 million worth of wheat in 1856.[17]

But the Erie Canal also opened up parts of the Mohawk Valley—Herkimer and Oneida and parts of Saratoga Counties—to dairy production for New York City. In these former wheat-producing regions, farmers turned their lands over to dairy production as the Genesee Valley came to dominate wheat cultivation. And the canal made it possible for the dairy farmers to transport their goods westward and down the Hudson. Mohawk Valley farms housed some of the largest dairies in the United States, containing herds of thirty to forty milk cows. The towns in this region exported 1,000 tons of cheese in 1832 and the small town of Steuben—the center of butter production—sent 150 tons of butter to be sold in Washington Market and its smaller counterparts.[18] Orange and Ulster Counties, north of the city, also continued to be major suppliers of milk, butter, and cheese to New York households. Meanwhile, ranchers in the Connecticut Valley of Massachusetts embraced improved fattening techniques and yielded larger droves of cattle bound for Gotham.[19]

Ohio got in on the ranching action as well. The Ohio Valley became a major thoroughfare for drovers, leading tens of thousands of cattle and hogs toward the Eastern Seaboard. These droves contained hundreds of animals traveling forty to fifty days across land to market in eastern cities. Observers along these routes commented on the heavy traffic of livestock, kicking up dust visible from a mile away.[20]

Distant farmers noted the commercial potential of the New York market. An article in the Charleston (SC) Mercury pointed to some local farmers who had shipped large quantities of fruits and vegetables to New York. Thanks to the "advantage of an earlier season," and the "facility of transportation by steamships," the article explained, "our Southern farmers and fruit culturists [can] anticipate the Northern crops." The paper thus urged local farmers and planters to cultivate fruits for the market, concluding: "with a favorable season, there is no crop that pays better."[21]

With distant hinterlands supplying less perishable foods, local farmers embraced intensive production of fruits and vegetables, abandoning grain and livestock. Long Island, New Jersey, and the Hudson Valley were dotted with market gardens that earned a lucrative trade catering to the markets of New York City.[22] These farms were not small affairs but rather major businesses. In fact, the farms immediately around New York City—commercial ventures of long-standing—became the most intensively cultivated lands in the nation. In 1852, John King, the president of the Queens County Agricultural Society, boasted: "Queens county cannot be interfered with in its prosperity, as long as there are in that metropolis (of New York) hundreds of thousands of mouths to be daily supplied, and hundreds of thousands of dollars to be expended for . . . fruits and vegetables raised out of season, and by artificial climates." The head of Staten Island's Agricultural Society made a similar claim, urging his members to take advantage of the island's proximity to New York and turn their "farms into gardens." Such a move, he concluded, would bring Staten Island's farmers into competition with those of New Jersey and Long Island in seeing great returns from agricultural output.[23]

In recognition of their market potential, the commercial farms near Gotham embraced heavy use of manures, paid laborers, irrigation, and tillage techniques to make their lands as productive as possible.[24] Farmers incorporated improvements in agricultural tools and machinery such as iron plows, harrows, mowing machines, and threshing machines, yielding better tillage and the faster processing of wheat. They took advantage of novel farming techniques such as soil improvement, the use of artificial grasses for better hay, and crossbreeding of livestock. Abandoning subsistence-plus lifestyles, local farmers purchased manufactured goods such as tools, clothing, and furniture, and turned their attention to commercial agricultural production.[25]

New York City was the center not only for distribution of farm products but also production of agricultural tools. And farms in the state took most advantage of new agricultural technologies. According to the 1860 census, New York State's farms had machinery valued in the amount of $29,166,695; the closest competitor was Pennsylvania, with a value of $22,442,842.[26] These businesses thus further connected New York City to its hinterlands. Manure serves as a good example. Companies like the Lodi Manufacturing Company (located in New Jersey) and its competitor the New-York Poudrette Company developed a marketable fertilizer (poudrette) made from peat, fish bones and, most important, the "night soil," or human waste of the city. "Night men" mined the "sinks," outhouses, and privies of the city and then transported their cargo to the poudrette works for processing and distribution to the farmers of the region. Difficult as it may be to imagine, human waste was a more valuable commodity than other organic matter in making fertilizer. In 1842, the New-York Poudrette Company took out an ad in the *New-York Tribune* to brag that, unlike its competitor the Lodi Manufacturing Company, the New York company did not depend on "a peculiar kind of peat" found on the marshlands of New Jersey where Lodi was located. Rather, the New-York Poudrette Company proudly reported, it was "paid for removing the contents of sinks, and has a great supply free of cost." The New-York Poudrette Company thus could offer a fertilizer far superior to the "poor sample of Poudrette" manufactured from New Jersey mud.[27]

Despite these claims, manufacturers, manure collectors, and the city government itself only scratched the surface of potential for human and animal waste in creating fertilizer. Most of the waste in the city either stayed in the streets where it rotted, or was collected and dumped into the rapidly polluting rivers, to the great chagrin of health reformers. In 1841, City Inspector John Griscom submitted a report to the city council decrying the waste and unsanitary effects of emptying the city's sinks. Griscom lauded the potentials of poudrette, whose value, he argued, "has been satisfactorily shown to be nearly 14 times that of common stable manure." Only the large cities offered the raw materials "in sufficient abundance to justify the manufacture," and yet, New York—"the largest city of this hemisphere . . . wholly wasted" its bounty.[28]

Apparently Griscom's letter went unheeded because the city did little to take advantage of poudrette's promise. Fourteen years after Griscom's filing, George Waring, who, after the Civil War, would lead, reform, and modernize the city's street-cleaning department, decried the waste of over $5 million annually in valuable fertilizer from the city and its surrounding communities. And *New-York Tribune* editor Horace Greeley declared the waste of waste "inexplicable stupidity."[29] The discussion of poudrette and manure in the press and city government documents shows an understanding of the interdependence of city and country even if, like today, they squandered the potential that recycling offered.

When applied, new fertilizers and farming techniques found success. Census returns from 1850 show that the highest producing farms in the state were completely concentrated around New York City. Queens County, New York County (Manhattan), and Kings County produced just over $300,000, $121,000, and $88,000 worth of market produce respectively. Westchester County returned just over $49,000 and Richmond County, or Staten Island, about $14,000 worth.[30] New York State had by far the most lucrative commercial farms in the nation. According to the 1860 census, New York State's fourteen-thousand-plus acres of improved lands were worth over $800 million, over a tenth of the total value of agricultural land in the United States. No other state came near New York in agricultural land value. The closest competitor was Ohio whose lands were valued at about $678 million.[31]

Technological improvements did not solely relate to transportation. They extended to food production and packaging as well. For example, farmers began to cultivate grapes and figs in hothouses; to preserve tomatoes in sealed packages; and to pack and ship on ice many varieties of fresh produce, fish, and game, in order to prevent spoilage.[32] In fact, while not as important as canals or railroads, ice made significant contributions to changing food production and distribution in New York. Again, this process both stemmed from and fueled demand. The availability of commercial ice increased after 1827, with the invention of the ice cutter and improvements in ice houses. The new ice cutter was a plow-like device, drawn by a horse across a frozen pond, eventually making a checkerboard pattern of deep grooves in the ice. Bars were set in the grooves, dislodging large blocks of ice that workers then floated to ice houses by the shore. By 1833, filling an ice house took much less time and 60 percent less money than before. The ice houses themselves were more efficient and better insulated, losing far less product to melting.[33]

Large ice companies formed in the northern United States, harvesting and distributing ice on a large scale to consumers around the country and beyond. In Cambridge, Massachusetts, the center of New England ice production, the ice harvest could yield forty thousand tons in six days.[34] New York's major ice concerns such as the Knickerbocker Ice Company, were located north of the city, along the Hudson River. Some upstate lakes were rimmed with several ice houses. For example, Rockland Lake, in Rockland County, supplied the city with more than half of the ice it consumed in the 1850s. The lake was surrounded by eight ice houses, each capable of holding thirty to forty thousand tons of ice.[35] During the annual harvest, hundreds of men cut, floated, and hauled large blocks of ice from the nearby ponds to the ferry landings and shipped it to Manhattan on large ice barges. There, the ice was sold to local individuals and businesses or shipped to other cities along the East Coast.[36]

The Knickerbocker Ice Company was the biggest in New York City, but it had several competitors, including A. Barmore & Co., C. R. Wortendyke & Co., and Turnbull, Ackerson & Co. In 1856, these companies produced over 285,000 tons of ice, almost all of which was stored in ice houses within the city to be sold to local customers.[37] By the 1850s, over a hundred ice wagons delivered thousands of tons of ice to the homes and businesses of

DRAWING THE ICE-BLOCKS TO THE ICE-HOUSE.

STORING THE ICE.

These images of ice harvesting, featured in *Appleton's Journal* in 1871, show the process of floating the harvested blocks of ice to the ice house, and the interior of the ice house where the blocks were stored. (Courtesy, American Antiquarian Society)

New York. An 1850 visitor to Fulton Market was amazed by the sight of "large square lumps of ice" that lay "glittering and smoking in the hot sun, on the dirty side-walk . . . as though they might just have fallen from a Swiss glacier."[38]

The availability of ice contributed to the increased use of refrigeration within market houses as well as restaurants, hotels, and private homes. The shift to ice dependence occurred quickly. Even as early as 1820, the Grand Street Market butchers petitioned the Common Council for permission to erect an ice house under the market structure. Beginning in the 1830s, butchers regularly stored their meats in ice-packed coolers that they kept in their market stalls.[39]

Inventors, manufacturers, and retailers began to develop and market refrigerators (what we would call ice boxes) to food purveyors in New York and other cities. Indeed, marketers and commentators positioned refrigerators as particularly valuable in the cities, where residents and retailers did not have fresh springs for drawing water or ice houses to keep their foodstuffs cool. Furthermore, the cities were the likeliest places to find reliable ice delivery, a prerequisite for regular refrigerator use.[40] For example, inventor Thomas B. Smith described his patent refrigerator, essentially a walk-in ice house, in *American Agriculturist Magazine* in November 1848, as especially useful to butchers, dairymen, grocers, and provision dealers, and in cities like New York, "where milk is kept on sale." Smith also suggested that a resourceful businessman could make a good living by purchasing his patent refrigerator and renting out storage space to local food vendors who wished to keep their products fresh and cool.[41] By the 1860s, market chronicler Thomas De Voe described refrigerators as "generally used by . . . butchers and housekeepers."[42]

These various new technologies and supply channels not only introduced novel food items to New York but brought back some older varieties that had grown scarce by the nineteenth century. For example, before the advent of steam transport, salmon was virtually impossible to find in the city's markets. But by the 1850s, salmon was a regular item in fishmongers' stalls and shops from March until September, though still quite expensive "on account of its scarcity, distance brought, and the difficulty of preserving them fresh and in good order," De Voe explained. Meanwhile, shad, once so plentiful that it was used as fertilizer, had become obsolete in New York by the early nineteenth century thanks to overfishing. But by the 1830s, it was again available, along with other varieties of fish "brought from the distance of 60, 80, and even 100 miles," explained Peter Cortelyou, the head of a Long Island fishery.[43] Likewise, formerly rare southern and even Caribbean fruits were a standard offering in New York's spring and summer markets. In 1856, Havana sent about six million oranges to New York City, along with dozens of cargoes of lemons.[44]

Beginning in the 1840s, the New York papers published weekly provisions reports which described the offerings in the public markets as well as prices and any remarkable items. These reports point to the new distances

## THE SHOW-CASE
# Iceberg Refrigerator.

Has plate glass on three sides, and furnishes to Florists, Fruit Dealers, Restaurateurs and others invaluable means for publicly and freely displaying in the window or at the door, choice Hot-house Fruits, Flowers, Game, or any other expensive and perishable article, without the speedy depreciation and loss that otherwise follows.

**No. 1.**—Black Walnut, 2 feet 11 in. long; 2 feet 11 in. deep; 4 feet 2 in. high. Show Room 12 cubic feet. Price.....$

*We can furnish them of any size or shape, either flat or square, for counters or otherwise, as may be wanted. Estimates furnished upon receipt of measurements and other particulars.*

This image of a showcase refrigerator explains its use to "Florists, Fruit Dealers, Restaurateurs," and others. *The Show-Case Iceberg Refrigerator.* Allegretti Iceberg Catalog, Trade Catalog, Manuscripts Collection, American Antiquarian Society. (Courtesy, American Antiquarian Society)

that food traveled before making its way onto the city's tables. The market reports of the *New York Herald* announced the arrival of shad from North Carolina, watermelons from Cuba, peaches from South Carolina, and oysters from Virginia.[45] One such reporter explained: "Thanks to the swiftest steamboats," from "the Gulf of Mexico to the Bay of Fundy," and to "our immense net-work of railroads all through the country," New York's markets saw fruits from the South a month before they were in season locally.[46]

The expansion of New York's food suppliers marked a very significant shift. For centuries, the vast bulk of New Yorkers' food had come from nearby producers, some of whom sold their own goods in the city's markets. But now the producer and consumer were often far removed from each other in proximity, but closer to each other in the time it took to ship foodstuffs. Thomas De Voe noted the distance of New York's food suppliers in 1865: "The variety, quantity, and quality of wild-fowl and birds . . . received in the public markets, especially of the city of New York is not surpassed in any other city in the world. The prairies of the West, the forest-regions of the North, the gulf coasts of the Northern and Southern States, and even European cities, all contribute to keep well supplied the wants of our citizen epicures, in every month or season of the year."[47]

Thanks to all of these developments, New York's food supply was more reliable and less seasonally dependent in the mid-1800s than it had been at the turn of the century. Meat serves as one example. In the early national period, seasonal fluctuations characterized the availability and consumption of different types of meat. While beef was in season year round, other red meats such as lamb, pork, and veal came into the market on a seasonal basis. But by 1867, these meats were in season throughout the year.[48] In the aggregate, antebellum New Yorkers continued to eat an impressive amount of meat. "In one year," *Leslie's Illustrated Newspaper* marveled, "New York eats 185,000 oxen, 12,000 cows, 550,000 sheep and lambs, 40,000 calves, and 200,000 hogs."[49]

As for produce, the city's markets were stocked with fresh fruits and vegetables throughout the year, from nearby in summer and far away in winter. During the prodigious summer months, when local farmers provided the markets with an abundance of produce, "garden truck of every hue and color, red and green and gold, sparkle and glisten on every side" of the markets, according to the *Herald*'s market report.[50]

The bouts of scarcity that had characterized the market fifty years before were less marked, and prices both of common and luxury foods had declined to bring many of them within the means of most New Yorkers. Furthermore, the diversification of sources for foodstuffs meant less potential for vagaries in price due to a shortage in one market. In December 1856, for example, *Leslie's Illustrated Newspaper* reported that "several attempts by the cattle brokers to control the market when a short Western supply has been looked for, have failed, owing to a large influx of State cattle."[51]

Commentators noted the reasonable prices of fruits, vegetables, and other market produce and hence their availability to a wide range of New Yorkers. For example, the *New York Herald* marveled that the city's residents enjoyed "luscious and health-promoting fruits" for much of the year and "at a cheapness which places them within the procurement of the very poor."[52]

Likewise, in 1856, *Leslie's* noted the relatively low prices of foodstuffs, including fish, butter, eggs, and vegetables. Potatoes, turnips, and other staples were very cheap at twenty-nine cents and eighteen cents per peck respectively. This circumstance, the paper concluded "will be good news for poor people."[53] In comparison, the more exotic peas could be had for thirty-one cents a half peck, artichokes eighteen cents per half peck, asparagus fifteen cents a bunch, strawberries ten cents per basket, and pineapples fifteen cents each, making these items luxuries available only to New Yorkers of means.[54] New York's artisans and laborers, who earned on average between one dollar and two dollars per day could probably not buy pineapples on a regular basis but could afford meat, fish, eggs, and a variety of fruits and vegetables in season.[55]

But the newfound abundance and variety came with some significant growing pains. New York's markets were literally overflowing. In the peak summer months, up to two thousand wagons of produce from local farms crowded the public markets. In addition, middlemen shipped in many thousands of barrels of produce from the southern states and islands like Bermuda and Cuba.[56] Produce sales were centralized at Washington Market by this point in time. New York's largest market handled over $17 million worth of vegetables and fruits annually by 1853, over three-quarters of it for the wholesale market. A year later, a letter to the *Herald* estimated a 1,000 percent increase in the volume of goods in Washington Market in the previous seven years.[57]

Washington Market thus was packed to capacity and unable to adequately distribute the food it gathered. "Complaints are continually being made that the market is insufficient for the business," noted a reporter for the *Herald* in 1848. "When it was constructed it was sufficiently large, but since that time the city has increased, and there is now no good depot for the sale of the innumerable quantities of provision which are daily coming in," he continued.[58] Country people jockeyed for space in and near the markets. Often they came up lacking and watched their inventory spoil on carts and wagons before they could unload their goods. These vendors fell easy prey to local forestallers who secured space in the markets by arriving before dawn, while the Long Island and New Jersey farmers were still waiting to catch a ferry to Manhattan. The forestallers offered below-market prices to the farmers who saw little choice but to accept the offers rather than dragging their produce back to their homes or, worse, watching it rot.[59]

Meanwhile, by the docks and extending outward into the Hudson River, hundreds of boats waited to unload their cargoes, sometimes in vain. The perishable produce, fish, game, and meat went to waste for lack of a

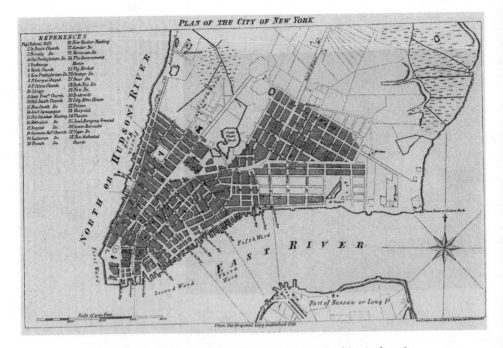

This map and the facing one show the geographic growth of the city from the 1790s to the 1860s. The map above shows the extent of the city, whose northern boundary extended to Chambers Street, above city hall. *Plan of the City of New York, 1789.* Lithograph by George Hayward. (Picture Collection, The New York Public Library, Astor, Lenox, and Tilden Foundations)

sufficient distribution system to unload the cargo and deliver it to the wholesale market. The scene at Washington Market was chaos. The docks, streets, and market houses thronged with people, carts, wagons, boats, and once lovely produce that could not find its way to the tables of Gotham.[60]

The markets also proved increasingly inhospitable to individual purchasers. The market buildings were unkempt and overcrowded, the surrounding sidewalks impassable due to the swarm of people, carts, boxes, barrels, and animals of various sorts. Journalists, travelers, reformers, and other commentators reported with shock and disgust on the condition of the city's once proud markets. "The dirt and filth in Washington market is past endurance," the *Herald* exclaimed in one representative comment. "It is too much filled up with all sorts of trash to get about in without much inconvenience. Either the market should be enlarged, or some truck excluded," the *Herald* concluded, explicitly noting the distribution bottlenecks that contributed to the markets' condition.[61]

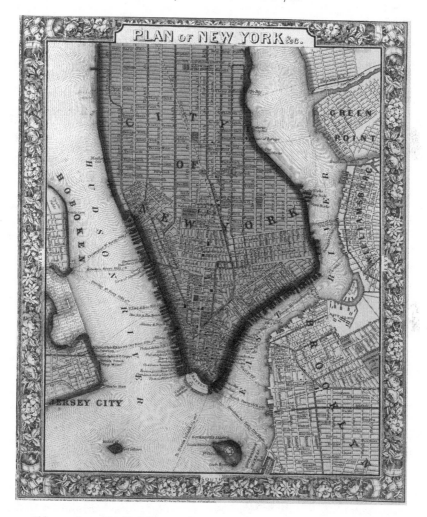

This map shows New York in 1863 when the settled area stretched even farther north than Fifty-Fifth Street, where it ends on this map. *Plan of New York, &c.*, 1863. Map from Augustus S. Mitchell, *Mitchell's New General Atlas*. (Picture Collection, The New York Public Library, Astor, Lenox, and Tilden Foundations)

Considering this state of affairs, it should come as no surprise that individual consumers increasingly looked to private food shops to supply their larders and tables. These shops had emerged in part to address rapid urban growth as the city transformed from the small walking city of the eighteenth century to the metropolis of the nineteenth. In 1800, New York's northern boundary had been Chambers Street. But by 1860, the city's settled area stretched up the island of Manhattan to Fifty-Fifth Street, about four miles north of Chambers.

Unlike their colonial counterparts, nineteenth-century merchants and professionals increasingly chose to set up residences away from their businesses.[62] Formerly situated in the "court end" of town, around the Battery and Bowling Green Park, wealthier homes were relocating to the tree-lined neighborhoods of the northern regions of the city such as Hudson Square, Greenwich Village, Gramercy Park, and Chelsea as well as across the East River in Brooklyn Heights. Industrial and transportation developments and urban rebuilding spurred this trend along. Omnibuses and street railroads, services priced out of the range of many New Yorkers but well within the means of the elite and middle classes, made commuting possible. The Great Fire of 1835, which destroyed large swathes of the city and necessitated the reconstruction of much of the downtown area, accelerated the separation of commerce and domesticity. Commercial structures replaced the burned-out residences in the former court end of town. Middle-class and elite families moved their residences from downtown—increasingly associated with commercial ventures and seedy homes—to new, leafy precincts on the edges of the city, associated mainly with people of similar economic circumstances.[63]

These geographic and demographic developments had a direct impact on New York City's markets. There were no public markets in Manhattan's newly settled areas. And the city did not build them. Harlem Market, located on 120th Street, was the only new market established above Fourteenth Street after 1830. And the only successful new retail market was Jefferson Market in Greenwich Village.[64]

The municipal government's decision to cease building new markets rested on a combination of politics and expediency. The patrician politics of the eighteenth century ceded in the antebellum period to the laissez-faire politics of the Jacksonian era. The city's patrician stance toward its markets and their vendors lost favor with the politicians and much of the public (though not with many of the licensed vendors) as the nineteenth century progressed. Practically speaking, building new markets was expensive and unwieldy as the city rapidly spread. Rather than engage in land surveys, hear petitions from residents, raise funds for markets, construct and regulate them, the Common Council found it far easier simply to offer provisional licenses to grocers and journeymen butchers to open private shops in the newer areas of the city that were underserved by markets.

Furthermore, the residents of these newer areas demanded immediate provisioners, not the slow process of building new public markets. As more

New Yorkers lived in market-less areas, they supported nonmarket food vendors who easily moved their shops and carts to new neighborhoods. Residents petitioned the Common Council to license butchers—both particular butchers and meat sellers in general—to operate in their neighborhoods. These petitions often met with success. For example, in 1821 Greenwich Villagers successfully petitioned the Common Council to secure a provisional license for butcher Richard Purchase. The council approved the license and, a few months later, an additional license for the presumably related Peter Purchase.[65] The number of petitions on behalf of unlicensed vendors seeking to sell goods outside of the markets increased exponentially in the early nineteenth century, from a handful to hundreds. The number of petitioners increased as well. For example, Daniel Hyde collected over one hundred signatures for his 1836 petition to expand his private meat shop on Christopher and Washington Streets in Greenwich Village.[66]

The Common Council recognized the creep of public sentiment in this direction in words as well as deed. A council member noted in 1841 that "it has become a burden to part of the community, by compelling them to go so far to find a market."[67] In addition to political leaders' and consumers' interest in more private provisioning options, many vendors themselves sought provisional licenses. Several of these butchers had served an apprenticeship but could not obtain a stall in the overcrowded markets. Joining their ranks were foreign-born butchers, especially German immigrants, who sought to break into the extremely competitive and insular community of native-born butchers that traced its roots back to the eighteenth century and earlier.

The Common Council began regularly to issue provisional licenses for meat sellers in neighborhoods with no convenient public market. Some butchers sought and received these licenses. Others just ignored the law altogether and sold meats outside of the markets—and the law. The city government turned a blind eye to its own regulations and frequently allowed unlicensed butchers to operate unimpeded. Henry Cornell was one example. Like many of his fellow butchers, Cornell was a victim both of the licensing system and the vagaries of urban growth. When populations shifted, markets closed in old neighborhoods and opened in newer, more populous ones. Thus, Spring Street Market closed in 1829 when its surrounding neighborhood became less residential and more commercial. Clinton Market, located on the west side between Spring and Canal Streets, replaced it. The Spring Street butchers petitioned the Common Council for stalls in the new market, and the council directed them to "buy in competition with the others." Stripped of his Spring Street stall, butcher Henry

Cornell claimed that he was unable to afford the price of the new stalls. So he opened a private meat shop, which he operated without a license. Many other butchers followed Cornell's lead, and meat shops proliferated around the city, coexisting with the markets and the provisional shops. On occasion, the city fined butchers for operating without a license, as evidenced by their petitions to have the fines revoked. But more often, the Common Council tolerated these breaches of the law.[68]

Private grocers also expanded their fresh offerings to include dairy, produce, meat, and fresh fruits and vegetables. This shift reflected another major change in food provisioning in New York City. In the early national period, private groceries had complemented the markets, selling mostly dry goods, preserved and processed foods, while the public markets carried fresh meats and produce. But as early as the 1830s, grocers supplied their customers not only with dried fruits, preserves, teas, and spices, but also dairy products, meats, and fresh produce. For example, at his grocery store on the corner of Spring and Crosby Streets, Charles Dusenberry offered a variety of nonedible dry goods as well as a significant range of edibles. In addition to the dried fruits, nuts, teas, coffee, wines, sugars, and spices that had been grocery-store standards since the eighteenth century, Dusenberry stocked cured meats, eggs, cheese and butter, fresh bread, and fresh fruits and vegetables.[69] A sense of the range of goods available in New York's groceries can be gleaned from grocer W. Locke's poetic description of his inventory:

> I have goods of all classes,
> Walk up and step up and get your 50 cent molasses.
> You can get ginger-bread, cakes, all you can swallow
> And eleven pounds of good sugar for one dollar.
> Fetch in all your butter and lard,
> Trade them for Goods at 10 cents per yard.
> All this is truth I declare,
> Here is the place to get your Queensware. . . .
> Please come, *do* come, and see,
> I will sell you half pound of good tea.
> We have pickles by the can, dozen, or jar,
> On hand plenty of good tar. . . .
> We will try to give you for dinner a good dish,
> And when you go home, sell you half barrel of White Fish
> We can please the young, and the old, and the dandy,
> And for babies always on hand plenty of candy.[70]

In the second quarter of the nineteenth century, Dusenberry, Locke, and other grocers like them expanded their stock so that they now competed with the public markets in terms of inventory and customers. By the 1850s, New York City was home to over 2,200 retail groceries and again, many New Yorkers patronized these private shops for their daily needs, rather than the public markets.[71] As southern visitor William Bobo explained it: "The regular markets could not supply every person in town by a long shot, consequently there are many other places where you can be pretty well supplied; there are several up town."[72]

These practices demonstrate how much the city's stance vis-à-vis food sales had changed from a generation before when the licensed butchers had a monopoly on fresh-meat sales in New York City. A highly skilled bunch, their position as kings of the markets was well established by the nineteenth century, and the government protected that position. But the antebellum city government was different from that of the early national period. With the expansion of the city's population and the granting of universal white male suffrage in 1826 in New York State, municipal politics became increasingly democratic. In the first decades of the nineteenth century the Common Council had been dominated by propertied men, professionals, and merchants. In the antebellum period, their numbers were cut in half as the council became a bastion of small entrepreneurs and craftsmen, including grocers, bakers, butchers, and saloon keepers.[73]

Representatives of the old guard lamented the democratization. The conservative newspaper *The New-York Tribune* critiqued the board of aldermen's "low and abusive language, bad grammar and still worse ideas."[74] But like it or hate it, the development represented a real and important realignment of politics and governance in New York City, and an important shift in the city's official stance toward its markets. Democratic politics of the Jacksonian era were inhospitable toward both patrician regulation and perceived monopolies. And the licensed butchers—who alone could lease stalls and sell meats in the public markets—were easily accused of benefiting from both.[75]

Not surprisingly, the licensed market butchers viewed the situation quite differently. They saw their livelihood and their craft tradition challenged by the private meat shops and the potential for deregulation. The licensed market butchers complained that unlicensed butchers were opening shops "in almost every part of the city with perfect impunity."[76] Some native-born butchers who expected to follow in their fathers' vocation (and even inherit their market stalls) were resistant as well to the inroads of immigrant Irish and German butchers into their trade. Native-born butchers joined with other workers to formally and informally protest the degradation of their trade, which they often blamed on the newer immigrants who had fewer skills and worked for lower wages. Native-born butchers were at the heart of the American Republican Party, a nativist party whose candidates won almost 23 percent of the vote for local officials in its first election in 1842. The party drew Protestant natives in the butchers' trade as well as other crafts such as shoemakers, tailors, and printers who blamed the degradation of their artisan traditions on immigrants, especially the Irish.[77]

Informal protests took the form of riots and mob violence as well as individual skirmishes involving fists, knives, and guns. The most famous and symbolic of these skirmishes involved the death of Bill "the Butcher" Poole at the hands of Lewis Baker, friend to Irish pugilist John Morrissey, Poole's longtime enemy and rival. At base, the incident was a fatal gun fight between two street rivals. But the murder and its aftermath were widely covered in the press and entered city lore through sympathetic vehicles like *"I Die a True American": The Life of William Poole, with a Full Account of the Terrible Affray in Which He Received His Death Wound*, published in 1855, or Herbert Asbury's later volume, *The Gangs of New York*.[78] In these works, in the working men's and sporting men's press, and especially in the melodramatic performances geared toward working-class audiences, Bill the Butcher was transformed from street thug to martyr and symbol of native and working-class pride in a rapidly diversifying and industrializing New York City. Bill Poole's image came to symbolize the shocks that attended the transformation of some of the oldest professions in New York City from artisan crafts to working-class jobs.[79]

In petitions to the Common Council, the butchers expressed nostalgia for the older era. They formulated a defense of their trade that was rooted in the market ideas of the eighteenth and early nineteenth centuries. Their complaints shine a light onto the shifting market ethos, away from the patrician stance of the eighteenth century, which saw market regulation as essential to the public good, and toward an era of laissez-faire, free market philosophy. Butchers evoked the language of rights and civic responsibility to defend their position. They argued that the laws regulating meat sales were central to the public interest in ensuring a healthful meat supply. Not only were the meat shops operating in open defiance of the law, the butchers claimed, but they were not subject to the inspections and oversight of municipal authorities, a role the licensed butchers thought essential to the public good. Their message was clear: government oversight of their trade was necessary to civic and physical health. They also complained that the city's failure to enforce the law was unfair, forcing them to pay large fees to the city for their stands while unlicensed butchers paid none.[80]

As a body, the press weighed in on the other side, charging that the laws regulating butchers and meat sales violated free enterprise and encouraged monopoly. The *Evening Post* accused the city's butchers of charging "monopoly prices."[81] Its Whig competitor, *The Tribune*, agreed that market prices were inflated as a result of city regulations.[82] Even the labor-friendly *Herald* chimed in, explaining that the city's licensed butchers purported to charge less than the private meat shops but in fact "shaved [the public] out of 3 ½ cents on the dollar" by charging a higher price on the final cuts than they quoted per pound.[83]

The press reaction suggests a significant movement away from the market ethos of the early republic. By the early 1840s, the licensed vendors stood accused of monopolistic practices and price fixing, counter to the public interest. Implicit in these arguments was the suggestion that the free market would better protect the public health and pocketbook than the regulated market system that had held sway for two centuries.[84] The *Herald* made this position explicit in 1842 when it recommended shopping at the (then still illegal) private meat shops, noting that "they undersell the regular butchers, and pay as much rent; besides, they are very convenient."[85]

Increasingly, the city government came to agree with this stance. In an 1842 meeting of the Common Council, one city alderman argued that the meat shops were necessary in the increasingly spread-out city and that "citizens will [not] allow themselves to be dragged for every pound of meat they want half a mile to market."[86] Residents agreed, continuing to petition the council to authorize provisional licenses for nonmarket butchers. More importantly, they voted with their feet, patronizing the shops near their homes—legal and illegal alike—and eschewing the public markets altogether.[87]

Finally, in 1843, the Common Council repealed the law that required that meats be sold only in the public markets. In so doing, the council effectively deregulated the retail side of the public markets, overturning centuries of civic oversight and centralization of New York's provisioning. The change to the markets followed practice rather than setting it. In other words, the city had paved the way for deregulation by failing to build new markets and opening space for butchers like Henry Cornell to operate illegal shops without punishment. Thus, when they finally legalized private meat shops, the municipal government was just formalizing an arrangement that had been operating informally for some time. After they became legal, the number of private meat shops exploded, from a handful to over five hundred shops by the 1850s. By midcentury, most New Yorkers purchased their meats from these private vendors.[88]

Many of the private meat shops were commodious and clean and offered convenient hours and delivery services to their customers. One such meat store was advertised for sale in the *New York Herald* in 1867. With its "splendid white oak figures; marble top counters and trays" and "desirable location," this "meat market" offered a significant contrast to the overcrowded, inconvenient public markets of downtown.[89] By the 1850s, the people most likely to frequent the public meat stalls were purchasers of large lots: the retail butchers who purchased meats wholesale at the markets and turned them over for sale in their retail stores, and the hoteliers and restaurateurs and boardinghouse keepers of the city. In a sign of the supremacy of the private meat shops, the city's newspapers began to include their inventory and prices in their weekly market reports.[90]

Butchers like Henry Cornell and Daniel Hyde and greengrocers like Charles Dusenberry began on the margins of the market economy, supplementary to the still-dominant public markets. But over time, they and other private food vendors moved to the center, replacing the market vendors altogether as a retail option. By the 1840s, many householders found it far more convenient and palatable to purchase their meats in the private shops rather than waking early and braving the increasing chaos of the public markets. Unlike the public markets where choice pickings were available from dawn until midmorning, local grocers had a good supply of foodstuffs throughout the day and in many cases were open until 10:00 p.m. In addition, the private shops provided services that the public stalls did not: delivery, later hours, and store credit. Retail food shops also came to distinguish themselves from the public markets by their comparatively calm, organized, and clean environments.[91]

Thus, John Pintard's habit of rising at dawn to visit the markets became a much less typical pattern for New Yorkers by the mid-nineteenth century. Individuals who shopped at the public markets increasingly came to be seen as quaint throwbacks. Thomas De Voe remarked on this reality. "The modern 'marketer,'" De Voe lamented, "will still occasionally observe some 'relics of the past,' who cling to the old custom taught them in their youth, perhaps, by an honored *sire*, who was not too proud to carry home a well-filled market basket, containing his morning purchase, which his purse or taste prompted him to select. These old fashioned ideas, alas! are all *lived down*."[92] Modern shoppers frequented local grocers and food purveyors for their provisions.

New York matron Caroline Dustan serves as an example. Dustan kept a record of her food-shopping excursions in the diary she kept in the 1850s and 1860s, much like John Pintard had done a generation before in letters to his daughter Eliza. Dustan's notations shed important light on the new food procurement patterns of mid-nineteenth century New Yorkers of means. Her habits are especially interesting when compared to Pintard's for they show some continuities but mostly changes to food shopping and eating from early national to midcentury Gotham. Like Pintard, Dustan was a woman of means with a varied diet. But thanks to her era, Dustan enjoyed a far greater range of foods than Pintard. Dustan recorded meals of roast beef, turkeys, ducks, and ham, lobster, veal pie, roast beef, shad, and lamb in season, fruits from strawberries to apples to pineapples, ice cream regularly in the summer, and candy and other sweets on various occasions.

Also like Pintard, Dustan had relationships of long-standing with a number of food purveyors. But Dustan had a greater variety of vendors to choose from—grocers, yes, but also confectioners, greengrocers, bakers, butchers, poulterers, and cake shops. The number of regular food sellers Dustan patronized dwarfed Pintard's two or three staple purveyors. In 1857 and 1864, Dustan regularly visited eight different grocers from whom she bought a range of foodstuffs, including butter—a frequent purchase—and cheese; produce like pumpkins, berries, muskmelons, apples, strawberries, tomatoes, lemons, pineapples, and other exotic fruits; crackers, eggs, rice, flour, cornmeal, and sugars. Dustan also received a regular meat supply from her grocers including beef, lamb, veal, turkeys, chickens, ham, and cured meats.[93] Thus, while Pintard's grocer supplied him with limited categories—primarily dairy products and preserved foods, Dustan's vendors offered her all kinds of groceries from dairy products to fruits to meats to dry provisions. While she mentioned the public markets, Dustan's relationship with them was the reverse of Pintard's. She bought most of her supplies at local retailers and supplemented on occasion with purchases at the public market. And on those occasions, she sent her servants to do her shopping at nearby Jefferson Market and, less frequently, the big wholesale markets downtown.[94]

In addition to her stable of grocers, Dustan had a number of regular specialty vendors including confectioners, bakers, and ice creameries. She purchased treats like jujubes, peppermint and lemon candy from confectioners Stuart's and Ridley's, both located downtown. And with surprising regularity, especially in the summer, Dustan bought ice cream from three different vendors—Pinsent's, Taylor's, and Lyon's. As for baked goods, Dustan found

Walduck's and Wall's to be the best source for cakes but purchased her pies at Turner's and donuts at Stewart's bakery.[95] Recourse to these vendors reflected another significant difference between Dustan and Pintard. Dustan enjoyed access to prepared and even manufactured goodies unavailable to Pintard. He too makes mention of baked goods and confections in his letters, but they are homemade by his daughter Louise, never purchased.[96] Dustan on the other hand not only purchased most of her sweets and treats but had several different specialty shops where she chose the best options for her table.

Dustan also took advantage of the conveniences these vendors provided, accepting food deliveries and keeping a credit account at various grocers, confectioners, and specialty shops.[97] For further convenience, she purchased items from hucksters and street peddlers who brought their baskets and carts to uptown neighborhoods to save residents a trip downtown to the markets. Each summer, Dustan dutifully reported on hearing strawberries, apples, raspberries, and other items "cried all day through the streets." Milk too arrived on a cart. While Pintard received his milk in barrels from the grocer, Dustan's milk was delivered to her door by the milkman who, on a particularly cold and snowy day in January 1857, delivered two days' worth of milk in case he could not get there the following day.[98]

Dustan was discerning about her vendors and their inventory. She was a careful shopper, comparing prices and quality of goods and commenting in her diary on whose butter was superior and whose was bitter, whose strawberries were expensive and whose were priced more reasonably. In her attention to these details, she was like Pintard, but she had a far greater range of options in terms of purveyors than he did a generation before, and she was able to vote with her pocketbook.[99]

The private shops also represented several layers of middlemen, unlike the one or two intermediaries at most between John Pintard and his food. Instead of the farmer-vendors of the early national period, antebellum commission agents, jobbers, retailers, and hucksters increasingly sold the agricultural goods that others produced. Householders developed relationships with local grocers, meat sellers, and fruiterers but in most cases, the proprietors of those shops were middlemen rather than producers. Thus, while Dustan had a personal relationship with her food vendors, a series of middlemen separated her from the original producer of the goods, some of which came from quite a distance. Certainly this was true of the itinerant fruit vendors who purchased their inventory from the public markets or even retailers, implying at least a four-to-five-degree separation between producer and consumer.

The distance was evident in other areas as well. Unlike Pintard, Dustan occasionally left the grocer's empty-handed because some provision—usually butter—had not yet arrived at the store. This situation occurred in November 1856 when the "boats had not come with butter" and in June 1857 when she went to the store for butter and learned that "rail butter came last week [but] was at depot still."[100] When the butter did not come in the following summer, Dustan's husband "went to look for Mrs. King's agent," suggesting that at least three middlemen (the agent, the grocer, and the dairyman) separated Dustan from her butter supply.[101] She also mentioned purchasing and eating foods from far away such as bananas, Havana oranges, and Nova Scotia salmon, implicitly acknowledging, even if she did not explicitly mention, or even consider, the various middlemen along the route.[102]

Clearly then, Dustan's food system was far more complex and varied than Pintard's. Her food-shopping habits show the distance food traveled, the separation between producer and consumer, and the reliance on local food retailers to provision the larders and pantries of New York's kitchens. Accounts by other New Yorkers of means show similar patterns. For example, like Dustan, Henry Ward Beecher visited his grocer for provisions when his wife and family went to the country, leaving him behind in Brooklyn. Beecher's grocer offered the same range of items as Dustan's purveyors. On his several trips to the local grocery, Beecher bought "six cantaloupes, as many tomatoes, and bread," as well as butter, eggs, salt and pepper, "a few crackers . . . and a few herrings," coffee and tea, sugar and milk. His grocer offered such a range of meats that Beecher was "staggered . . . a little" by the quantity available. But he settled on "two beefsteaks and five pounds of mutton-chop," which he had delivered to his home an hour later.[103]

In uptown neighborhoods, local provisions stores completely replaced the public markets. As Dr. Joel Ross explained in his 1851 description of New York: "It has become so fashionable to have a meat-shop on almost every corner and fruits and vegetables in almost every grocery, and fish and oysters well nigh swimming through the streets that our large markets are to some extent foresaken." Not just fashion but convenience guided these residents who could now "step out of their houses slipshod into an adjoining meat-stall, and step back again, almost at the same breath, to find the steaks all ready to leave the gridiron." This situation was especially suited to busy midcentury New Yorkers who "hardly have time to carve, or chew, or swallow, much less to go far to market," Ross concluded.[104]

By the end of the 1850s, a consensus had formed in favor of private food shops for householders. The New-York Times summed up the situation in a small item in 1858, explaining: "most market stuffs can be bought cheaper of the grocery stores two or three miles up town, and in the suburbs of Brooklyn, than of the retailers in either Fulton or Washington Market." According to the *Times*, private shops were not only more convenient and cheaper but "the purchaser is rather surer of an article of good quality in the places first named than in the markets."[105] This editorial reflects a complete reversal of the rhetoric about markets from the period of the early republic. While earlier observers had marveled about the quality of market produce, by midcentury such approval was reserved for private shops. Indeed, the *Times* became a major proponent of private food shops (or private markets, as the paper called them), going so far as to demand the abolition of the public-market system in favor of a network of private shops throughout the city.[106]

And what of the public markets? While private shops moved from the margins into the center of Gotham's food sales chain, the public markets did not disappear. To the contrary, they shifted to a wholesale function, serving as a central supplier for towns and cities within the United States and beyond as well as the restaurants, hotels, and retail food shops of Gotham.[107] Wholesale markets like Washington and Fulton thus continued to play a vital role in provisioning New Yorkers even though these residents rarely visited the markets personally.

In fact, the markets served a national and even international function as New York City became the central hub of the nation's export and reexport trades. Barges, wagons, sloops, and carts sidled up to the markets and unloaded goods bound for customers from New York City and the world. In 1853, sales at Washington Market—the largest in the nation—exceeded $28 million. Some individual market vendors enjoyed sales of over $200,000 per year.[108] Crowded, bustling, and spread out along several city blocks, the market took up a large portion of the lower west side of Manhattan. The old market structures held more than five hundred stalls, plus the dozens of booths that lined the sidewalks around the market structures. On landfill to the west of the original market stood "West Washington Market," which held an additional four hundred stands.[109]

Fulton Market, the city's second-largest wholesale depot was the city's fish market par excellence, supplying local customers, institutions, and even the vendors at Catharine and Washington Markets. Fulton was well suited to this purpose because of its position directly on the East River, convenient to the fishing "smacks" as the boats were called, which arrived daily laden with fish from local waters. About 150 water vessels arrived at the Fulton Market daily in 1853, carrying anywhere from 20 to 120 tons of live fish.

This 1866 image from *Harper's Weekly Magazine* shows the growth of Washington Market and its extension to the surrounding neighborhood. The expansion of the market is especially marked when contrasted with the 1829 image of Washington Market depicted in chapter 1. *Washington Market, New York City.* (Picture Collection, The New York Public Library, Astor, Lenox, and Tilden Foundations)

These smacks unloaded their cargo onto one of the two hundred "fish cars" lined up along the docks at Fulton Market, from which fish was dispensed to the market stands. Each car could hold about seven thousand pounds of fish.[110]

In addition, Fulton received shipments from commission dealers who transported fish to market from the New Jersey coast by steamboat to the New York market. Many of the boat owners also shared in one of the twelve fish stands in the market proper. They did an annual business of well over $1.1 million. In addition to the fish stands, Fulton Market had eight stands for the sale of shellfish such as clams, scallops, mussels, lobsters, and oysters, which were sold out of the shell to hungry patrons for immediate consumption. In all, the fish market at Fulton conducted a trade of close to $1.5 million per year in the early 1850s.[111]

Some intrepid individuals still bought fresh foods at the large public markets. But the bulk of market business transpired between midnight and 7:00 a.m. and catered to the wholesale trade. Washington Market butcher M. J. Sturges, for example, sold exclusively to "hotels, restaurants and private families who market largely," according to an 1860 advertisement. Sturges's customers included some of the most famous restaurants in New York, including Windust's, Gosling's, and Florence's, as well as several other market butchers and the Atlantic and Gardner Hotels.[112]

As in the early national period, the choicest shopping at the public markets still occurred very early in the morning. But now the task was completed not by individual householders or even their personal servants but by proprietors of and agents for the large hotels, groceries, restaurants, and meat shops of the city who perused the freshest, ripest, most delectable, and most expensive of the markets' offerings. In 1905, New Yorker John Sturtevant recollected half a century before, seeing the market gardeners head to Washington Market every day at around 4:00 p.m. to grab a space from which to sell their produce the next day. He wrote: "Lines of wagons from the Market Gardens within twenty miles of the city" thronged the streets around the markets. The farmers camped out near the market, sometimes paying someone to watch their cart while they caught some rest in a nearby hotel. For those seeking entertainment instead of sleep, nearby saloons stayed open all night to serve the country people. At 1:30 a.m. they hit the streets, "ready for the 'Green Grocers' who arrived about this time for their daily supplies."[113] Along with the truck farmers came the butchers bringing meat from the slaughterhouses.

Other wagons quickly followed, some loaded with poultry, game, fish, and other market goods but many of them empty, carrying agents and representatives of the greengroceries, meat shops, and food stores of the city and suburbs ready to load their wagons up and stock the shelves of their shops. At the break of dawn, the hoteliers and restaurateurs arrived. These shoppers for "the great hotels and caterers for the 'palatial mansions' gather up the choicest loins and most thoroughly perfect vegetables," explained *Appleton's Journal*, "and what is left, with the bloom of freshness gone, is turned over piecemeal to an humbler class of customers, and quite another set of dealers"—the secondhand vendors of fruits, vegetables, and meats.[114] By 8:00 or 9:00 a.m., the marketing was finished.

As *Appleton's* suggested, the hoteliers and restaurateurs chose the freshest and most novel items, not trusting the choices to agents or delivery services. Chronicles of the markets mentioned the fastidiousness of the city's fine restaurant and hotel keepers in exploring the choicest produce of the markets. (Interestingly, this reputation was in direct and marked contrast to the female boardinghouse keepers who were known for trying to find the cheapest that the market offered, which rarely was the best.) These accounts also indicate the volume of wholesale business conducted at the markets. An

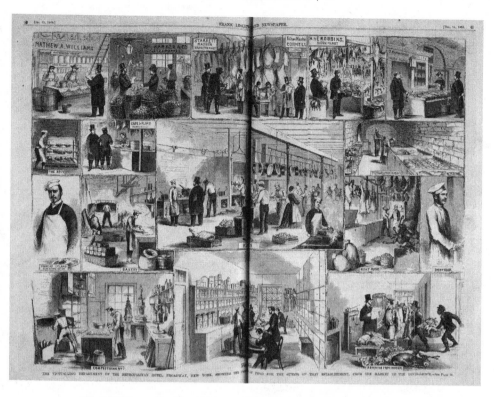

This 1860 illustration from *Frank Leslie's Illustrated Weekly Newspaper* shows the process of purchasing and preparing food for the hotel ordinary, from visiting the various stands at Washington Market to preparing the food in the various culinary departments of the hotel. *The Victualling Department of the Metropolitan Hotel, Broadway, New York.* (Courtesy, American Antiquarian Society)

1850 article in *Frank Leslie's Illustrated Newspaper* accompanied Warren Leland, the commissary-general at the Metropolitan Hotel, one of New York's best caravanseries, to Fulton Market for his daily visit. Beginning at four in the morning, the tour made stops at a butcher, poulterer, produce vendor, fishmonger and separate shellfish stand, a mutton seller, and a smoked meats purveyor. Leland bought thousands of items, including 544 pounds of beef loins and ribs, 372 pounds of turkeys, and 5,000 oysters. The quantity and variety of his purchases—made on a daily basis—show not only the abundance and variety in the markets—even in December—but also the abundance and breadth of hotel and restaurant cuisine.[115]

But most New York consumers were as removed from the displays of Fulton Market as they were from the kitchens of the Metropolitan Hotel. By the 1850s and accelerating past that point, New Yorkers' food supply and their relationship with it had been transformed. Long gone were the market patterns of the early national period, when individual householders rose with the sun to get to the market and find the choice pickings, meet directly with farmer-purveyors, and see foods only when they were locally in season. Now, New Yorkers bought food that was harvested, hunted, slaughtered, and packaged far away. And, if they could afford them, they enjoyed fresh delicacies year round.

Today the locavore movement has gained a following, and New Yorkers of a certain class place a value on having direct relationships with the farmers and producers of their foodstuffs. These concerns would have made no sense to New Yorkers of the eighteenth century, for whom all food was local. But in the nineteenth century, producer and consumer moved farther and farther away from each other. Midcentury New Yorkers purchased their food from local retailers, located in neighborhoods throughout the greatly enlarged metropolis. They rarely visited the public markets, which largely served a wholesale clientele and which presented an increasingly unpleasant environment for the individual purchaser. As a result, New Yorkers' relationship with the food they ate—and the individuals who grew, produced, and processed it—became increasingly distant both literally and figuratively. The foodways of midcentury New Yorkers were thus closer to our own than they were to those of their parents and grandparents.

This situation garnered attention in the popular press of the time. Some commentators already expressed nostalgia for the days when individual consumers had a more personal relationship with their food and food providers. *Leslie's Illustrated Newspaper*, for example, remarked that many New Yorkers had no sense at all of where their food came from, nor did they care. The offerings at Fulton Market, *Leslie's* noted, the "mountains of fish, flesh and fowl . . . are quite extraordinary, and the way they are constantly replenished would afford many interesting incidents, which would strangely surprise dull people, who literally pay no heed to where their food comes from, provided it gets safely and thoroughly cooked out of the kitchen."[116] Similarly, the *New-York Times* pointed out that "apart from those whose business brings them in direct contact with the market," very few people 'have any idea of what those great depots of meat and vegetables are, whence the inhabitants of the City obtain their daily dinners."[117] These assessments would have shocked an earlier generation of New Yorkers, who visited Fulton Market weekly or even daily.

*Leslie's* lamented the removal of the consumer from food production and processing and urged a visit to a public market—again, a quotidian event for earlier generations—to witness "a store of nature's wealth . . . that would astonish every one not initiated into the mysteries of feeding a great city." *Leslie's* wondered if the "dainty ladies" of the uptown districts "have ever seen vegetables, fish or flesh in their natural state—that is, unprepared for the table."[118] In another article, *Leslie's* congratulated the Astor House Hotel for establishing its own farm and dairy in the 1850s, noting that appetites were better and more healthily satisfied when people knew the derivation of their foodstuffs. "It adds no little keenness to our appetite," *Leslie's* remarked, "when we know that everything we eat is the produce of our own farm—that it is all fresh, pure, and consequently wholesome."[119] Again, this type of argument is strikingly modern and would have a place in many of today's contemporary periodicals. But the issue it addresses—the early industrialization of foodstuffs and the removal of producer from consumer—goes back well into the nineteenth century.

The press reflected the position of other New Yorkers, especially those whose livelihoods had been affected by the market transformations. Butcher Thomas De Voe's voice had the most reach thanks to his history of New York's public markets, *The Market Book*. In his volume, part chronicle and part lamentation, De Voe complained bitterly about changes to market laws and practices and the reliance of most New Yorkers on private shops over public markets for their daily needs. Of the meat shops, De Voe noted that they might carry the same meats as those displayed in the meat stalls of the public markets "but never the variety, quantity, or with the same chance for cheapness, or choice." Furthermore, De Voe suggested the public markets were best at safeguarding the public, asserting: "citizens and others can be best protected and accommodated in public markets . . . and more especially when the products are obtained from the first hands."[120]

Implicit in De Voe's critique was a sense of a lost style of life, a lack of connection between the consumer and his food. De Voe missed the disappearing custom of visiting the markets regularly, illustrated in John Pintard's letters to his daughter Eliza. No longer, De Voe sighed, did the householder visit the markets early, taking advantage of the opportunity to "select the *cuts* of meat wanted from the best animals; to meet the farmer's choice productions, either poultry, vegetables, or fruit, and *catch* the lively, jumping fish, which, ten minutes before, were swimming in the fish-cars." Instead, householders relied on servants, middlemen, and even paid market assistants who, in the market-oriented spirit of the times, bought from those that would "give them the largest percentages" rather than the highest quality.[121] De Voe also decried the lack of connection between the vendors and the food they sold, reserving his greatest derision for the local street peddlers whom he accused of either selling inferior goods to those available in the market, cheating their customers with "false-bottomed measures, short weights," or quickly retreating before purchasers detected that the articles they had just purchased were "stale or unfit."[122]

De Voe did not single out the immigrant background of many of these peddlers or the new butchers, but he certainly was aware that German and Irish immigrants dominated the grocery and, increasingly, the butchering trade in New York City. Even if implicit, the attack on street peddlers and unlicensed butchers was a recognition of a changing food landscape in New York City, not just in terms of the derivation of the product but in terms of the ethnicity of the vendors and purveyors, a shift from native-born dominance of the trades to immigrant control. This dominance paralleled the population of the city itself as the nineteenth century progressed.[123]

Perhaps the most iconic New York butcher of the nineteenth century, Bill "the Butcher" Poole, serves as an example of this transformation. Scholars have accurately analyzed Bill the Butcher's life and, especially, his death as a symbol of native-ethnic tensions and the rough-and-tumble nature of working-class life and culture in antebellum New York City.[124] But Bill Poole represents even larger forces in the city's political economy, serving to illustrate the transition from a preindustrial, artisan economy and culture to an industrializing, laissez-faire one.

Poole's life and career trajectory hewed to traditional patterns of artisanal experience in New York and other communities in the early national period. At eight years old, Poole followed his late father into the butcher's trade, entering into an apprenticeship with Washington Market butcher William Berriman around 1831. Poole's apprenticeship with Berriman presumably offered the young orphan a means of support and oversight. After finishing his apprenticeship, Poole gained a butcher's license from the city. In 1847, William Poole, butcher, appears for the first time in the City Directory. The following year, he obtained his own stand in Clinton Market and, by 1850, procured a lease for stand number 10 in the prestigious Washington Market.[125] Poole's ability to garner a stall in the competitive market where the supply of licensed butchers greatly exceeded the number of market stalls likely owed to his social and political connections. Poole forged these connections in part through his family's generations-long inclusion in New York's butchering community. In this way, Poole served as a throwback to the past. (Incidentally, so too did Thomas De Voe, whose father and brothers were all butchers as well.)

But the future had arrived by 1843, when the city abandoned its centuries-old market laws and traditions and sanctioned the opening of private meat shops, operated by retail butchers. When the municipal government overturned these laws, it made official what had been customary for years. Beginning in the early nineteenth century, unlicensed butchers began taking advantage of loopholes in the market laws and an increasingly laissez-faire position on the part of the city government vis-à-vis the public markets. These artisans operated a network of private shops in newer neighborhoods on the city's edges. Many of these shops' owners were immigrants, recently arrived to the city from Germany, Ireland, and other ports. While they had trained in the butcher's trade in their home countries, they did not rise, as Bill Poole did, through the artisan butchers' community of New York. Thus, they did not have the connections that aided Poole and his colleagues in obtaining stalls in the public markets or breaking into the social world of the city's butchers and so resorted to opening shops outside of the market networks.

We cannot know whether Poole's nativism stemmed from his resentment toward the encroachment of foreign-born competitors into the butcher's trade. Some New York artisans saw the de-skilling of their trades during the antebellum period and blamed the deterioration of their craft not on large economic and technological forces but on foreign competition for jobs.[126] But butchering remained a highly skilled trade in the mid-nineteenth century and could yield a fine living for its practitioners. Poole himself was relatively well off, maintaining his stall in Washington Market, as well as a saloon on Broadway and Howard Street, and his private residence on Christopher Street in Greenwich Village, "one of a neat row of small brick houses, respectable outside and comfortable within," according to the *New-York Daily Times*.[127]

Nonetheless, while Poole and his colleagues remained financially stable, there was no question that their trade and its place in the city's political economy were transformed over the first half of the nineteenth century. By 1855, the year of Poole's death, the licensed butchers had lost their sanctioned monopoly over meat sales in New York City and with it their vaunted position at the top of the public-market hierarchy. The market butchers still maintained a good livelihood but faced significant competition from private, neighborhood-based butchers, many of them foreign-born. The public demanded options closer to home in private shops rather than be limited to the increasingly cacophonous and chaotic public markets. And the municipal government, rather than seeing the public markets and their vendors as a public good worth protecting, increasingly ignored their own market laws and structures and opened the way for a proliferation of private, extra-market food sellers throughout the city.

These changes both stemmed from and reflected a significantly enlarged food economy in antebellum New York City. Thanks to transportation and technological change, the city's markets had grown in just a few decades from local suppliers into food wholesalers to the nation, drawing and centralizing foodstuffs from around the country and even the world. These developments in turn affected where New Yorkers got their food, both in wholesale and retail terms, as well as the lives and livelihoods of those who produced it. New York's food revolution was under way.

# THREE

# "Monuments of Municipal Malfeasance": The Flip Side of Dietary Abundance, 1825–1865

In the middle of the nineteenth century, *Harper's Weekly* magazine proclaimed New York City's food markets the best in the world. "From its metropolitan situation," the article explained, "New York City . . . has greater facilities for obtaining every kind of provision, and in quantities that surfeit the demand." Everything, in short, "that can appeal to and gratify the epicurean sense," was made available in New York's markets by the technological marvels of the early nineteenth century.[1] And yet, while the public markets were overflowing with beautiful and abundant foodstuffs, the setting for that produce was abominable. The *Harper's* reporter who marveled at the superiority of New York's market offerings called the market buildings "a disgrace to the city." And journalist Junius Browne offered a similar assessment: "The domestic markets of New-York are the best, and the market-houses the worst, in the country," he wrote. "They remind one of delicate and delicious viands served on broken and unwashed dishes and soiled table-cloths."[2] By the 1840s, this kind of criticism of the markets was uniform and overwhelming.

Thus, New York City's nineteenth-century food supply embodied a paradox. Thanks to technological and industrial developments, New Yorkers had access to a more abundant, varied, and reliable food supply than ever before. By midcentury, New York was the wholesale food center of the nation; its residents reaped the benefits of this development. The wealthiest New Yorkers enjoyed the most varied diet but the new abundance touched all but the very poorest. And yet, these benefits were unevenly spread. More than a generation before Mark Twain coined the phrase "the Gilded Age," New York had developed into a city of marked contrasts. These contrasts were part and parcel of the city's growth into a metropolis and related to how and where people lived and worked, and what and how they ate.

During the first half of the nineteenth century, New York City experienced the greatest period of demographic growth in its history. The city's population doubled every decade, mainly due to immigration, especially from Ireland and Germany. The commercial and industrial sectors exploded, and Gotham's economy suffered the boom-bust vagaries of early industrial capitalism. The city's social structure reflected capitalism's extremes as well. The middle class and the wealthy saw a rising standard of living and access to conveniences unknown to their parents and grandparents. But the disparities between the haves and have-nots grew evermore stark in antebellum New York, and the food supply reflected the imbalance.

Demographic growth, along with transportation improvements like the omnibus and street railroad, contributed to the geographic spread of the city as well. Middle-class and working-class neighborhoods emerged in northern neighborhoods like Greenwich Village, Gramercy Park, and Chelsea. And the old walking city ceded to a spatially stratified metropolis. The stratification of neighborhoods according to class and function occurred simultaneous with and coincidental to the deregulation of the public markets and the privatization of food retailing. Class and geography thus worked together to determine the quality of the food supply to which an individual New Yorker had access. By the 1840s, gross disparities existed in terms of the environment and inventory of private food shops. Wealthy and middle-class New Yorkers could frequent fine grocery stores in their uptown neighborhoods and, if they had the means, could access an unprecedented variety and abundance of foodstuffs. But poor and working-class New Yorkers, whose ranks were ever growing in the second half of the nineteenth century, had far fewer options. Tenement groceries were often glorified liquor stores. The food they did sell was notoriously adulterated, tainted, and rotted, as was the merchandise of many street peddlers, scavenged from the markets and streets and sold in the poorer wards of the city.

The public markets, once celebrated as civic treasures, became symbols of municipal corruption in the mid-nineteenth century. They offered the most abundant and diverse array of fresh food in the world. But distribution channels were poor and by the time the food traveled out of the market and onto the tables of New Yorkers, it was often a far inferior article to what it originally had been. Furthermore, as the distance between producer and consumer grew wider, middlemen stepped in, driving up the prices of foodstuffs so that New York offered the most diverse and abundant of options but also the most expensive. Again, those with the means could afford a cornucopia, but those without experienced a declining rather than an improving food supply in the nineteenth century.

Worse than the neglect on the part of the municipal government or individual food vendors was the outright corruption and malfeasance that contributed to the disparities in the food supply. Filthy slaughterhouses in the center of city neighborhoods, incidents of market-cornering that drove up prices of both common and luxury food items, a complete lack of regulation of private food shops, and food scandals that highlighted both corrupt government practices and the shocking disregard of the city's industrial food producers were emblematic of the era and of the unsavory flip side of abundance.

Class and social status had always determined one's access to food, of course. Even in the eighteenth century when the public markets had served all New Yorkers, only the wealthiest could afford the best the markets had to offer. But two things happened in the nineteenth century to make the contrasts starker. First, the middle and upper classes experienced a significantly better standard of living than their parents and grandparents. Comforts and conveniences such as gas lighting, plumbing, heating, and even refrigeration became available to New Yorkers of means over the first half of the nineteenth century. But the poorest New Yorkers were excluded. Their neighborhoods and homes grew increasingly crowded, and the living conditions worsened at the same time that middle-class and wealthy homes and neighborhoods improved.[3]

Second, as the food supply grew more complex, those with access to cash and fine-food suppliers were in a far better position than those with little money and a reliance on tenement grocers and street peddlers. To reiterate, in the eighteenth century, all New Yorkers had shopped at the same public markets. They did not purchase the same items or even shop at the same time; rather the root of the food supply was shared, and it was regulated by the city. But in the nineteenth century, the city abandoned strict regulation of the markets. The result was a free-for-all. When the city intervened in the markets, it was often to line the pockets of the members of the increasingly corrupt municipal government, which took advantage of the market fee structure to enrich itself and Tammany Hall. Aside from government neglect and corruption, the rapid growth of the city contributed to problems with the food supply, including distribution bottlenecks and inadequate market accommodations. Thus, the quality of the food at the source worsened for poorer New Yorkers compared to their wealthier counterparts. As New York developed into a metropolis, its food supply was characterized by limitations as much as possibilities.

By the 1850s, New York City was home to over two thousand groceries. These stores represented a significant range, from the fancy shops of Broadway to the tenement groceries of Five Points, which served more liquor than fresh food. Deregulation, city growth, and government neglect contributed to a real disparity in the quality of New York's food shops and their inventory in the antebellum era. In some respects, these developments adversely affected overall food quality and access even for those of means. For example, deregulation of the butchers led to less oversight of the meat supply in general. Consumers of all stripes thus had to be more zealous in inspecting their own meats for purchase.[4]

But more than ever before, geography and social class were intertwined in the antebellum city. And since residents now purchased food in shops near their homes rather than at the public markets, the geography of food provisioning was class specific as well. As is the case today, poorer wards had insufficient options in terms of food shops compared to middle-class and elite neighborhoods. The Fourth Ward, for example, had one "place where articles of food are sold" for every 164 inhabitants. But the ward housed one liquor store for every eight inhabitants. In 1851, each block of the notorious Five Points slum housed an average of twelve stores that sold liquor. As a point of comparison, the notably salubrious Fifteenth Ward, located in and around Greenwich Village, had half the number of "drinking shops" as the Fourth Ward but several "well kept private markets," according to a report by the Citizens' Association.[5]

Drinking shops, private markets, liquor stores, groggeries, groceries. The terminology became muddled as the nineteenth century progressed. In part, this confusion was linked to the transformation of the image of the grocer as he moved into the center of food retailing in New York City. In the eighteenth century, grocers were neutral figures, selling dry goods, sundries, and preserved foodstuffs from local and foreign sources as well as wines and liquors. But with the nineteenth-century temperance movement and the geographic stratification of the city, the grocer's image changed. Increasingly he was portrayed as a nefarious figure who plied his customers with adulterated liquor and other vices. A distinction arose between "family grocers" and liquor grocers. The first group sold a range of fresh produce, meats, and dairy products as well as grains, coffee, teas, and other dried and preserved foodstuffs. They might still *sell* liquors and wines but, if they wanted to maintain a reputable grocery, they would not *serve* alcoholic beverages on the premises. A few industrious grocers even advertised themselves as "temperance groceries," avoiding liquor sales altogether.[6]

The very terminology applied to the antebellum grocer reflects the class associations drawn around liquor, temperance, and even family at this time. The geographic stratification the city was experiencing was rooted not only in spatial and population growth but also in the formation of particular and distinct working-class and middle-class cultures. While the idealized middle-class culture was organized around family and home, male working-class culture and conviviality often focused around the saloon and grog-shop. While it had a working-class component, the temperance movement, like most antebellum reform movements, was dominated by the middle class and promoted bourgeois values such as moderation and self-control.[7] Thus, the terms "family" and "temperance" in the description of certain groceries were not neutral but rather value- and class-laden associations.

Contemporaries understood these associations and shared a mostly unwritten understanding about the distinction between "family groceries" or provisions stores and the corner groceries, which were just another name for grogshops. The New-York Tribune made this distinction explicit when it responded to a complaint from a reader that its forthcoming feature on the "liquor groceries" would paint even the reputable among these businesses in a poor light. The Tribune responded that it would go forth with its story on the liquor groceries, explaining: "No one will be green enough to confound a regular family grocery or provision store with the liquor grocery. The real family grocer sells no liquor at his counter." In the same paper, an advertisement offering a "family grocery" business for sale stipulated: "Will not be let for a rum-shop."[8] Likewise, in reviewing the sanitary conditions of the notably healthful—and wealthy—Twelfth District in Greenwich Village, sanitary inspector F. A. Burrall, MD, asserted that the corner groceries "exert[ed] the worst influence . . . upon the health of the community." But among the "mostl[y] commodious," and even "some spacious and elegant" stores, he counted "49 groceries of all kinds," assuming his reader instinctively understood the difference between the corner and reputable groceries.[9]

In fact, so common were the family groceries that few contemporary descriptions of them exist, unlike their more seamy corner-grocery cousins. But references to "spacious," "respectable," or "elegant" groceries were frequent in the press. And fine or family grocers advertised themselves as such. For example, in their review of holiday advertisements offering holiday gifts for sale, both the Times and the Tribune included a section on "Groceries, Confectionary, &c." These establishments offered "Fruit, Teas, Figs, Almonds, Chocolate, Coffee, Cheese &c. wherewith to fix up 'the table,'" and "fresh fruit from the tropics, the dried substantials of southern Europe, the fancy fabrics of our sugar workers &c. &c." Likewise, among the retail stores on the ground floor of the Fifth Avenue Hotel was William H. Jackson & Co., grocers, "the largest retail grocery in the country." No Five Points rookery, this fine shop "comprises a stock of the choicest articles to be found in the market," including "the many little delicacies so desirable in travelling," an ad extolled. The hotel shop catered to the traveling public while Jackson & Co. had a separate uptown branch on Twenty-First Street and Sixth Avenue for a more local clientele.[10]

Distinct from these respectable groceries were the "liquor groceries" that dotted the poorer wards of New York. These establishments sold drinks by the glass, which patrons imbibed on the premises, and took advantage of loopholes in blue laws that allowed grocers but not saloons to operate on Sundays. At the end of the grocery counter in these establishments would be found the "inevitable bar," one account explained, where each person who entered would indulge in a "consolatory drink."[11] Grocers often served adulterated liquor: straight alcohol colored to look like brandy or cognac or some other libation. Tenement districts abounded with these groceries and, indeed, a surfeit of groceries was one marker of a slum neighborhood, much like a concentration of liquor stores is a marker of poor neighborhoods in today's cities. This situation prevailed even as early as the 1820s, as George Catlin's famous image of the Five Points slum demonstrates. Notice the number of "grocery" signs affixed to the buildings on the famous five-point intersection.[12]

In fact, many corner groceries were essentially bars that sold foodstuffs as well. These shops contained some food and other sundries: "A few maggoty hams and shoulders, half-a-dozen bunches of lard candles melted into one, some strings of dried onions, a barrel No. 3 mackerel, some pipes and tobacco," according to journalist George Foster. But "above all," Foster explained, they offered "two barrels of whisky—one colored red with oak juice and sold for 'first-rate Cognac brandy,' and the other answering with the most limpid assurance to the various demands for gin, Monongahela (whiskey) or schnapps." German immigrant Frederick Bultman described his cousin's Five Points Grocery where he stayed upon his arrival to New York in 1850. "The volume of business on the grocery end of the store was rather small but the other end of it was equal to a little gold mine," he explained.[13]

Evenings at the corner groceries gave up any pretense to food provisioning. After 10:00 p.m., the *New-York Times* noted in its "Walks among the New-York Poor," "the corner groceries are crowded with drunk parties, op-

This famous image of the Five Points intersection by artist George Catlin shows
the large number of grocery-groggeries in the area. *Five Points, 1827.*
By George Catlin. (Collection of the New-York Historical Society)

erating as makeshift saloons." George Foster indicated that the groceries
turned into saloons and all-night gambling dens "as soon as the shutters
are closed at night."[14]

Author Frank Beard offered another evening scene at the liquor groceries in his 1866 exposé *The Night Side of New York,* describing the Avenue A
grocery of Mike Lynch. Beard's description suggests the permanency of the
bar, which "runs the depth of the room . . . its bright slab . . . a solitary, carefully polished oasis in this desert of dirt and rust." A screen separated the
bar from the back room, which served as a saloon. The clientele of the grocery consisted of "newly-fledged thieves; hardened rogues; souls that have
blood on them; dirt-begrimed menders of the highway. . . . Young roughs,
haggard with the furors of dissipations. . . . Old men, silvered with hoary
locks . . . grinning with toothless gums." This "motley-dressed band" was
gathered for the entertainment of a bloody cockfight. Beard's exposé also
points to the strong connections between the groceries and the increasingly
rough-and-tumble politics of the city. "Mike Lynch" (a pseudonym) was not
only the owner of this particular grocery but also "an ex-city official, a rov-
ing politician [and] a foreman of the late fire department." Liquor groceries
hosted vices other than drinking, gambling, and blood sports. They also
drew in prostitutes, according to George Foster, "who fortify themselves
with alcohol for their nightly occupation."[15]

The prostitution, gambling, and drinking that occurred in these shops offended middle-class propriety, and middle-class reformers and observers maligned the tenement groceries. But for the residents of immigrant neighborhoods, especially Irish-born New Yorkers who had fled unrelenting famine, these shops offered unimaginable gustatory plenty, even if the quality of that abundance was low by middle-class standards. In a discussion of Crown's Five Points Grocery that he wrote for the *Tribune*, George Foster described the overcrowded quarters and substandard food of the infamous establishment. But he also suggested abundance in describing the "piles of cabbages, potatoes, squashes, eggplants, tomatoes, turnips, eggs, dried apples, chestnuts and beans [that] rise like miniature mountains round you." "The cross-beams that support the ceiling" Foster continued, "are thickly hung with hams, tongues, sausages, strings of onions and other light and airy articles, and at every step you tumble over a butter-firkin or a meal-bin." And the packed shelves were "filled with an uncatalogueable jumble of candles, allspice, crackers, sugar and tea, pickles, ginger, mustard, and other kitchen necessaries."[16]

Furthermore, the groceries served as important points of social and political contact in the growing immigrant wards of the city. Grocery owners—like their saloon-owning counterparts to whom they were closely aligned—were linchpins of the immigrant working-class community. Owning a grocery along with running a saloon and heading a volunteer fire company were among the routes to power in the nineteenth-century political machine. Mike Lynch, the pseudonymous owner of the Avenue A groggery mentioned above, was one of a number of city officials involved in the grocery trade. When Tammany politicians and ward bosses visited Five Points or the Tenth Ward, they stopped at the groceries to meet their constituents. Fernando Wood, Tammany politician and mayor of New York in the 1850s, and himself a former grocery owner, would go "among his constituents in the lower parts of New York" and "[hold] his levees in beer saloons and Dutch groceries," a guide to New York's sunshine and shadows explained. And while the groceries' entertainments offended the sensibilities of middle-class reformers, they offered an important social outlet to their patrons.[17]

All that said, the food that the corner groceries sold *was* frequently second-rate, spoiled and stale, and of questionable nutritional value. An article in the reform journal, *Harbinger*, complained of the "liquor groceries'" stock: "The butter, eggs, lard, salt fish and meat sold here are . . . generally stale and rancid, unfit to sustain life, and highly conducive to disease, and constantly keeping the neighborhood predisposed to take the first epidemic that arrives, in its worst and most malignant form." Years later, sanitary inspector Dr. Ezra Pulling reported on the grocery found in the notorious Gotham Court tenement in the Fourth Ward slum. The food for sale included "partially-decayed vegetables, rather suspicious looking solids, bearing respectively the names of butter and cheese, and decidedly suspicious fluid bearing the name of milk," as well as beer and liquor.[18]

Sanitary reformers blamed the tenement groceries for contributing to epidemic rates of disease and mortality in poorer neighborhoods by selling rotted fruits, vegetables, and meats. Reporting on conditions in the overcrowded, poverty-stricken Fourth Ward, located east of city hall, near today's Chatham Square, Dr. Pulling claimed that the food for sale in these establishments was "unfit for human sustenance." Among the items he singled out as particularly problematic were decaying pickled herring, left out in buckets in the open air; rotted vegetables; "sausages not above suspicion"; and "horrible pies, composed of stale and unripe fruits." Pulling and his colleagues blamed the small groceries and their rotting merchandise for epidemic malnutrition and a variety of gastrointestinal disorders.[19]

In addition, reformers and other middle-class observers blamed the liquor groceries for a host of evils found in tenement districts, from violence to gambling to disease. Located at the center of social life in tenement neighborhoods, these establishments contributed to the neighborhood "grow[ing] filthier and filthier, and its inhabitants more besotted and depraved," George Foster wrote. The very fact that the groceries were a center for food purchases and also sold liquor made them problematic. As Foster lamented: "They afford facilities for drunkenness to thousands of husbands, wives, and children, who otherwise might not be tempted." The easy pickings, in other words, encouraged dissipation.[20]

Liquor grocers also came under attack for extorting their poverty-stricken customers since they retailed items by the piece instead of in bulk, driving up the price of an item by as much as three to four times, or more. Patrons were lulled into paying usurious prices because, as George Foster explained, they lived "from hand to mouth," buying food and liquor "not only from day to day, but literally from hour to hour." In addition to the high markups, liquor groceries were renowned for cheating customers at the scale through false weights and sticky measures that held on to a portion of the purchase.[21]

The groceries were not the only institutions that reformers critiqued. The pushcarts and peddlers who sold food largely to the poor were also singled out. Reformers ascribed the high mortality rates in antebellum New York City to these unsanitary food vendors and the rotted, stale, and otherwise unhealthy food they offered for sale. Reformers blamed the carts for a host of gastrointestinal issues, including cholera, diarrhea, and dysentery.[22]

These reformers were concerned about the food supply of poorer New Yorkers in terms of its quality but also its conditions of sale. In fact, an interesting cultural trope developed during this period whereby the environment in which one made purchases (food or otherwise) served as a class marker. More specifically, purchasing food, clothing, and other goods from peddlers and carts became the province of the working classes and the poor while the middle and upper classes made their purchases indoors. This distinction did not exist in the colonial and early republican periods, especially not for food since the public markets—which were by definition outdoors—serviced the food needs of all New Yorkers, regardless of class. But as food sales became privatized and neighborhood-focused, more privileged New Yorkers were serviced by indoor shops—fine, private grocers and even private indoor markets. Meanwhile, the streets of the poorer neighborhoods were filled with pushcarts and street vendors who sold inferior merchandise at lower prices.

This situation did not only apply to food. The wealthy also purchased clothing, dry goods, and consumer products in private shops and even early department stores such as A. T. Stewart's Marble Palace, where the shopping environment became as important as the merchandise. Their less fortunate counterparts, meanwhile, purchased a variety of goods from the pushcarts and peddlers in their tenement neighborhoods.

This indoor-outdoor class distinction was not lost on contemporaries, who in fact confirmed their own biases in their descriptions of outdoor food options. For example, Junius Browne described the varied merchandise of the ubiquitous street vendors of New York City, who offered "every kind of low-priced article, from a dog-eared volume to a decayed peanut." Browne was careful to locate these vendors geographically on "Park Row and Bowery," declaring "those quarters . . . the best adapted for street-venders, who in Broadway rarely find purchasers except among strangers and the transient class that believe they must buy something when they come to the Babel of Manhattan."[23] In other words, the outside vendors were located geographically and symbolically in the city's working-class quarters. Likewise, the *Times* noted that food purchased outside in the Bowery was cheaper than in Broadway shops but "surer to bring on a cholera morbus."[24]

A second-generation Italian New Yorker recalled that unlike nonimmigrant families, "we had a bread man . . . and a fruit and vegetable man, a watermelon man and a fish man. . . . Americans went to the stores for most of their food—what a waste."[25] This account highlights both the indoor-

STALE-VEGETABLE DEALER.

STALE-MEAT BUYER.

These 1872 images from *Appleton's Journal* editorialize about the honesty of market vendors and the poor quality of their foodstuffs. The first depicts a "Stale-Vegetable Dealer," the second a "Stale-Meat Buyer." (Courtesy, American Antiquarian Society)

outdoor class distinction *and* the very different perspective immigrant and working-class shoppers had of their shopping options compared with that of middle-class reformers. Where one group saw opportunity and abundance, the other saw rot and filth. This distinction was not completely cut-and-dried, of course. Itinerant vendors of fresh foods visited the wealthier neighborhoods of the city, as Caroline Dustan's diary attests. Dustan recorded hearing the street peddlers crying "Strawberries!" and "Raspberries!" through her Greenwich Village neighborhood in the 1850s. But Dustan made the vast majority of her food purchases from private indoor shops rather than street vendors. In tenement wards, the situation was reversed.

In truth, many middle-class reformers saw rot and filth even in the food supply available to New Yorkers of means. For example, proponents of regulation argued that the city's laissez-faire attitude compromised the quality of the meat supply. Even before the city changed the market laws to allow private meat sales, the Common Council's Market Committee complained that the (still-illegal but clearly sanctioned) private meat shops offered inferior meats. "In several instances," the committee explained, "the carcasses of animals which have died, either from disease or some natural cause, have been cut up and offered for sale at some of the shops."[26] After the licensing changes, the situation worsened as the city failed to inspect even the public-market butchers. According to the superintendent of markets in 1847, fewer than half of the city's 426 private meat shops paid their fees and kept up their licensing. The situation was exacerbated by the city's decentralized slaughterhouse system, making inspection of meat processing as inefficient as that of finished meats.[27]

While some market butchers sold substandard meats, by far the worst sanitary conditions existed in the tenement groceries and the pushcarts that sold food mainly in tenement districts, where the poorest New Yorkers lived. And the cheapest cuts of meat were also likely to be the lowest quality so the poor suffered disproportionately as a result of price point as well. While no prior golden age of meat quality existed, meat selling and quality control clearly grew more complex after the city altered its market laws in the mid-nineteenth century. This complexity undoubtedly contributed to increasing disparities in the quality of food available to poor New Yorkers and their wealthier counterparts and the need for more discernment in general for the meat shopper concerned about quality.[28]

Substandard meat was certainly a problem. The tainted product that evinced the loudest and most sustained concern, however, was milk. By the early nineteenth century, the city was urban enough that backyard cows were a relic of the past and New Yorkers relied upon regional dairies for their milk products. Westchester, Orange, and Ulster Counties were the mainstays for milk production in the early national period and were joined by parts of the Mohawk and Saratoga Counties after the opening of the Erie Canal. But, increasingly in the nineteenth century, dairies within the city limits supplied milk to New York City households. These dairies were usually attached to distilleries, and the cows were fed the cheapest and most convenient food their owners could find: slop that was made up of the mashed grain waste of the distillery, and kitchen scraps culled from the city's garbage. Distillery cows lived in crowded and dirty conditions and received no exercise and limited air. Distillery dairies were found throughout New York City and Brooklyn but by the 1850s, the two largest in New York were Johnson's Distillery and Stables at Sixteenth Street on the Hudson River and Moore's on Thirty-Ninth Street between Tenth and Eleventh Avenues.[29]

Distillery cows were decidedly unhealthy. The bovines suffered from rotten teeth, soft hooves, ulcerated bodies, patchy hides, and crowded conditions. In a very modern twist, the cows received inoculation against a common cattle disease that no doubt was exacerbated by their crowded and unsanitary environment. Cows often developed an infection at the injection site known as "stump tail." According to one report: "The marks of a slop-fed cow are so distinct, that were an inmate of the Sixteenth-street stables to

These woodcuts from *Frank Leslie's Illustrated Weekly Newspaper* illustrated the newspaper's 1858 exposé of the swill-milk dealers. They show the exterior and interior of Moore's distillery stables at Thirty-Ninth Street and Tenth Avenue and the sickly condition of the cows. (Courtesy, American Antiquarian Society)

This illustration from *Frank Leslie's Illustrated Weekly Newspaper* shows the progression of the condition of cows' hooves, from the healthy one on the left to the typical swill cow hoof on the right. (Courtesy, American Antiquarian Society)

escape, she might, like a State-prison convict, be detained and brought back by a stranger without advertisement or description of the fugitive."[30]

New Yorkers with the means and inclination could contract with dairies outside of the city to get their milk. But the majority of the milk came from within the city limits. The railroads, which allowed for the quick carriage of fresh milk to the city from the country, did introduce more "country milk" into the city but the distillery dairies increased even more quickly. Plus they sold a cheaper variety of milk than the country dairies so they were the only option for the city's poorer households. The milk industry notoriously engaged in fraudulent practices. Even some carts that purportedly carried milk produced on upstate farms in fact sold distillery milk, procured within the city limits and falsely labeled. An 1853 report on the milk supply in New York found that New Yorkers consumed almost one hundred million quarts of milk per year. About thirteen million of these quarts were transported by railroad from the upstate counties. The remaining eighty-seven million quarts were supplied by distillery dairies. The report estimated that four thousand cows were stabled in the city of New York for commercial milk production, half in distillery stables and the other half in cheap stables throughout the city. They were universally fed a diet of distillery slop, twenty-five to thirty gallons per day, the report asserted.[31]

If the owners had supplemented the swill with grain and hay, the cows' diet may have been sufficient to offer a decent milk supply. But owners saw little profit and therefore little incentive to offer the cows any food other than the distillery slop. The distillery milk thus was contaminated at the source. Dealers made it worse by doctoring the milk to improve its appearance, adding water, colorants, chalk, flour, starch, magnesia, molasses, and even eggs. Worse yet, according to one agricultural journal, some city grocers "literally manufacture the milk . . . 'out of the whole cloth,'" using watered-down cornmeal mixed with a drop or two of milk. In many cases, they then loaded it onto carts labeled "Pure Milk" or "Orange County Milk" and delivered it to homes and grocers throughout the city. On occasion, these distilleries even sold milk to dairies in Orange County as well as Long Island and New Jersey. The horrors of swill milk did not stop with the milk itself. Once they dropped dead from their poor diet, harsh treatment, and cramped living conditions, distillery cows were sometimes slaughtered and their meat sold to grocers, meat shops, and even market butchers.[32]

Amazingly, the distillery dairies operated out in the open. The fact that cows fed on a diet of distillery waste was not in and of itself scandalous. The owners and operators of the distillery dairies, along with many city officials, defended the quality of the milk produced in their establishments. But reformers, doctors, and health professionals had expressed concern for decades about the poor quality of the milk sold to New Yorkers. The outcry against tainted milk began in earnest in the late 1830s.[33] In 1841, reformer Robert Hartley, the secretary of the Society for Improving the Condition of the Poor, wrote a treatise on milk that included a condemnation of the swill-milk industry. Hartley pronounced the acceptance of swill milk as an equal article to the milk produced by grass-fed country cows, "a fatal delusion." Indeed, Hartley suggested that until he exposed the distillery dairies in a series of articles that he had published in 1836 and 1837, the public had never even considered the issue at all. By the 1840s, he argued, "the public has been *beguiled* into the support of the slop-milk business." He continued: "Its mischiefs were not even suspected," for "who could have imagined, that under the disguise of so bland and necessary an article as milk, was lurking disease and death?"[34]

The milk that the distillery cows produced was clearly (to medical professionals and reformers) inferior. The liquid was spiked with alcohol, and so thin and devoid of cream that it could not even be made into butter or cheese. Doctors blamed swill milk for a host of medical issues, including dysentery, diarrhea, and a range of other gastrointestinal disorders as well as compromised immunity in general. Anyone who drank swill milk suffered from its effects. But children paid a disproportionate cost, based on the amounts of milk they drank and their increased susceptibility to illness, given their still-developing immune systems. Doctors decried not only the swill-milk vendors but also the mothers who relied on cows' milk instead of nursing their children. Reformers and doctors blamed swill milk in part for the extraordinarily high childhood mortality rate in the city—one in five children died in infancy.[35]

The children of the poor were especially vulnerable since middle-class and wealthy families could afford to order weekly deliveries from the farms of Westchester and Orange Counties, sources (usually) of truly pure milk. In a letter to *Leslie's Illustrated Newspaper*, which launched an exposé into the swill-milk industry in 1858, Dr. Edward H. Parker noted that the children in his private practice did not ingest swill milk. But he did treat patients at a public dispensary, including "1500 children of the poorer classes—just those whose parents are most likely to be purchasers of . . . impure milk." In some cases, the families were so poor that even swill milk was out of range except for infants, for whom it was their primary source of "nutrition." Not surprisingly, the meat of distillery cows was also far more likely to land on the tables of the poor rather than middle-class or wealthy New Yorkers who, as a rule, purchased their meats from more reputable sources.[36]

These types of practices—selling tainted and spoiled food, cheating customers, inflating prices—were exactly the justification behind the municipal oversight of the food supply from the seventeenth through the early nineteenth century. But the mid-nineteenth-century city government was far less interested in regulating its markets and food vendors than its predecessors. By the mid-nineteenth century, the traditional, patrician government of the early republic was replaced by a machine-dominated politics, reliant on immigrant voters and other recently enfranchised groups. Tammany Hall—the main Democratic machine—solidified its position with the election of Fernando Wood as mayor in 1854. Other political groups vied with the club for power, sometimes successfully, including the rival Mozart Hall, which Tammany defector Wood helped found in 1857. But Tammany ruled New York City governance—from the mayoralty down to the ward bosses—for the rest of the nineteenth century. Supporting its programs and lining its pockets with money skimmed from municipal coffers, Tammany used public works as fences for its illegal activities. The municipal corruption affected the public markets as it did most public institutions.[37]

Even though the city government moved toward a laissez-faire stance in the nineteenth century in terms of regulating the food supply, it continued to collect fees and issue licenses to vendors (whether in the public markets or private stores). Thus, corrupt city officials stopped overseeing the quality of market products and at the same time used the market fees and licensing structure to enrich themselves and the political machine. Indeed, under Tammany Hall, the very structure of governance led to corruption vis-à-vis the food supply. Patronage politics ensured that those in charge of the markets, of measures, and the public health were not medical professionals or even bureaucrats but instead Tammany men, rewarded with titles like "city inspector," for their loyalty to the machine rather than any particular qualifications. The city inspector, who oversaw the food supply, was paid by market and other fees rather than by a straight salary. So the temptation was great to line his pockets with kickbacks from market vendors.

Furthermore, the municipal structure did not keep pace with the rapidly growing metropolis so this one individual had charge of an unwieldy department which oversaw markets, weights and measures, street cleaning, *and* the public health. An 1853 article in the *Herald* explained that while the market laws were very stringent, in practice, "they are dead letter, for they are seldom or never carried into execution." This task would be impossible, the *Herald* posited, because only two clerks were charged with the "herculean task" of regulating the markets, including collecting rents, preventing monopolies, keeping the markets clean, enforcing all market-related laws and ordinances, and reporting all violations to the district attorney. All this for the princely salary of $500 per year.[38] Even the most organized and least corrupt government might have lost track of one or two of these duties.

Unfortunately, in many cases, market corruption was quite purposeful. Tammany officials sold market stands that did not exist and extorted fees from market vendors. Country produce vendors were especially vulnerable to shakedowns because they paid daily fees for the right to sell their merchandise in or near the market houses. The daily nature of the business made it far easier for corrupt officials to demand bribes from the produce vendors than it would have been to take kickbacks from butchers, for example, who essentially owned their stalls and leased the space on an annual basis.[39]

Furthermore, there was very little paper trail so inspectors and market clerks could easily cook the books. As the city inspector explained: "No record was kept of the occupants of the various stands, and the receipts from the markets were set down in a lump. The clerks of the markets then seemed to have entire control, and gave the use of stands to whom they pleased, at what rents they pleased, and in some cases, perhaps, without any rent at all."[40] The situation was exacerbated by the strong ties between the members of the city council and the markets; many aldermen were themselves market men.

An 1857 case illustrates these practices. At the tail end of that year, market vendor James O'Reilly accused a group of city officials of building thirty to forty stands west of Washington Market and selling them for $250 to

$850. In addition to several aldermen and councilmen, the petition implicated the city inspector George Morton and the clerk of the market, Matthew Greene. The land was set aside for market wagons, but the councilmen sold off lots for country people to erect proper stalls. This might have seemed a fine improvement except that the councilmen pocketed the money, and the country vendors had no official right to build the stands that they paid for. It was akin to selling the Brooklyn Bridge ten years before that span was envisioned.[41]

The investigation into this case exposed what we would see today as a major conflict of interest. The very same aldermen charged with overseeing markets had stands within them. At one point, their colleagues in the city council accused them of hampering the investigation. The accused councilmen defended their actions as business as usual, a form of "honest graft" that machine politicians would defend throughout the nineteenth century. Questioned about repeated charges of fraud and illegal sale of market stands, city inspector Morton acknowledged that individual city officials profited personally from the sale of city property. However, he saw no wrongdoing since the lands in question were "used for refuse" or "a nuisance," and speculators who sold stands there generated revenue for the city and for themselves. The investigating committee agreed with their argument and exonerated the officials of any wrongdoing. This type of market extortion and fraud occurred repeatedly in the ensuing years.[42]

Reformers, editors, and other observers launched vitriol at the markets themselves and at the city officials who were charged with overseeing these important institutions but instead neglected them, or exploited them for kickbacks. In an 1852 editorial celebrating the dissolution of the corrupt Common Council, the New York Herald referred to the government's exploitation of the markets. The paper explained that the "late Common Council" had resolved to rebuild Washington Market, "at the frightful expense of $375,000, which, according to past experience, will turn out, before the work is complete, to be $500,000." The Herald pointed out the connections between former council members and the contractors to whom they awarded the job. The paper also reprinted a speech from the mayor acknowledging that in recent years, the markets have been a drain on the treasury rather than a boon because of the actions of corrupt officials. An 1860 letter in the New-York Times put the situation more succinctly, describing the public-market houses as "filthy monuments of Municipal malfeasance and infamous jobbery."[43]

Market vendors were not alone in paying the cost of corruption. The markets themselves suffered from the combination of neglect and exploitation and so did the quality of the foodstuffs sold within. First, the markets were grossly overcrowded and because the city did not build new structures or oversee old ones, there was not nearly enough room for all of the vendors who came to sell their goods. Carts, barrels, wagons, and their merchandise spilled out onto sidewalks and into the streets. Thoroughfares and pathways were made impassable and retail stores near the markets inaccessible to deliveries and to customers. Vendors and store owners complained about the negative impact of market disorganization on their businesses. For example, in an 1857 case, cartman William Hawks claimed that the market wagons blocked the streets around the market houses, adding hours onto his efforts to reach the main store for which he carted goods. And in February 1858, petitioners testified in front of the committee that the "unsightly sheds and market stands" disrupted business and obstructed the sidewalks for pedestrians and the streets for vehicles.[44]

The owners of these carts, and leasers of these sheds and stands, also argued that the government's disregard of its own regulations led to their exploitation by forestallers—individuals who bought up market produce and resold it at higher prices. There was a fine line between forestaller, huckster, and official agent for far-off suppliers. And as the distance between consumer and producer grew over the course of the nineteenth century, this line became more blurred.[45] During the colonial period, local farmers had often sold their own goods on certain market days. But as their farms became larger and more productive, they came to employ agents. Commission agents were even more important for the distant producers of the South and the Caribbean who clearly were not bringing their own produce daily to sell in the New York markets.

Even though they contributed to the lengthening of seasons and a more reliable food supply than in the preindustrial era, these commission agents and other middlemen drove up the prices of produce and other market goods. An 1852 editorial in the *New-York Daily Times* complained that forestalling (or huckstering, as they called it) had gone national with the recent rise of the railroads. "Orders go out in every direction," the *Times* explained, "to buy, to buy quickly, to buy at an advance of the local demand, to buy anyhow." The odd result was a contradictory combination of abundance and higher prices.[46]

These inflated prices were passed on to the second middleman—the grocer and meat-shop proprietor—who in turn passed them on to his customers. The *Times* noted that wholesale prices of fresh foods were reasonable, but the retail prices "tell a very different story." The disparity, the newspaper explained, stemmed from the surfeit of "middle gentlemen," who were "too numerous by half." The *Tribune* struck a similar tone, complaining that the middlemen forced a "tax upon every consumer of food of at least twenty-five per cent upon all the purchases of daily marketing."[47]

Just as the grocer was transformed from a neutral to a despicable figure in the early nineteenth century, so too the figure of the huckster evolved. By the mid-nineteenth century, hucksters were often depicted—by other market vendors and by certain editors—not as desperate women and children but as middlemen and speculators who drove up the price of staple foodstuffs. The *New-York Tribune* blamed the "market-huckster" for rising prices in the markets, excoriating these "huckster-gladiators," who "would be glad to shut out all the shopmen," compelling local vendors to offer their inventory to the hucksters, driving prices and profits up even further. Journalist George Foster also lambasted the hucksters in his "New York Slices" piece on the city markets. Conflating them with forestallers, "buying up large quantities of fresh articles, when they are low, and keeping them until a rise, when of course they are stale and unwholesome," Foster declared the hucksters and their practices "the greatest evil connected with our Market System." Thanks to these voracious middlemen, Foster determined, shoppers paid a 15 to 50 percent markup, often for inferior or stale foodstuffs.[48]

As for the country vendors, they resented the forestallers as competition not only for market customers but, more important, for market space. Forestallers did not operate under the same constraints as the farmer-vendors, who had to bring their goods to market daily via ferry and increasingly failed to find space in or near the markets to sell their goods. This situation was exacerbated by the shifting policies of the city government's Markets Committee on whether vendors could bring their carts and wagons to the markets, and where they could stand with them. Since forestallers either lived locally or purchased goods to sell from farmers within the city, they did not face the difficulty of traveling long distances (from Long Island or New Jersey farms, for example) and thus could reach the markets earlier than the legitimate country sellers.[49]

The Markets Committee received repeated petitions and letters outlining these complaints. A petition signed by ninety-five farmers and submitted to the Common Council on May 29, 1843, serves as an example. The petitioners claimed that speculators had completely overtaken the space set aside for their use in Washington Market and designated "the Country Market." "After riding fifteen or twenty, and some of us thirty miles at night, it is in vain that we apply to the Clerk of the Market as he says there is no room. and we must find a place where we can," the petitioners explained. But if they stood their ground inside the country market, they were "in danger of being assailed and our things upset and in some cases destroyed by the speculators." The legitimate vendors were thus forced out onto the sidewalks where additional dangers lurked, including angry store owners whose businesses they blocked, runaway carts that threatened to run them over, and exposure to the elements. The petitioners begged for a separate country market where they and their merchandise would be safe.[50] These same competing interests had characterized the market economy of the early national period. But in the antebellum era, the city government grew less responsive to vendors' demands for protections of their trade and more supportive of individual enterprise.

The press also reflected the changing attitude. In a sign of how much the tides had shifted since the early national period, the *Times* excoriated the market gardeners who demanded space within the public markets to sell their goods. In a series of petitions, the farmers argued that they suffered at the hands of forestallers and hucksters to whom they now were forced to sell their goods because there was no room in or near the markets to sell them directly. As they had many times before, the farmers asked the city government to set aside land for this purpose. Unlike earlier commentators who argued that the country vendors should have space near the markets to sell their products, the *Times* saw the vegetable vendors and their stands as a "nuisance which ought to be abated." Rather than seeing them as a class worth protecting, the *Times* wondered, in a series of editorials on the matter, why farmer-vendors should be afforded special privileges.[51]

The *Times* also rejected the farmers' claim that they were being squeezed by middlemen, arguing that raising vegetables for the market was a lucrative and reliable trade and "those who engage in it can very well afford to pay for all the accommodations which the nature of their business requires." The newspaper concluded that these market men should stop demanding special privileges and start renting private stores from which to sell their merchandise, like grocers and other food vendors. Such a move would eventually spell the end of the public-market system, which the *Times* recommended since the paper found the private food shops clearly superior to the public markets.[52]

In addition to the people and goods that filled the markets to bursting, garbage, filth, and trash also lined the market stalls, aisles, and streets. As the largest and most important marketplace, Washington Market was often singled out. As early as 1842, for example, the *Herald*'s market reporter proclaimed Washington Market a "disgrace to the city," and "an unfit place."[53]

The *Herald* continued to cry out against market conditions for years, and its rival newspapers weighed in as well. In an 1853 editorial, the *Times* described Washington Market as a "receptacle for filth, a nest of crime, and in every respect a nuisance to the city." Two years later, the *Times* referred to the market as "a huddle of decaying old sheds, low, rickety, unsightly, tumble-down, overcrowded, filthy and inconvenient." The *Times* cited "the dirt and filth, the dust, the broken street, the utter want of order, the absence of all attempt to preserve a decency of exterior, or even to give to the articles exposed for sale an inviting appearance." And in an 1860 letter to the same paper, demanding market reform, the author described the markets as "inconvenient, badly managed, [and] illy constructed."[54]

Washington Market was not the only market that came under withering attack. By the 1860s, one commentator described the once celebrated Fulton Market as "a disgrace to a civilized community." But these complaints went unheeded and the markets remained in a deplorable state. An 1872 assessment in *Appleton's Journal* rehashes the same complaints about the markets that had been issued for decades, describing Washington Market as "little else than a series of inconvenient labyrinths and rude pens," and declaring it "one of the most unsightly places that can be found in any Christian community."[55]

Reformers and doctors feared the impact of the deteriorating markets on the quality of food supply and on public health. The Citizens' Association singled out the markets as some of the worst public nuisances contributing to the high mortality rate and poor sanitary conditions in the growing metropolis. In 1866, one in thirty-five New Yorkers died annually. As a comparison, in the early twenty-first century, that number is closer to one in 135. Filthy streets piled with waste and garbage, lack of proper sewage removal, livestock and slaughterhouses located in crowded neighborhoods, and nuisance industries such as bone-boiling and fat-melting within the city limits contributed to illness and high mortality rates.[56]

But the public markets and food supply were implicated as well. In 1859, in a sign of primitive medical knowledge as well as concerns about health, the *Herald* worried about the potential for "malaria and contagion" offered by the "impure atmosphere" of Washington Market. And health reform groups like the Council of Hygiene and Public Health were troubled by the market's leaky roof, warped floors, and poor drainage leading to filthy standing water in the gutters surrounding the market houses.[57] Throughout the 1840s, 1850s, and 1860s, the Common Council (and its 1852 replacement, the board of supervisors) fielded proposals to rebuild, repair, and remove the city's largest markets—Fulton, Catherine, and Washington, but few of these resolutions ever saw fruition.[58]

Given the corruption and inefficiency of the city government, some reformers called for privatization of the entire food system, eliminating government involvement altogether. These reformers recommended privatizing the public markets and leaving regulation and oversight to the invisible hand of the market.[59] But this solution was never enacted. Privately owned markets did eventually emerge in New York City, such as the Broadway Market on Forty-Fourth Street and the Manhattan Market on Thirty-Fourth Street, opened in 1871 and 1872 respectively. But these markets were failures, owing to a combination of vendor and customer disinterest and intimidation on the part of public-market vendors and the Tammany politicians who wanted to maintain their kickbacks from the public markets.[60]

Like the markets, the problem of the milk supply was exposed, debated, and ultimately left unresolved in the mid-nineteenth century. Newsman Frank Leslie exposed the conditions of the distillery stables to a horrified public in a series of articles in his *Illustrated Newspaper* in May 1858. *Leslie's* coverage strikingly foreshadows exposés of poor practices in the food industry from Upton Sinclair's 1906 *The Jungle* to Michael Pollan's 2006 *Omnivore's Dilemma*. Armed with artists' depictions of the sickly cows, filthy stables, and inhumane conditions, *Leslie's* spent months raking the muck of the city's dairy-distilleries and milk delivery routes. The newspaper reports showed diseased and ulcerated cows living in inhumanely cramped and filthy conditions. At Moore's stables on Thirty-Ninth Street, a *Leslie's* reporter attested, the cows were "literally imbedded in filth and manure" and their hair came off in clumps in his hand. They had ulcerated tails and in several cases no tails at all. Many of the cows were so sickly that they could not even stand up and yet when they died, they were butchered and their meat sold to the city's residents. In addition to the conditions in the stables, *Leslie's* reported on the frauds perpetrated by the distillery dairies who loaded swill milk onto wagons labeled "pure country milk," or "Westchester County milk." A reporter explained: "There was a wagon painted blue and gold, with the words 'F. Willibrand, Morrisania, Westchester county,' inscribed on it. The cans in it had just been filled with the swill milk, all ready to dispense the contents in the city as 'pure country milk.' Upon my asking if that was what they called pure milk one replied, 'Yes, sir,' while the crowd yelled and groaned around us."[61]

*Leslie's* also marshaled medical evidence and testimony about the poisonous nature of the distillery milk. The paper claimed that one in five of the city's children did not live past infancy and that the swill-milk purveyors were mainly to blame. Dr. Conant Foster attributed a host of medical problems to distillery milk, including "diarrhoea, dysentery, cholera infantum . . . chronic dyspepsia, and scrofula, and tubercle—perhaps even the seeds planted of hereditary disease." Foster's colleague F. H. Dixon, editor of the medical journal *Scalpel*, concurred and optimistically opined that if the swill-milk stables were obliterated, childhood mortality could be cut in half.[62]

Again, the public knew about the distillery dairies. But they were shocked at both the conditions of the stables and the fact that distillery milk was being passed off as the purer, country variety. After *Leslie's* began its exposé, the public demanded action. The city council appointed a committee of aldermen to investigate the source of the city's milk supply and the conditions of the distillery stables. The investigating committee raided the city's two main swill-milk stables—Johnson's and Moore's—then held hearings, interviewing the milk dealers, medical authorities, and Frank Leslie himself.

Not surprisingly, as was the case with the market investigations, the swill-milk investigation of 1858 was a sham from the beginning. Two of the aldermen leading the investigation, Michael Tuomey and E. Harrison Reed, had strong ties to the swill-milk dealers: Tuomey, known as "Butcher Mike" as a child for selling meats out of a market basket in the Fourteenth Ward, owned a grogshop on Grand and Elizabeth Streets. And Alderman Reed was also a butcher.[63] *Leslie's* labeled Tuomey, in particular, "the most honest, barefaced, shameless rascal of the three, for he showed his swill milk proclivities from the first." *Leslie's* surmised that Tuomey "got himself appointed as the Chairman of the committee, in order to protect his chums and patrons, the distillery owners and swill milk vendors, from the consequence of an honest inquiry." By the time the committee raided the distilleries, the owners had scoured their stables and gotten rid of their most diseased cows. Tuomey was widely believed to have tipped off the swill-milk men. Indeed, *Leslie's* obtained a signed affidavit from a witness who claimed to see Tuomey visiting the homes of some swill-milk dealers the night before the committee visited their stables, presumably warning them to clean up their premises.[64]

The hearings also were less than neutral. In an editorial, *Leslie's* declared them "An Inquiry into the best Method for whitewashing Iniquity and perpetuating Poison." The editorial accused the aldermen of glad-handing the distillery men, allowing them to defend their product (the superintendent of the Sixteenth Street stables claimed he raised four children on swill milk). Typically, the swill-milk dealers argued that their milk was in fact a healthier article of food than the milk produced by grass-fed cows in the city's rural hinterlands. One dealer stated that he had worked in Orange County dairies for a time but left because it was hard to sell quality milk from those areas. They were so far away, he argued, that the milk spoiled before it reached its customers in the city. The city stables, he claimed, thus offered a healthier source of milk for local customers.[65]

The transcripts published by the board of investigation show the aldermen's bias in favor of the milk dealers and their antagonism toward Frank Leslie and the medical professionals who exposed the evils of swill milk. Indeed, in many cases the committee struck a tone that suggested they were *representing* rather than *interrogating* the swill-milk dealers. Hardly adversarial, they led the witnesses to defend and support the safety of swill milk and the health of the cows who produced it. A telling example occurred when Alderman Tuomey was questioning a carpenter who worked in Johnson's dairy. "You didn't ever see any ulcerated cows there, did you?" asked Tuomey. "*Did* you ever see any ulcerated cows there?" Alderman Reed corrected his colleague.[66]

Meanwhile, the aldermen grilled the doctors who testified about the ill effects of swill milk, such as Dr. John W. Francis, who argued that "it is impossible that either the milk or the flesh of these animals can be nutritive." Reed browbeat Dr. Francis, arguing that the doctor's evidence about children sickening from swill milk was hearsay and that he could not tell if it was swill milk or country milk which was the more deleterious article. "Would not country milk that had been milked over night, and when it came to the citizens here, half sour, perhaps, would it not be as likely to produce disease as the swill milk?" asked Reed. When Francis held his ground, Reed and Tuomey allowed the milk dealers' lawyer to interrogate the doctor, a move that had Frank Leslie himself on his feet issuing objections. To no avail. Furthermore, Leslie was enraged that the investigation focused mainly on a couple of stables rather than the swill-milk trade in general. In particular, the investigators ignored the many small stables in the city and in Brooklyn, which *Leslie's* found were even filthier than the stables under investigation.[67]

Doctors who were more sympathetic or even supportive of swill milk, such as Dr. John Shanks, received notably gentler treatment from the Investigating Committee. Shanks's contention that swill milk was a "harmless beverage" was based on secondhand analysis but unlike that of Dr. Francis, the committee accepted his "hearsay" evidence unchallenged. They also allowed Shanks to make frankly preposterous characterizations of the neighborhoods that housed the swill-milk distilleries: fetid, polluted industrial areas on the city's waterfront. When asked: "[Do] you think stables of that kind should be permitted, in a sanitary point of view, in a densely populated city?" Shanks replied: "Not in the centre of a *densely populated* city, perhaps, but located as they are on the edge and border of a river, where they are constantly kissed by the breezes from the opposite shore, I think that is a delightful location!" When pressed on the problem of bad odors from industry blowing into the neighborhood, Shanks responded: "I think it is a rather *musky odor—agreeable.*"[68]

The swill-milk investigation highlights the distance traveled from the colonial and early republican eras, when a patrician municipal government engaged in strong oversight of the public markets and food supply. This point was not lost on Frank Leslie, who evoked the language of civic responsibility in his critique. "What is the use of city government," *Leslie's* editor asked in an early article about the swill-milk horrors, "if not to protect the innocent and unwary from impositions?" It was the job of city leaders, *Leslie's* argued, to oversee and regulate the vendors who supplied New Yorkers' daily necessities. But the municipal government had abdicated this responsibility. Private interests were superseding the public good, *Leslie's* complained. "There is no city in the world where there is so little generous active public spirit as in New York, " the editorial concluded.[69]

Other reformers also noted the decline of civic virtue and public responsibility vis-à-vis the food supply. The state of Washington Market was particularly embarrassing since its decline occurred at the same time as some notable municipal successes, including the creation of the Croton water system and Central Park. But these two large public works projects turned out to be the exception that proved the rule. Croton represented an ending, rather than a beginning—a relic of the patrician government of the early national period. The municipality of the early republic produced city hall, the 1811 Grid Plan, and the Erie Canal, all of which envisioned a strong government hand in internal improvements. But Croton's $12 million price tag, which increased the municipal debt by a factor of eighteen, scared conservatives, bankers, and New York politicians, who would not embark on a public works project for another fifteen years.[70] That project—the monumental Central Park—was indeed a striking success. But the park was developed under the oversight of a state agency, the Central Park Commission, and therefore protected from the corrupt influences of Tammany Hall.[71]

As for the swill-milk scandal, Leslie's impassioned pleas went unheeded. The committee came back with a verdict favorable to the swill-milk dealers. The report found that the stables were stuffy and that the cows were packed in too tightly but approved of the general conditions. They recommended that the stable owners improve their ventilation and give the cows more room within the structures. But they both allowed the swill-milk stables to remain open and argued that they found no evidence that swill milk was harming New York City's children. In fact, they maintained that "the chemical analysis establishes the fact that there are no deleterious or poisonous substances either in the milk secreted by these swill-fed cows, or in the swill upon which they are fed."[72]

Not everyone on the investigating committee agreed with these assessments. Charles Haswell, the lone councilman on the committee (the rest of the members were aldermen), issued a minority report, in which he argued that the distillery cows *were* diseased, that their milk was sold to an unwitting public and, as bad, so was their meat. Haswell went far beyond his colleagues in his resolutions. Not satisfied to stop just at cleaning up the distillery stables, he called (unsuccessfully, of course) for an ordinance banning the stabling of more than two cows south of 125th Street. But the board of health accepted the majority recommendations. Adding insult to injury for *Leslie's* and the reformers, the board never followed through on enforcing implementation of even the mild improvement measures recommended by the swill-milk-sympathizing committee.[73]

The swill-milk scandal did have an impact on the milk supply of the city, but not for those most affected by swill milk. As soon as *Leslie's* exposed the conditions and constitution of the swill milk and the stables where it was produced, New York's non-swill-milk dealers began to take out ads in the back of the newspaper assuring the public that their milk was pure, from Orange County farms and not from the city's distillery dairies. Other milk interests, such as the recently formed Borden's Milk Company, plugged their evaporated and concentrated milk as healthful, commercial alternatives to the tainted local milk. And restaurants and hotels assured the public that their milk had always come from reliable and healthful sources outside of the city limits. For example, the Astor House Hotel announced in a notice in *Leslie's* that "all the milk used here comes from a farm carried on for the sole and express purpose of furnishing MILK, VEGETABLES, POULTRY, EGGS, AND PORK to this Hotel."[74] Thus the groups that most benefited from the increased attention to tainted milk were the middle- and upper-class customers, who could seek and afford alternatives, and the producers of those alternatives who found new marketing opportunities. Meanwhile, the poor denizens of New York City ingested tainted milk for another generation.

The major fallout of the 1858 swill-milk controversy was political rather than legislative, an indication that the public was a step ahead of its representatives on this food-health issue. Aldermen Tuomey and Reed both lost their bids for reelection in 1858. Indeed, while Tuomey briefly regained his seat in 1876, he was forever marked with the stain of the swill-milk controversy. His 1878 run for city coroner failed when voters were reminded of his association with the 1858 scandal.[75] But New York's milk supply remained tainted for decades to come. The *New York Observer and Chronicle* accurately predicted that "in a few weeks the excitement will subside, families will take the same kind of milk of other dealers, with 'Pure Orange County Milk' on their carts, and all will go on as before."[76] And so it was. After the initial shock over the distillery dairies subsided, the public and its elected officials returned to other concerns and the swill-milk industry continued to operate in New York.

The lack of progress is evident in subsequent exposés of the swill-milk dairies. After the 1858 swill-milk investigation concluded, sanitary reformer Dr. Samuel M. Percy worked to investigate the distillery dairies. The doctor went undercover, assuming various identities, including a farmer selling cattle, a butcher looking for beef, and a grocer seeking a pure milk supply. Percy pursued his investigation for six years, visiting the distillery dairies, their environs, and the homes of their customers. The doctor, his cover apparently blown, was granted a cold reception. On at least one instance, he was pelted by offal, and at two stables, the burly "milk maids" threatened to throw him in the vats filled with cattle excrement. When he published his findings, Percy documented the same shocking conditions that Frank Leslie's reporters and artists had exposed five years before. And he found the same lack of response from the city council and its board of health which, despite the evidence provided them, never held hearings on the subject.[77] Given the city government's patent disinterest, Percy, like other reformers of his day, took his case to the state legislature, where legislation at last occurred. In 1863, the state finally outlawed swill milk.

The law was an important step but, unfortunately, it lacked teeth. While it made it a misdemeanor to sell unwholesome or adulterated milk, it failed to define what it meant by "adulteration" or "unwholesome," thus giving much leeway to the distillery dairies. For example, a municipal judge found that the addition of water was not an adulteration. And despite some cooperation from the mayor and police, lax enforcement ensured the continuation of swill-milk practices.[78]

In fact, the 1865 report of the Sanitary Committee suggests how little enforcement there was. Inspector James L. Little, MD, decried swill-milk distilleries, exposing these "detestable establishments," including the still-extant Moore's, one of the main targets of *Leslie's* investigation, which was located in his district. Like Frank Leslie almost a decade earlier, Little described the poor ventilation, the crowding of the cows, and their diseased conditions. Little also condemned the marketing of diseased milk to poor families, particularly children, and the sale of the meat from these diseased cows "of course to the poorer classes."[79]

Tainted milk remained a problem in New York City for the rest of the century. Only in the 1890s did philanthropist Nathan Straus and the Henry Street Settlement House work to provide pasteurized milk to the children of the poor, helping to address the extraordinarily high infant-mortality rate. And the Progressive Era of the early twentieth century saw true and lasting reform in pure-food-and-drug laws at both the local and national level. The Progressive-era reforms did not, as some historians suggest, emerge anew from industrial growth of the late nineteenth century.[80] Rather, the United States Department of Agriculture and the Pure Food and Drug Act developed from a long history of food issues and scandals daring back to the 1830s in New York City.

Reform of New York's food supply in general would also await another era. The market houses remained an embarrassment to the city throughout the nineteenth century and indeed worsened before they improved in the twentieth century. Grocers and other food retailers continued to sell substandard food in the city's poorer wards. And the pushcarts and peddlers that sold food to New York's poor multiplied, crowding the streets and sidewalks of tenement neighborhoods.

The unprecedented variety and abundance in New York City's mid-nineteenth-century food markets had an unsavory flip side. In many ways, the markets and their problems served as an index to larger challenges faced by New York's leaders and residents as the city emerged as the nation's metropolis. Gotham's public markets shifted from celebrated landmarks to emblems of municipal corruption and neglect. This transformed image was rooted in part in Tammany Hall's stance toward its public markets. At best, the city council embraced a laissez-faire position in keeping with the spirit of the times. The councilmen assumed the free market would better serve the public good than strong government oversight. At worst, corrupt officials saw in the markets opportunities to line their pockets through graft, kickbacks, and shakedowns. Even if Tammany had wanted to continue regulating the markets, the distribution channels that worked in the early republic were grossly inadequate in moving fresh food from the ships and trains that brought it to the city into the markets themselves. The neglect of the markets extended to other areas as well, most notoriously the city's milk supply. Drawn from the distillery dairies of the city but sometimes passed off as the "pure country" variety, the milk that the city's residents drank, especially the poor, contributed to epidemic rates of gastrointestinal disorders and in many cases, death.

The increasing contrasts in the city's class structure, between the haves and the have-nots, were reflected in the food options available to them. As the city grew, class and geography became evermore intertwined in determining one's access to healthy and affordable foodstuffs. Wealthier New Yorkers shopped in private markets and meat shops near their homes on the outskirts of the city. These neighborhood groceries offered convenient hours and services and sanitary environments to their customers. But the tenement groceries that dotted the poorer and working-class wards were another animal entirely. These corner groceries often served more liquor than foodstuffs, and the food they offered was frequently stale, rotted, and otherwise substandard. Middle-class reformers demanded change, including legislation regulating the milk supply, a return to better oversight (or alternatively, privatization) of the city's markets, and prosecution of corrupt officials. But their efforts bore little fruit in the first two-thirds of the nineteenth century. And while later reforms improved New York's food supply, the class divisions that emerged in the midst of New York's food revolution remained solid. Indeed, the strong connections among class, geography, and food quality—rooted in these early years of metropolitan growth—remain a central issue in New York City today.

# FOUR

# "To See and Be Seen": Restaurants and Public Culture, 1825–1865

"Restaurants abound"! proclaimed the New York-based magazine *Home Journal* in 1854. "They are the daily resort of hundreds of thousands of all classes of citizens. Many go nowhere else for breakfast, dinner, or supper." Fifteen years later, New York journalist Junius Henri Browne proclaimed the ubiquity of Gotham's restaurants: "Go where you will between the hours of 8 in the morning and 6 in the evening," Browne asserted, "and you are reminded that man is a cooking animal. Tables are always spread; knives and forks are always rattling against dishes; the odors of the kitchen are always rising."[1]

These descriptions suggest the central role of restaurants in the business and social life of mid-nineteenth-century New York City. But in fact, the map of New York dining looked very different just fifty years before, when taverns and pleasure gardens were the only venues available to New Yorkers seeking commercial meal options. Along with changes to its retail provisioning sector, the growing metropolis of New York developed a new institution—the restaurant. Restaurants addressed a practical need—feeding the thousands of businessmen, tourists, and shoppers who crowded into the city's commercial downtown after the 1830s. But restaurants did far more than administer an undistinguished mass of food to a hungry populace. They quickly came to serve other, more symbolic needs as well. Restaurants grew up with the city itself and became entrenched in the landscape of New York. As such, they provided a staging ground for social interactions and stratification, for gender mores and conventions, and for working out social relationships and public behavior in the increasingly complicated metropolis. They were among the quintessential urban institutions of the nineteenth century and in accommodating their growth and proliferation, New Yorkers created a new urban culture.

Indeed, restaurants both reflected and helped to shape a new public culture in nineteenth-century New York City. In eighteenth-century New York and other American cities, taverns contributed to a lively public sphere. Like the London coffeehouses studied by German scholar Jürgen Habermas, taverns provided a space for the exchange of ideas and a gathering place for information and news. They thus offered fertile ground for the questioning of authority and governmental decisions, practices that were crucial to the eventual formation of democracy.[2]

But in the nineteenth century, the public sphere contracted. Historian Mary Ryan addresses these shifts in the American city. As industrial capitalism took hold in the nineteenth century, Ryan suggests, business owners sought ways to maximize profits that conflicted with the free space and discourse of Habermasian civil society. The open discourse and free exchange found in taverns and coffeehouses was ceded to semipublic spaces such as department stores, hotels, and sanitized public amusements that straddled the line between the private world of the home and the public world of business. Women played a crucial role in the creation of this semipublic sphere for it was their patronage that savvy entrepreneurs sought. Theater impresarios, hoteliers, and department store mavens like A. T. Stewart crafted spaces in the public sphere but removed from its most unsavory elements. In these highly regulated venues, according to Ryan, rules of conduct and strictly defined functions allowed ladies to socialize comfortably with little threat to their bodies or reputation.[3]

Restaurants represented an equally important semipublic space. As New York's restaurant sector grew larger and more diverse, restaurants became segmented along class and other lines. Rules—tacit and explicit—emerged to police such spaces and became part and parcel of the restaurant experience. Restaurants served as important spaces of social articulation—stages for acting out status and conspicuous consumption. Historian Rebecca Spang argues a similar role for the late-eighteenth-century French restaurant. Rather than serving as a place of dialogue and discussion, the French restaurant was about consumerism and spectacle.[4]

Restaurants played an important role in cementing New York's public culture. First, they helped shape New York's business life at a crucial point in the city's commercial development. Business transactions occurred over restaurant meals, and the very existence of restaurants allowed merchants, lawyers, clerks, and others to continue the workday uninterrupted. Second, restaurants provided New Yorkers of various backgrounds with the opportunity to dine out. Those of different class, gender, and ethnic identities did not necessarily share common *space*—specialized restaurants quickly emerged to cater to different groups of New Yorkers. But they did share a common experience—eating and socializing among strangers in public. In restaurants, they confronted new aspects and characteristics of metropolitan life including extremes of wealth, evolving class and gender mores, and commercial activities such as gambling and prostitution. They practiced new behaviors around food-related consumer items and participated in particularly urban forms of interaction.

New York's restaurants were part of a constellation of consumer leisure venues. In concert with department stores, luxury hotels, theaters, and brothels, restaurants formed an increasingly active and interactive consumer culture that touched almost all of the city's residents and visitors in one way or another whether as diners, as staff, or both. But perhaps more than any other institution, the nineteenth-century restaurant shaped and reflected New York's metropolitan public culture because such a wide range of restaurant types emerged. Virtually every New Yorker at every level of the social scale experienced restaurants in some form. The next closest institution in this respect was the hotel, whose common rooms and lobbies hosted public events.[5] But even with their reach, hotels did not touch the daily lives of such a broad range of New Yorkers as did restaurants.

In the growing metropolis, restaurants became important social spaces, not only gathering places for acquaintances and friends to share a meal but also venues where people learned how to interact with strangers in a convivial way. In this sense, restaurants served like many public and semi-public spaces in today's metropolis—the subway, the office building, even the neighborhood—where people become familiar with strangers, passing and greeting the same people on frequent occasion but usually not really interacting with or learning anything about each other. As Junius Browne explained, "Restaurants in New-York create singular companions," bringing together people who would not come together in any other situation. "Faces become familiar at a table that are never thought of at any other time. You know the face, as that of your brother, or father, or partner; but when it turns away into the crowd, you never suspect, or care, or conjecture where it goes, or to whom it belongs."[6] This experience was an important locus of civil society; it served as one basis of a shared public culture even in an increasingly segmented and divided populace, and it formed the roots of New York's modern restaurant and metropolitan culture.

The concept of a restaurant—a free-standing establishment that serves meals to customers from a fixed or rotating menu—was a relatively new one in the early nineteenth century.[7] The very first restaurants emerged in eighteenth-century Paris not as a place but as a thing—a restorative broth served to the sick in guild-operated establishments. From these early foundations grew the Parisian restaurant, the template for those that opened across the Atlantic in the nineteenth century.[8] The French influence on restaurants cannot be denied. On a very basic level, some of the earliest American restaurants were started by French immigrants in cities like New York, Boston, and Philadelphia. By 1810, the New York City Directory listed five free-standing "victualling houses." Many of the early eating houses were French-owned and French-inspired, including Delmonico's, which opened in 1830. But while Swiss brothers John and Peter Delmonico revolutionized fine dining in New York and the United States at large, they did not introduce the concept of the free-standing restaurant to the United States. In fact, the earliest-known American restaurant was not even in New York; it was Julien's Restorator, a full-scale French-style restaurant that appeared in Boston in 1794.[9] So New York certainly did not invent the American restaurant. But by the 1840s, Gotham bypassed all other cities as the center of American restaurant activity. New York had more restaurants, boasted greater variety, and catered to a wider diversity of people than any other US city. Moreover, New York restaurants both pioneered and cultivated the culture of eating out as well as set the standard for restaurants in cities around the country. And while New York's restaurants were undeniably influenced by their Parisian predecessors and counterparts, New York would develop its own particular and unique restaurant culture.

The first area where New York diverged from Paris was in the origins of its restaurant sector. New York's restaurants emerged to fill a need but not a medicinal one. They arose to serve the growing number of residents and visitors seeking meals away from their homes and hotels. In the eighteenth and early nineteenth centuries, New York's merchants and laborers worked in or near their homes, and they returned home for meals.[10] But by the 1820s, a large population of New Yorkers worked downtown and commuted from their homes in the growing residential neighborhoods on the city's edges. Too far from home to return for the midday meal, they began to seek dining options near work.

Many potential restaurant patrons lived not in private homes but in hotels and boardinghouses. Such living arrangements became an integral part of American urban life in the nineteenth century. These practices originated in the housing crunch and expense of buying a home in New York City. In the 1850s, renting even the "narrowest and shabbiest lodging for a family" cost $100 to $150 per year and a middle-class house between $500 and $700 per year to rent or $3,000 to $5,000 to own, according to the *Times* and *Tribune*.[11] Setting up housing in a hotel or boardinghouse offered a more affordable option. Between 1830 and 1860, permanent residents occupied half of the hotel rooms in New York. One English visitor noted: "At some of the principal hotels you will find the apartments of the lodgers so permanently taken that the plate with their name engraved on it is fixed on the door."[12]

More common than hotel living was boardinghouse residency. These establishments ranged from the genteel to the seedy, and they formed a core institution in nineteenth-century New York. The expanding sector of white-collar clerks especially relied on this type of living arrangement. These young, single men entered the city in large numbers in the early nineteenth century, bound for work and training in the countinghouses, offices, and warehouses of the bustling port. Rather than establishing homes of their own, they settled in boardinghouses with other, similarly situated young men. Indeed, historians estimate that one-third to one-half of nineteenth-century urbanites lived in such lodgings.[13] Another housing option, one explored exclusively by poor and working-class New Yorkers, was the tenement or rental unit. But not until after the Civil War when French flats—large apartment units in big, residential buildings—became acceptable living accommodations for middle- and upper-class New Yorkers did the boardinghouse lose its predominance as a housing option in New York and other US cities.

Boardinghouse living and commuting contributed to the growth of New York's restaurants, a fact noted by observers of the New York scene. *Putnam's Monthly* attributed the proliferation of eating houses to the increasing distance between the downtown business district and the residential areas "up town, and across the East and North Rivers, and down the bay to Staten Island." Likewise, in an article subtitled "How New Yorkers Sleep Uptown and Eat Downtown," the *New-York Daily Times* described the large market for diners in the downtown eating houses. Their clientele included "the thousands of active working people who are engaged in various avocations downtown" but "have their homes far up town, or in the neighboring Cities of Brooklyn, Williamsburg, Jersey City, or some other suburb." Alternatively, commuters might carry their lunch and eat in or around the office. But, as the *Times* put it, "tin dinner-kettles, and little provision baskets are carried by comparatively few."[14]

For many of these men then, eating out became a daily occurrence. Calvin Pollard, a New York City architect who lived on Twenty-Second Street and worked downtown, was such an example. Pollard noted daily dinners (the midday meal) in his 1841–1842 account book, usually at the cost of 12.5 cents. In 1849, George Templeton Strong wistfully recalled the "fashion of former times," when one returned home to dine. Strong complained of "this ruinous business of lunching at Brown's and dining at Delmonico's and trespassing on my viscera in all sorts of ways." And John Stubbings Webb, a clerk for a British metals firm who lived in a Brooklyn Heights boardinghouse and commuted to his job in New York City, likewise ate dinner out every day. In an 1853 letter to his parents, he described his daily schedule, which included proceeding to an eating house for dinner each day at 1:00 or 2:00 p.m. By the 1860s, the *Tribune* estimated that one-quarter of the eight hundred patrons at One Chatham Street eating house were "regular customers."[15]

The growth and popularity of restaurants reflected a real change in the daily lives of many New Yorkers. Just a generation before, they took every meal at home in the company of family. Now, many men ate at least five meals a week among strangers in commercial venues. Mealtimes changed as well to accommodate urban growth and the new institutions that catered to it. When men returned home for the midday meal, it was the most substantial of the day. At the end of the workday, families ate a small supper of cold meats, soup, cheese, and bread. By the 1840s, this option was an impossibility for many. Thus, men of the middle and upper classes took their dinners at the public dining houses while their wives and children ate a small meal of breakfast leftovers at home—an early form of lunch. The dinner hour was pushed back to the early evening, and families either had supper at nine or ten o'clock or did away with this meal altogether.[16]

Not just local commuters but travelers to New York sought restaurant options as well. Some of these visitors were accustomed to European hotels, in which meals were served to order and paid for individually. American hotels, on the other hand, customarily followed the pattern established in taverns of offering a table d'hote. Under the table d'hote plan, diners ate precooked selections family-style, rather than choosing from a menu. Meals took place at set times and were included in the price of lodging, a practice called the "American Plan," and hotels that followed it were known as American Plan hotels.

With the growth in both the number of foreign visitors to the city and the incidence of permanent residency in New York hotels, more hotels adopted the European model. This process evolved in the three decades before the Civil War. Guests of European Plan hotels paid for meals separate from their lodgings. They could thus opt to take their meals in the hotel's restaurant, in their rooms, or off premises, and pay accordingly.[17]

As more hotels switched to the European Plan, some hoteliers opened free-standing restaurants to serve both their own guests and those of other hotels. In 1852, hotelier W. G. Dunlap advertised the opening of Dunlap's Saloon, a restaurant attached to his hotel. As the advertisement explained, the proprietor was moved to do so "in consequence of the guests at Dunlap's Hotel being for some years exposed to the inconvenience of procuring their meals at other saloons." And in 1857, the venerable Astor House announced the addition of "an entirely independent" restaurant to its hotel, "for merchants doing business in its vicinity." The Astor House's restaurant was immediately successful. On the first day, it attracted seven hundred patrons and quickly grew to accommodate twelve hundred a day. While the American Plan hotel persisted throughout the nineteenth century, European Plan hotels became an important presence on the New York hotel scene by the 1850s and further contributed to the growth of free-standing restaurants, both in the same structure and separate from the hotels.[18]

From a handful of options in the 1830s, New York quickly became a restaurant town. A tourist's guide to the city published in 1847 estimated that there were about one hundred restaurants in New York, plus the "Oyster Houses and Cellars, which are numerous in all quarters of the city." And by the 1860s, Junius Browne claimed that Gotham had five thousand to six thousand different restaurants. *Putnam's Monthly* suggested that "nearly half the people of New-York dine out every day of the week," including "almost the entire male population of New-York [who] dine 'down town.'" The breadth of dining options by the 1850s led clerk John S. Webb to conclude: "The perplexity as to where you shall dine in New York is not because you cannot find a place, but from the choice and variety of places."[19] Restaurant districts and rows began to emerge, on Nassau Street downtown, along the Bowery, and up the spine of Broadway.

Restaurants and their patrons quickly started to sort themselves. Certain restaurants served specialized clienteles. For example, Windust's, its walls lined with playbills, clippings, and theater images, was the headquarters to New York's theater crowd for years. Located on Park Row near the Park Theater, this restaurant's patronage included actors, artists, musicians and their fans, as well as journalists from the nearby newspaper offices. Particular restaurants served tourists, merchants, mechanics, artisans, sporting men and bachelors, and families. The city housed Italian restaurants as well as other ethnic offerings that represented "all the different tribes of Scandinavia and Germany." And at least one restaurant catered to "'the upper ten' of sabledom," New York's wealthy African Americans.[20]

This map depicts the eating houses, oyster houses, confectioners, and coffeehouses of New York City in 1835, according to their listing in the New York City Directory. (Map by Ben Benjamin)

Even children ate at New York's restaurants, a practice that evoked interest and comment from several observers. These comments suggest the early incidence of children and families dining out socially and while traveling as well as the extension of restaurant dining into various segments of New York's population. But at this point, it was mainly the children of the wealthy who patronized Gotham's restaurants. Many more children were involved in the service side of public dining in New York: peddling food items on the streets, serving as runners in restaurant dining rooms, or performing menial jobs in the back of the house. [21]

Overall, by the mid-nineteenth century, New Yorkers of virtually every

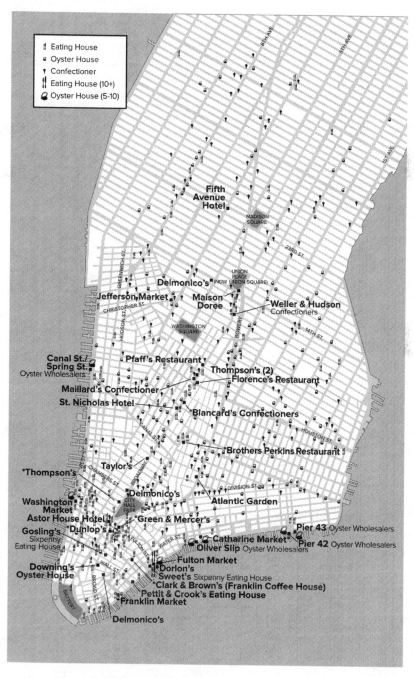

This map depicts the eating houses, oyster houses, and confectioners of New York City in
1865, according to their listing in the New York City Directory. Locations marked with
an asterisk were closed by 1865 but are referenced in the chapter text. All other locations
were extant in 1865. Note the proliferation of restaurants between 1835 and 1865 as
well as the development of restaurant districts around Nassau Street, Bowery, Chatham
Square, the spine of Broadway, and near the public markets. (Map by Ben Benjamin)

background ate meals in restaurants or worked in some type of public accommodation. "A half million people, of all ages, sexes, colors and conditions depend upon the eating-house for their daily bread," the *New-York Tribune* remarked in 1866. These five-hundred-thousand-plus people did not all dine at the same restaurants or rub shoulders together, of course. "Some of [them] live luxuriously," the *Tribune* explained, "tickling their sensitive palates with delicate meats and wine." But others cram "their stomachs with the coarsest and grossest food which the pinched purse can afford . . . [to] satisfy the inordinate cravings of that terrible hunger which only the street pauper knows." In between could be found a variety of diners and a range of restaurants that catered to them. This assessment was repeated in a good number of midcentury descriptions of New York City's restaurants.[22]

The hierarchy of restaurants was an important aspect of New York's public culture. Restaurants spelled out where one fit in the social structure. Early on, this sorting was largely about means rather than social codes—if you could afford to dine at Delmonico's regularly, you were probably able to do so—but it served an important role in both shaping and reflecting the class structure of mid-nineteenth-century New York City. In 1848, journalist George Foster categorized New York's restaurants into three tiers. The bottom tier consisted of the "Sweeneyorum," a downtown eating house. In the middle was "Browniverous," a mid-priced chophouse. And at the top: the "Delmonican," modeled after Delmonico's, the exemplar of fine dining in the United States throughout the nineteenth century.[23] Foster's taxonomy serves as a useful tour through the restaurant culture of antebellum New York.

The Sweeneyorum referred to one of the most common restaurant types in antebellum New York, the sixpenny eating house, so named because the main dishes cost six pence. These short-order houses, including Sweeney's, Johnson's, Dunlap's, and Sweet's, catered to an all-male clientele drawn from Manhattan's commercial district around Wall Street and Lower Broadway. Their proprietors such as Daniel Sweeney, Rufus Crook, and Foster Pettit made a name for themselves in the nineteenth century as savvy entrepreneurs who saw a market and profited handsomely from it. For example, Rufus Crook, the owner of various sixpenny houses, amassed a fortune of $100,000 by his death. Eventually Crook graduated from short-order establishments to open some more leisurely restaurants in the downtown district.[24]

Given their novelty and popularity, restaurants provided entrepreneurial opportunities to many others as well. According to one account, opening a restaurant "afforded the surest means of making a fortune out of a comparatively small beginning." Newspaper ads placed by entrepreneurs seeking partners in restaurant ventures support this claim. An 1855 ad in the *New York Herald*, for example, sought a partner in an "oyster, eating and drinking saloon," with potential "receipts from $14 to $23, day and night." Another ad in the same paper promised "at least $5000 a year, clear profits" for a partner in "one of the best paying restaurants, located in the greatest thoroughfare in this city." Five thousand dollars appears to have been a magic number, proposed in several ads as profits to restaurant proprietors.[25] That said, restaurants were—as they are today—volatile businesses with high turnover and a sketchy success rate. "Many signs are taken down after a few months' airing and stowed away in garret or cellar among the dusty relics of untimely ventures and fruitless, extravagant hopes," the *New-York Tribune* lamented.[26]

Sixpenny restaurants shared a similar arrangement to each other, a template followed by other kinds of New York restaurants: a large, rectangular room with tables for four arranged in long aisles. In some cases, the tables were booths or "boxes" that lined the sides of the room, again separated by a long aisle. Some eating houses also had counters that ran the length of the room. Waiters, usually of Irish descent or African American, stood along the aisles, ready to take the orders of hungry and hurried patrons. In place of a printed menu, a "large white placard," or chalkboard outside the door displayed the meal options and prices—six pence for a small steak, three cents for a cup of coffee—or waiters called them out. After taking orders for standard offerings like roast beef, boiled mutton, lamb, or fish, these servers shouted them to the runners who conveyed them to the kitchen. The runners then delivered the preprepared meals in a flash to diners who quickly bolted them down, paid their bill, and left, usually within thirty minutes of their arrival.[27]

Not surprisingly, these venues were crowded, chaotic, and loud, according to all descriptions of them. Knives and forks made an "amazing clatter," as did the waiters who "bawled out in a loud voice, to give notice of what fare was wanted," one diner recalled. The pace involved an "extraordinary bustle," with patrons eating as quickly as possible. Customers swallowed their food "with a strange, savage earnestness, and in silence." The close quarters and assembly-line atmosphere presented, to one observer, "a most uncomfortable spectacle." Another visitor described the rapid turnover: "We were not in the house above twenty minutes, but we sat out two sets of company at least." A template was set for these establishments in the 1830s, and the script varied little even decades later. Even the prices remained the same.[28]

In fact, the standardization of restaurant prices suggests the growth of an organized industry by the early 1850s. Restaurant owners cooperated with each other in setting prices, addressing licensing issues, and dealing with crises such as the shortage of specie in New York in 1851 and again in 1862. In 1852, the owners of several sixpenny houses got together and raised prices to nine pence to deal with the increasing cost of supplies. Customers did not protest or demand a lowering of prices, but they countered the higher rates by ordering fewer side dishes, thus offsetting any additional profits the proprietors might have gained. Before long, the managers of the cheap eating houses agreed to return their prices to six pence. Likewise, the specie shortages led restaurateurs to issue coupons for meals so their customers could pay for a sixpenny or shilling plate without having to scrounge for elusive coins. And in 1852, restaurant and saloon owners got together and set a price standard for liquor offerings in response to new licensing laws that raised their operating costs.[29] New York's restaurants also carried on a high volume of business and moved a huge amount of product. In 1855, the *New York Journal of Commerce* reported that some of the downtown houses served one thousand to two thousand people daily. In a single month, patrons of one restaurant "devoured . . . 11,842 pounds of meat, 1,485 pounds of fish, 158 bushels of potatoes, 2,760 loaves of bread, 6,472 quarts of milk, 2,959 pounds of sugar," [and] 1,336 pounds of butter."[30]

In many of these early restaurants, food was secondary to other factors—speed, convenience, and cheapness. In fact, the cuisine left something to be desired. George Foster described it as "generally bad enough—not nearly equal to that which the cook" of a wealthy home "saves for the beggars." Foster particularly singled out the "disgusting masses of stringy meat and tepid vegetables." *Harper's* "Man about Town" decried the "black, elastic substance, known as a small steak," and the "balls of a species of vegetable putty, which figured as potatoes." And another diner complained that all of the dishes shared the same bad taste, a sure sign "that they have all simmered together in one omnivorous oven." These critiques aside, many sixpenny houses continued to do a brisk business, in part because the patrons of these establishments never sought a fine-dining experience. Their goal was to eat on the quick and cheap, and then return to work. "The downtown eating houses are a place where a man seizes a hasty lunch, bolts it and runs off . . . rapidly" the *New York Herald* explained.[31] These accounts suggest that the short-order restaurant was not a place of easy sociability, but rather of expediency, akin to today's fast-food restaurant. In the fast-paced world of New York commerce, this type of restaurant served an important role for on-the-go New Yorkers.

Indeed, the sixpenny houses encouraged and even cultivated the rushed, slovenly eating habits ascribed to nineteenth-century Americans in general and New Yorkers in particular. Descriptions of eating habits in restaurants and public dining rooms provided both amusing and evocative illustrations of the pace of daily life in New York City. In Gotham, the center of American finance, commerce generally superseded dining enjoyment. English tourist Horace Batcheler remarked that New Yorkers eat "with a despatch beyond my powers of mastication . . . and it frequently happens that you meet the parties who arrived the same hour with yourself coming out of the dining-room as you are about to enter."[32]

Descriptions of this type continued with little change throughout the nineteenth century. For example, in 1868 the *Tribune* presented a typical downtown diner:

> Sharp, nervous, and pulse at 98, [he] rushes into the saloon, drops into the chair . . . shouts "roast beef and coffee" to the nearest waiter, looks twice at his watch in the minute he is gone; then hitches up his cuffs, salts and peppers his beef, and, grasping knife and fork, attacks it as though it were alive and it was doubtful which would eat the other first. He flushes his coffee in the second attempt, demolishes a dessert ordered in advance, wipes his mouth with a handkerchief in lieu of a napkin, seizes his check, slaps down his change, and is off almost before you have begun your dinner.

This common assessment of the brisk dining habits of New York business-men reflected the quickened pace of the commercial metropolis. These ac-counts give a definite sense (one that still persists to this day) that New Yorkers did not have time to enjoy breakfast or lunch because they had to get back to work. Contemporaries recognized this point specifically. The *Tribune* described the downtown restaurants as "rooms where the busy, hur-rying money changers are lunching." These diners "have known all the vicis-situdes of the stock gambler's life," and "can never be withdrawn from its seductions," the *Tribune* explained.[33]

Restaurants thus quickly became an integral part of New York's burgeon-ing business culture and among their central institutions. As George Foster put it: "New York could no more exist without her Eating-Houses, than you, dear reader, could get along without your stomach." And New York memoirist Abram Dayton opined: "Eating-houses . . . may be alluded to collectively as one of the stepping-stones, which cropped out as, by degrees, primitive Gotham gave way to metropolitan New York."[34]

But the sixpenny refectories were hardly the only eating-house option.

For those who craved a more leisurely pace, a second type of all-male restaurant emerged on the scene, the Browniverous on Foster's taxonomy. Owned and operated by English immigrants, establishments like Clark & Brown's (aka the Franklin Coffee House) were "quiet, cozy places." They featured sanded floors, English prints on the walls, and steaks to order. Chophouses served as a bastion for English expatriates in Manhattan as restaurants would do for a host of other immigrant New Yorkers. Chophouses were somewhat similar to the short-order houses, but the pace a bit slower, the menu a bit more official. "The chief difference to be noted between the two is that . . . at Brown's the waiters *actually* do pass by you within hail now and then," George Foster explained. Brown's (a separate establishment from Clark & Brown's) also offered a printed menu and slightly higher prices than Sweeney's. While they were a cut above the sixpenny houses, the chophouses were still very unassuming. They offered a few dishes—"roast beef very rare and cut in thick slices, or a beefsteak scarcely warmed through, English plum-pudding," and of course English ale—and eschewed the pretenses that would attach to first-class restaurants like Delmonico's. Samuel Ward disparagingly recalled "the democratic nonchalance of the service" at chophouses like Clark & Brown's, and Brown's.[35]

If the distinction between Brown's and Sweeney's was merely one of degree, that was certainly not true of the top tier of Foster's taxonomy—the Delmonican. As New York's restaurant sector grew more established, some restaurants emphasized gastronomical luxuries over mere convenience. Delmonico's was the ultimate example of these first-class restaurants. But the dining rooms of the city's palace hotels served as important precursors. Beginning in the 1830s with the Astor House, the grand hotels placed a premium on luxury and cutting-edge technology, offering their wealthy guests a new standard in service and comfort. The dining rooms sat at the center of these palaces for the people.[36] One European traveler described American hotels simply as "giant feeding places," ignoring the range of other services the hotels provided, including lodging.[37]

The hotel ordinaries followed the model of colonial taverns, offering a table d'hote, where, again, various dishes were precooked and delivered to the dining room en masse. Guests chose individual meals, which waiters carved, dressed, garnished, and plated at the sideboard. But there the comparison with the rustic tavern ended. The giant hotel restaurants provided as much opportunity for showing off as they did for eating. Patrons participated in a highly ritualized dining performance, replete with props, dress, and prescribed roles. The hotel waiters performed a military-style drill, choreographed to the head waiter's whistle, which signaled them to deliver dishes to diners, uncover them with a flourish, and stand at attention through the seven courses that typified a hotel meal. The dining performance extended to the dress of the patrons, the tables, and the room itself. Some of the female patrons "appear in a different dress at every meal, and in point of elegance and costliness of attire, they went beyond anything in my poor experience," marveled Astor House guest William Chambers. Meanwhile, the long tables that seated hundreds of guests were covered with the finest linen, cut glass, porcelain, and silver. At each place lay a menu card, itself a new prop. The Astor House had its own printing press for the exclusive purpose of producing these daily menus.[38]

Unlike the traditional taverns, with their rustic settings, the hotel dining rooms were among the most lavishly decorated spaces in all of New York. Black walnut tables and velvet-covered chairs filled the dining room at the St. Nicholas Hotel. Gilded mirrors hung on its walls. And twenty-four marble pilasters supported the frescoed, twenty-foot-high ceiling. This immense fifty-by-one-hundred-foot room was, *Putnam's Monthly* reported, "an exquisitely beautiful example of a banqueting room, and shows to what a high condition the fine art of dining well has already been carried in this city." Indeed, *Putnam's* argued that the dining room decor if "lively and cheerful" offered an "essential aid to digestion."[39]

Meanwhile, the hundreds of hotel diners enjoyed some of the finest cuisine available in the city. The bills of fare were extensive. A guest at the St. Nicholas marveled at the number of dishes offered, including "our choice of two soups, two kinds of fish, ten boiled dishes, nine roast dishes, six relishes, seventeen entrées, three cold dishes, five varieties of game, thirteen varieties of vegetables, seven kinds of pastry, and seven fruits, with ice-cream and coffee." Dinner was the most extravagant meal served at the hotels but other repasts were similarly prodigious.[40] As early as 1843, the Astor employed three chefs including a "a Frenchman for the side dishes, an Englishman for the roast meats, and an Italian for the *patisseries.*"[41]

But guests enjoyed far more than fine food. A diner at the public table sat among hundreds of others who like him wished to "sun [themselves] in the public gaze." Dining out in the hotel ordinaries became an event unto itself in antebellum New York, an entertainment rather than just a meal. As one contemporary proclaimed in 1844: "The going to the Astor and dining with two hundred well-dressed people, and sitting in full dress in a splendid drawing-room with plenty of company—is the charm of going to the city!" In comparison, theaters, shopping, and sightseeing were "poor accessories to the main object of the visit." Dining was not a private act or a family occasion but a public event and, according to some observers, the more public, the better. "The distinguished, the fashionable, the dressy and handsome," the *New York Weekly Mirror* proclaimed, "all dine . . . *at the public table.*"[42] As they did so, they socialized and participated in a performance of conspicuous consumption.

This show took place on the stage of the hotel ordinary, which emphasized space and display, as well as culinary excellence. The hotel ordinaries defined luxury dining, and hotel dining was among the most refined activities available to antebellum New Yorkers. "The days have gone by," the *New-York Tribune* noted, "when quiet comfort, mere neatness, and a good table were sufficient." According to the *New York Weekly Mirror*, the Astor House was "a perfect mirror of the fashions in costume, the luxuries, conveniences, comforts, manners, refinements, beauty, and elegancies of the 19th century."[43]

The rituals and furnishings of New York's grand hotel dining rooms thus represented something new—the public, commercial meal as opportunity for conspicuous consumption among strangers. As New York society grew more complex, the hotel dining room and the luxury restaurant served an important role in delineating the standards of decorum and display for New York's elite and those aspiring to join their ranks. In this way, the restaurant experience was sacralized along the same lines as the theater and other amusements in the mid-nineteenth century. The theater once offered entertainment for all classes under one roof. But as the nineteenth century progressed, it became segmented according to class, with plebian theaters located in separate structures and neighborhoods from elite and middle-class ones. Elite theaters increasingly required not just higher prices of admission but also stricter codes of conduct than working-class theaters, which hewed to older practices—bright lights in the house and a high level of interaction between audiences and actors.[44]

Restaurants also enforced a class hierarchy with the most exclusive not only charging more money but requiring knowledge of codes and rituals for inclusion. Among these codes and rituals was an ability to understand the menu—often written in French. A diner needed to make sense of the various accoutrements—utensils, linens, serving dishes—that covered the table. And he or she needed to feel comfortable interacting with servants since the elite restaurants employed large waitstaffs, themselves versed in a complex code of conduct.[45]

If the hotel restaurants introduced dining as spectacle to New Yorkers, Delmonico's perfected it in a free-standing setting. This famous restaurant began as a modest affair, a confectionery shop opened by Swiss brothers Peter and John Delmonico in 1827. During this nascent period, expectations

This wash drawing of the Delmonico brothers in their William Street restaurant shows a rare interior view of the early Delmonico's. Its simplicity of decor would be eclipsed by midcentury by the opulence associated with the Fourteenth Street branch. (Collection of the New-York Historical Society)

for restaurants were significantly lower than they would become in subsequent years. "Two-tine forks and buck-handled knives were not considered vulgar then," explained memoirist Abram Dayton, and "neither were common earthenware cups and plates inadmissible."[46]

In 1830, the Delmonico brothers expanded their operation into a restaurant on the Parisian model, hiring a French chef and a staff of waiters who prepared and served a wide selection of hot meals. The emergence of a proper restaurant in New York was novel enough that the *New York Gazette* made note of it. In 1830, the newspaper announced that a French restaurant had opened in Charleston and bragged: "we have one in this city" too, "kept in the true Parisian style—at Delmonico's, No. 23 William Street."[47]

At first, Delmonico's catered mainly to foreign expatriates but eventually, the restaurant "attracted the attention, tickled the palate, and suited the pockets of some of the Knickerbocker youths, who at once acknowledged the superiority of the French and Italian cuisine as expounded and set forth by Delmonico," Dayton recalled.[48]

Delmonico's patrons celebrated the restaurant's service, appointments, and food. An 1840 visitor lauded the host, John Delmonico, who "will talk with you in all the civilized languages, and serve you a dish after the manner of any christian country." The details of service included "the whitest napkin, coolest ice, and the best *demi tasse* of coffee . . . this side of Constantinople." And the rich furnishings consisted of mirrors, marble, gilding, fine fabrics, crystal, silver, porcelain, and linen.[49] These descriptions reflect the changing scene in New York City's restaurant culture, the shift from eating to dining in New York fostered by the hotels, Delmonico's, and eventually, other first-class restaurants.

By the 1840s, Delmonico's was *the* destination for downtown merchants as well as the go-to caterer of New York society. The restaurant had developed a national reputation as "beyond . . . question, the most palatial café, or restaurant on this continent."[50] Boosters in cities around the country used the famous New York restaurant as a benchmark against which to compare their culinary offerings. At this point, the restaurant's main operations had moved to Morris Street and Broadway, just south of Chambers, and Lorenzo Delmonico, the nephew of the founders, was overseeing the daily operations. In addition to its epicurean contributions, Delmonico's added to New York's antebellum public culture first by serving a wide swathe of New Yorkers in its various dining rooms and second by offering an important space for political and business transactions.

Even within Delmonico's one structure, though, a hierarchy of diners existed. Memoirist Samuel Ward recalled the differing populations at Delmonico's in this era. Downstairs were clerks and scribes on one side and journalists and politicians on the other. A small, intimate dining room served middling merchants. Meanwhile, on the top floor, in the "superb and luminous" main dining room, "men of distinction in every pursuit and profession, save the church" gathered for meals. The luminaries who dined upstairs included department store maven A. T. Stewart and *New-York Times* editor Henry S. Raymond, dining with politicians of various levels. Evenings brought a whole new and more profitable clientele, including stockbrokers, bankers, and journalists.[51] The restaurant also hosted private dinners and catered the biggest social events in New York, including the visits of the Prince of Wales and Charles Dickens.

The Delmonicos took cues from the hotel dining rooms—emphasizing space, performance, and fashion. But Delmonico's departed from the hotel model in several crucial ways. First, the restaurant was a free-standing establishment, separate from any lodging space (although the Delmonico family did eventually open a hotel on Broadway that also housed one of their several restaurants). Second, they abandoned the ordinary format; guests could choose their meals from a menu of options, prepared to their order, a practice known as the "French style" of service. Indeed, Delmonico's was one of the few free-standing restaurants in antebellum New York to print actual menus rather than listing the offerings on a chalkboard. And these menus were vast. Even as early as the 1830s, the menu, printed in French and English, consisted of eleven pages and included an astonishing 346 entrées, eleven soups, twenty-four liqueurs, fifty-eight wines, and an extensive list of side dishes and desserts.[52]

Delmonico's presented a distinctive environment, the opposite of the sixpenny houses where customers bolted their meals with no attention to taste or decorum. At Delmonico's, as at the hotels, patrons dined, their experience including not just the food but the service, atmosphere, accoutrements, and the ability to see and be seen within the walls of the famous restaurant. Of the space itself, Foster noted that the restaurant was "equal in every respect in its appointments and attendance . . . to any similar establishment in Paris." Similar to the hotel ordinaries, the midcentury Delmonico's had a lavish atmosphere with its frescoes, mirrors, gilding, and other sumptuous appointments.[53]

One paid a high price for Delmonico's service and atmosphere. Dinners started at two dollars in the 1850s, two days' wages for the average manual laborer of the time. But it all fit with the restaurant's role as stage for conspicuous consumption. Customers could count on a high level of attention from Lorenzo Delmonico and his skilled staff. While the waiters at Sweeney's and even Brown's were comically inattentive, at Delmonico's the waiters seemed to predict customers' needs before they were even uttered. "Without seeming to observe you, [they] are always at your elbow just at the moment you are beginning to think about wishing for something," explained one patron. In contrast to the cacophonous short-order waiters, Delmonico's servers were "noiseless as images in a vision," evincing "no hurry-scurry of preparation." Rather, they "glide about as noiselessly as ghosts." Abram Dayton concurred, impressed by "the absence of bustle and confusion," and a lack of "boisterous commands." If "our best American hotels were the palaces of the people," Samuel Ward exclaimed, "he might have added that Delmonico's was their Paradise."[54]

Delmonico's also provided a stage for the articulation of power and prestige in the growing metropolis. Political functions and dinners for visiting dignitaries took place at the restaurant. And politics was a point of discussion at its tables. For example, a reporter for the *Herald* visited Delmonico's to gauge public opinion on who would be elected mayor in 1856 and found it "thronged with patriots of various political proclivities, most of whom seemed to agree upon the certainty of [Fernando] Wood's election." When Wood was reelected three years later, after being turned out of office for a year, he received the election returns in a private room at Delmonico's.

Beyond these public affairs, the very act of dining at Delmonico's conveyed status upon the diner, a position that contemporaries acknowledged explicitly. As Abram Dayton explained: "To lunch, dine, or sup at Delmonico's is the crowning ambition of those who aspire to notoriety."[55] Indeed, by the mid-nineteenth century, patronizing Delmonico's had become an important marker of status and cosmopolitanism for New Yorkers and Americans at large, completing "the metropolitan education of an intelligent visitor, foreign or American," according to Samuel Ward.[56]

By midcentury Delmonico's had four locations, including two near Wall Street, one on Lower Broadway, and one on Fourteenth Street. The downtown branches served the business elite while the uptown location catered to the evening crowd. Delmonico's shared the apex of New York's culinary hierarchy with a few other restaurants including Blancard's and La Maison Dorée on Union Square. But Delmonico's, which now had its main branch on Fourteenth Street, remained the "*ne plus ultra* of restaurants."[57]

New York had developed so complex a restaurant culture as to defy George Foster's early three-part categorization. In the interstices between and beneath Sweeney's, Clark and Brown's, and Delmonico's were dozens of other choices. But while almost everyone in midcentury New York could participate in some way in its restaurant culture, New Yorkers of various stripes did not necessarily come together in common spaces. Indeed, the growth of the city's restaurant sector allowed for a complex social ordering. Price served as an obvious class delineator. Working- and lower-middle-class New Yorkers—those earning between one dollar and two dollars per week—simply could not consider Delmonico's or other fine restaurants, where a meal cost more than their weekly wage. But they could afford the occasional six-cent meal at Sweeney's or even a twelve-cent dinner at Clark and Brown's chophouse. Oyster saloons and coffee shops offered less expensive options, selling entire meals for a few cents.[58]

An 1868 illustration in *Harper's Weekly* magazine demonstrates the contrast between commercial dining options for wealthy and poor New York-

This 1868 illustration from *Harper's Weekly* shows the contrast between a Broadway ice creamery and a Bowery ice cream stand. Patrons are enjoying the same food item but in very different settings. (Courtesy, American Antiquarian Society)

ers. The image juxtaposes a group of poor children patronizing an ice cream stand on the Bowery—the main entertainment zone for working-class New Yorkers—with a genteel Broadway ice cream saloon. On the right side of the picture, a shabbily dressed ice cream vendor stands over a barrel, serving a group of children whom contemporaries might have described as street urchins. Dressed in rags and holding brooms and other tools, the young customers compose a decidedly ungenteel picture as they stand on the crowded street devouring their freshly scooped ice cream cones. If their appearance did not give away their class status, their manner of eating surely would have. For no self-respecting young lady or gentleman would have eaten anything on the streets, let alone out of a cone. The latter would be more likely to frequent the venue pictured on the left. Here, the marble floor, mahogany tables, crystal dishes, bright lighting, and well-dressed patrons suggest a very different atmosphere for eating the very same item.

The text alongside the image highlights the class differences attached to the venues. "The picture," it reads, "presents most admirably the contrast . . . between Broadway and the Bowery, those two great arteries of the city, filled almost to bursting with such different blood." While "each scene is a very frequent one," the article continues, "you never see the Broadway character in the Bowery, and the Bowery waifs do not deign to lunch on Broadway."[59]

Southern visitor William Bobo made a similar distinction between the fashionable ice creameries of Broadway and the plebian ice cream shops (which sold nothing else) of Chatham Square, at the foot of the Bowery. The Chatham Square shop drew Bowery boys and girls. These patrons, Bobo explained, "are not dressed, nor do they act like those in Broadway; they are entirely a different class of the *genus homo.*" And yet, Bobo went on to explain, they shared similar pursuits in different venues; "they walk the street, spend their money and time in the same sort of pursuits, yet they are different and widely so."[60]

Of course, many New Yorkers experienced the city's restaurant culture not as patrons but as workers. A typical restaurant in the 1860s required a staff of thirty-four people including twelve waiters; separate cooks for meat, vegetables, soup, griddle cakes, and "meat to order"; carvers; a coffee boy; a knife boy; dish washers; laundresses; and firemen to kindle the grill fire; according to the *New-York Tribune*. Restaurants and catering provided one of the few routes to economic and social mobility for black entrepreneurs, and some of the most well-known New York food entrepreneurs were African American, including famed oysterman Thomas Downing, whom merchant Philip Hone referred to as "the great man of oysters." A far greater number of African American New Yorkers served as waiters and cooks in New York's restaurants, along with Irish immigrants. "Female waiters" were still novel enough to merit special attention in travelers' accounts, such as that of William Ferguson, who remarked on the attractive, smartly dressed "girls" who waited tables at the Clarendon Hotel.[61]

Restaurant and other workers also frequented the restaurants that emerged in working-class neighborhoods. For example, the Bowery, the main entertainment zone for laboring New Yorkers, became associated with its numerous eating houses and oyster saloons. Many Bowery restaurants gained a dubious distinction as "cheap and nasty" establishments. A description of one such venue featured "blotched table-cloths . . . afflicted with the disease of chronic mustard-stains," waiters dressed in threadbare uniforms, and an atmosphere redolent with a "fatty vapor." Meanwhile, the patrons sported "close-cut hair, bloated, whiskerless faces, lowering, cruel eyes, and a general expression of vice and villainy."[62] In short, the cheap and nasty restaurants earned their nickname.

The cheap and nasty restaurants evinced particular concern because they were among the few inexpensive, free-standing general restaurant options.

Oyster cellars offered cheap meals but not as much variety as a regular restaurant. And the short-order houses did a brisk lunch business but did not offer much in the way of dinner. An 1859 article in the *Herald* complained about the dearth of decent inexpensive restaurants in New York and the surfeit of "cheap and nasty" options: "We must dive into oyster cellars, or be bored at hotel tables, or disgusted with dirty table cloths, unclean and stupid waiters," the newspaper lamented. The *Herald* called for reasonably priced restaurants with clean and comfortable accommodations and respectful and efficient waiters. Restaurant proprietors began to emphasize the cleanliness of their establishments in order to distance them from the reputation of the cheap and nasty.[63] Thus, a new type of restaurant began to emerge: the inexpensive yet respectable establishment. These restaurants would really proliferate in the second half of the nineteenth century.

Cleaner and more palatable than the cheap and nasty restaurants were the German beer gardens, which began to open along the Bowery after the 1840s. Here, entire German families thronged to "eat their national food, or an approximation thereto, drink their lager bier . . . and indulge in uproarious conversation and laughter, in which the shrill treble of childish voices is frequently caught varying the guttural monotony," the *New-York Tribune* remarked.[64] The lager beer saloons and their German patrons were among the few places in New York where married women and families dined for the pleasure of the event, and around liquor (or beer), while maintaining respectability. Given a cultural pass, the German hausfrau could eat sausage and sauerkraut in a barroom and hold on to her virtue. Her American-born counterparts did not enjoy the same dispensation.

In fact, gender and class conventions worked together to mark certain restaurants and behaviors as respectable and therefore acceptable for middle-class women who were concerned about their reputations when frequenting commercial entertainments. As New York's restaurant sector expanded, genteel women began to partake. The daily activities of middle-class and elite women included shopping, which took them from their homes on the residential outskirts into the commercial downtown. Like their husbands and fathers, many of New York's women of means thus found themselves too far from home to return there for the midday meal. But the restaurants that emerged to cater to them set and followed particular strictures of behavior, decor, and even food that became important elements of Gotham's restaurant and public cultures.

From an early point in the city's history, some public dining options existed for women. Colonial taverns had separate spaces where ladies—a category of social distinction—could attend balls and assemblies with a male escort. And late eighteenth and early nineteenth-century pleasure gardens served genteel refreshments to a mixed clientele. Indeed, these venues sometimes depended on ladies to ensure the respectability of their establishments.[65] In early nineteenth-century Gotham, confectioneries and coffee shops joined taverns and pleasure gardens in catering to the ladies' trade. Opening in the 1820s and early 1830s, Thompson's, Contoit's, and Delmonico's were among the confectioneries that set aside tables and chairs for female customers. And when the grand hotels began to open in New York in the 1830s, they provided segregated space for ladies' dining rooms, restricted to women and to men accompanied by a lady.[66]

Despite this history, when free-standing restaurants began to proliferate in New York, most of them excluded women. Some, like the sixpenny houses, prohibited women by policy. In other cases, social conventions made some restaurants off-limits to ladies. George Foster noted that entering a certain ice creamery required climbing a flight of steps. Since doing so meant lifting one's skirts above the ankles, this means of entry was "of course, not to be tolerated in good society." Nor, for the same reason, did respectable ladies descend into restaurants, eliminating a good number of establishments that were located underground, including the city's ubiquitous oyster cellars. Another sure way to guarantee that genteel women would avoid a restaurant was to serve liquor. It was not until later in the nineteenth century that "saloons" came to refer specifically to drinking establishments. In the antebellum decades, the word applied to many large, commercial amusement venues, including billiard, bowling, ice cream, oyster, and eating saloons. Definitions aside though, the line between a restaurant and a drinking saloon was a fine one, and a lady who cared about her reputation would not risk entering the latter. And restaurants that courted the ladies' trade forwent hard drinks for delicate patrons.[67]

As a demand arose for free-standing restaurant options for women, entrepreneurs, happy to take advantage of this new market, began to open establishments specially earmarked as ladies' eateries. This description was used interchangeably with ice creameries, or ice cream parlors, since the ladies' eateries served the frozen treat, along with pastry and light meals. The menus included items such as ice cream, oysters, eggs, boiled and broiled meats, and chocolate but pointedly avoided liquor.[68]

Ladies' restaurants began to proliferate in the 1830s. Thompson and Son's Restaurant, opened in 1827, billed itself as "the first saloon established in this city for the accommodation of ladies." By the 1850s, several ladies' eateries operated in the city. *Carroll's New York City Directory to the Hotels of Note, Places of Amusement, Public Buildings . . . Etc.,* published in 1859, listed five "Saloons Suitable for Ladies," including Maillard's, Gosling's, Thompson's, Weller's, and Taylor's.[69]

Some restaurant proprietors also advertised accommodations for ladies and families separate from the male-defined areas of the restaurant. In 1842, oysterman Thomas Downing advertised the opening of a Broadway branch of his famous oyster house. "I have . . . a set of furnished rooms in the upper stories," he announced, "with a private entrance as well as from the saloon, for the accommodation of private parties and families." Similarly, Brother Perkins's restaurant offered a separate entrance for families, "so arranged as to communicate with the street, independent of the main saloon, and where persons can be as private and retired as by their own firesides." And Green and Mercer Coffee and Dining Rooms touted its dining room for ladies, with its own entrance and overseen by Mrs. Mercer.[70]

These establishments offered private entrances to create a symbolic break between the public street and the semipublic restaurant, had female managers as well as patrons, and sought to replicate the home "fireside" to create a suitable environment for genteel women. Furthermore, by admitting only ladies and their guests, these restaurants aimed to make their patrons feel comfortable dining in public without compromising their reputations. As one New York guide explained, at these establishments, "our wives and sisters may visit without being compelled to mingle with miscellaneous society."[71]

Semipublic spaces in the nineteenth-century city acted as a third realm, between the public and private. As historian Mary Ryan explains, activities and behaviors were regulated by explicit rules and unspoken custom, allowing for suitable interactions among strangers.[72] Thus, middle-class women could enjoy commercial amusements while maintaining safety and respectability. Indeed, gender worked in both directions in this process. Respectable spaces welcomed ladies and, in turn, the presence of ladies lent respectability to a venue. On railroads and steamboats, in hotels and department stores, spaces were delineated "ladies" spaces either by name or by convention. In many cases, the ladies' accommodations were the most opulently furnished and well-appointed rooms in the building, akin to a private parlor. By creating a parlor ambience in terms of decor and manners, the ladies' restaurants established themselves as respectable and genteel settings. Indeed, in time some ladies' eateries even came to be called parlors, the ice cream parlor being the prime example.[73]

In New York's growing consumer culture, as an increasing number of goods came into the reach of people of varied means, space and accoutrements became important ways of signaling a place as socially proper. Hence as more and more female, middle-class New Yorkers began to partake of public, commercial amusements, the atmosphere of those amusements grew particularly important in delineating these venues as respectable. Ladies' eateries thus distinguished themselves through design. Fitted up with marble floors, gilded walls, and plush draperies, these restaurants astonished visitors.

Taylor's, the premiere ladies' restaurant in 1850s New York, was so richly furnished that English guest William Chambers wondered if "some will think [it] much too fine for the uses to which it is put." Chambers's compatriot Isabella Bird described it as "a perfect blaze of decoration . . . a complete maze of frescoes, mirrors, carving, gilding, and marble." A wall of mirrors on one side reflected a wall of windows on the other. The back wall featured a stained-glass window, flanked by fountains. Crimson-painted and gold-trimmed Corinthian columns stretched to the twenty-two-foot-high frescoed and gilded ceiling. Classical bronze statues kept watch as waiters rushed orders of oysters, omelets, sandwiches, eggs, coffee, hot chocolate, and ice cream to the black walnut tables that filled the room. The restaurant also boasted the largest pane of glass in New York City. Taylor's served gentlemen as well in a separate dining room.[74]

Taylor's main competitor was Thompson's. Both establishments originally operated as ice cream shops and grew into vast and opulent full-service restaurants that catered to refined ladies and their escorts. Over the years, Taylor's and Thompson's vied with each other in terms of space and service, to attract the ladies' trade. By the 1850s, that competition included opening entirely new outlets, far larger and more extravagant in furnishings and appointments than their predecessors. Thus in 1851, Thompson's opened a new location, a stone's throw from Taylor's, on Broadway. This new Thompson's was, according to one account, "rebuilt in splendid style, and hence has been more attractive in its appearance than Taylor's." But not for long. Two years after the new Thompson's debuted, Taylor's followed up, establishing a much enlarged space, fabulously called Taylor's Epicurean Palace, just a few storefronts away from Thompson's.[75]

The opening of the new Taylor's restaurant, at 365 and 367 Broadway, attracted much notice and was accompanied by an eleven-page promotional pamphlet. Filled with adjectives like "sumptuous," "magnificent," "immense," and "brilliant," the pamphlet devoted most of its attention to describing the furnishings, decorations, and expense of the building and very little time to the food served there. Journalists and visitors agreed that

Taylor's Epicurean Palace was among New York's most extravagant and impressive venues. One account called it "the most spacious and elegant restaurant in the world." A notice in *Gleason's Pictorial* marveled at the restaurant's cost (more than $1 million) and its capacity (over eight hundred persons), its daily expenses of $600 and its receipts of $900 per day on average. Likewise, *Leslie's* swooned over the expense of decorating the restaurant's ceiling ($17,000) owing to the copious gilding and unique decorative molding. The restaurant served three thousand patrons per day, including many women in need of a rest after hours of shopping at A. T. Stewart's department store, located just a few blocks away.[76]

Another way that ladies' restaurants ensured decorum was to demand particular behaviors of their patrons. Taylor's and similar establishments were the opposite of the sixpenny houses with their cacophonous din, rushed pace, and hideous manners. "The room is darkened—ladies love such subdued atmospheres," George Foster began his description of "the fashionable lunch for upper tendom," in a ladies' eatery. In place of the ear-splitting noise that characterized the downtown eating houses, in the ladies' eatery "low-voiced orders [were] entrusted confidentially to the waiters." Mrs. Bird described the atmosphere as "redolent with the perfume of orange-flowers, and musical with the sound of trickling water, and the melody of musical snuff-boxes."[77]

The links among gender, respectability, and the restaurants point to another important interplay between restaurants and public culture in New York. More than any other semipublic space in the city, the restaurant brought together women and men in a commercial space of entertainment. So defining the boundaries of respectability was particularly important here, especially for those women who were concerned about their reputations. At the same time, if a restaurant permitted too many non-respectable behaviors or patrons, it lost its respectability as well. While middle-class men could engage in non-respectable behaviors and remain respectable themselves, the same was not true of their wives, mothers, and daughters. Restaurateurs thus were careful to maintain boundaries and to police behaviors within their spaces to ensure the maintenance of social conventions. Tunis Campbell pointed to this need in his 1848 *Hotel Keepers, Head Waiters, and Housekeeepers' Guide* when he instructed: "Ladies who may be traveling alone should not be left to come to the table without being seen by the proprietor, and brought in and seated." Campbell thus reminded his readers that it was their responsibility to vet the female patrons of their establishments to be sure that they were not introducing a non-respectable element to their dining rooms.[78]

It was not only that ladies traveling alone were suspect. Restaurants garnered concerns about respectability in part because so many restaurants hosted less than respectable activities. Providing a space for men and women to interact socially in public, commercial spaces, restaurants offered temptations and lures even for the most virtuous. Thus, even the wholesome ice creameries had a taint of lasciviousness. Men were not admitted to Taylor's and Thompson's main dining rooms without a female escort. But, contemporaries intimated, there was no guarantee that a woman's companion was entirely proper. Describing a fashionable ice creamery, George Foster admitted that most of the patrons were "correct and commonplace." But a close look revealed some suspicious pairings, such as a middle-aged couple who were "evidently man and wife," but "not *each other's!*" The ice creamery offered them an easy cover for an illicit rendezvous. The ice creamery's location downtown provided extra security to the clandestine couple, since it was situated near businesses that would draw each to the neighborhood, a millinery shop for her, a dentist's office for him.[79]

Another commentator pointedly described the ice cream saloons as "a trysting ground for all sorts of lovers," including young singles courting each other and middle-aged marrieds besotted by other people's spouses. The *New-York Times* explained that Taylor's "always maintained its popularity, in spite of (or perhaps because of) rumors that it afforded most elegant opportunities for meetings not entirely correct." In addition to young couples, Taylor's also drew women "whose business it was to frequent public places, and who were not over particular as to the company they kept." Junius Browne also commented on the role of restaurants in hosting inappropriate dates. In this case, he referred to the uptown restaurants, where women were permitted to dine with male escorts. "How few of the fashionable wives that sup up town after the play or the opera, sup with their husbands!" Browne exclaimed. "Their husbands may be there; but they are with other women."[80]

The *Times* argued for the impossibility of effectively policing improper behavior in a crowded, diverse metropolis. As the newspaper explained, the proprietor could not be blamed since "our most frequented places are always selected by the evil disposed for assignations, and even our churches are not exempt from such contaminations."[81] This explanation for how Taylor's could maintain its respectability even in the face of less than respectable behavior speaks to the complex ways that restaurants played into New York's public culture. It also suggests the reasons why restaurants were such fraught spaces for respectable people in general and ladies in particular.

Furthermore, as dining out—and conspicuous display—became more entrenched in the life of New York society, upper-class ladies managed to maintain their status despite questionable behavior. After all, the need to maintain one's reputation for status purposes was more important for middle-class New Yorkers who sought to gain entry to the halls of power and respectability than it was for their elite counterparts who had already gained admittance.[82]

Here, respectability and wealth were inextricably tied together. The rendezvous that Browne, Foster, and others described at Taylor's and the uptown restaurants were carried on by society women and their consorts, not by middle-class women. For the latter group, restaurants were both a novel and interesting form of entertainment and convenience on the one hand and a minefield to navigate on the other. Faced with this paradox, many middle-class women in the antebellum period simply chose to eat at home or frequent a handful of "safe" restaurants. Strictures relaxed a bit in the postbellum period and more restaurant options for respectable middle-class women emerged, but in the antebellum years, relatively high prices assured that ladies' lunchrooms catered mainly to middle-class and elite women. Many working-class establishments were restricted to men, by policy or by custom. Only at the end of the nineteenth century, with the rise of cheap amusements, did working women gain a real foothold in the city's commercial entertainments.[83]

The tension among respectability, entertainment, and commerce came up as well in the restaurant type most associated with New York City in the antebellum period—the oyster cellar or saloon. Emerging on the scene in the 1830s and proliferating throughout the subsequent decades, the oyster cellars of antebellum New York were that era's counterpart to today's pizza parlors. Oyster eating, particularly in the ubiquitous cellars, was emblematic of New York's burgeoning consumer and entertainment culture.

Travelers to New York rarely failed to comment on the city's renowned bivalves and to visit the legendary establishments that served them. One of the most famous, Charles Dickens, described the signs hanging outside of oyster cellars announcing "'Oysters in every Style,'" remarking, "They tempt the hungry most at night, for then dull candles glimmering inside, illuminate these dainty words, and make the mouths of idlers water, as they read and linger." Oyster cellars could be found all around New York with the highest concentration on Canal Street, near the Bowery. They were identified by a red-and-white-striped balloon hung outside, illuminated during open hours, which lasted well into the night. Most oyster cellars offered what was known as the "Canal Street Plan." For a few cents, one could eat all the oysters he could stomach. Proprietors purportedly punished overly greedy eaters by slipping a bad oyster into what would surely be their final order of the evening.[84]

Like Delmonico's and Taylor's, some oyster houses distinguished themselves by their fine appointments and reputations. African American oysterman Thomas Downing pioneered the respectable oyster cellar in New York City. A Chesapeake transplant to New York, Downing became the preeminent oyster caterer in the antebellum period. The son of free blacks, Downing learned how to harvest oysters on his parents' land on the Virginia coast. In 1819, he traveled to New York City, bought a small boat, and began selling oysters that he gathered from the shores of the Hudson. By 1825, Downing had earned enough capital to open an oyster cellar on Broad and Wall Streets. His Broad Street shop, opened in the 1830s, was among the most famous oyster restaurants in New York until its closing in the 1860s. Downing catered to the business and political elite, their friends, and even their wives for his oyster saloon was one of the few in the 1830s and 1840s that accommodated women, provided they had the proper escort.

Downing's example shows both the limits and possibilities for African American entrepreneurs in antebellum New York. By entering into a service occupation—cooking and waitering were acceptable jobs for African Americans within the white power structure—Downing found a niche for himself without upsetting racial conventions. But that niche placed him at the helm of a restaurant, which offered a public space for politicians and businessmen to gather. It thus offered him access—if not entry—to the highest political and social circles in the city. At his death, the *New York Herald* explained: "The fact that he was of African descent abated in no degree the regard in which he was held," and so many "gentlemen" requested to attend his funeral that his family held a special viewing at St. Philip's Episcopal Church. Downing also grew personally wealthy through his restaurants, becoming a central member of New York's antebellum black elite, a vestryman of St. Philip's and an advocate "for the elevation of the colored race," according to his obituary in the *Times*. Upon his death, Downing had amassed a "large fortune" of over $100,000. Downing was certainly not the only African American New Yorker of his time to make money from a food trade. According to an 1860 survey, two of the three richest black New Yorkers were waiters. The other was a cook.[85]

Other oystermen, white and black, followed Downing's lead, opening high-end oyster saloons that eschewed private rooms and bawdy behaviors. Again, space, accoutrements, and behavior played a role in distinguishing respectable oyster saloons from non-respectable ones. "Fitted up with great luxury—plate-glass, curtains, gilding, pictures, &c.," these "fashionable saloons," chronicler Thomas Nichols explained, served oysters "in every style and in great perfection." Preparations included raw, fried, or stewed, as in the oyster cellars, but diners could also enjoy scalloped oysters, oyster pie, fish with oyster sauce, and even poached turkey stuffed with oysters. Located on the street level rather than underneath, these venues were "frequented day and night by ladies as well as gentlemen."[86]

Other oyster houses skirted the line of respectability. "Thieves, burglars, low gamblers, and vagabonds in general . . . haunt these quarters," sneered George Foster, describing a Five Points oyster cellar. Meanwhile, their "'pals' are up-stairs carrying on the game of prostitution." Even some oyster cellars on fashionable Broadway were pits of iniquity according to Foster, catering to "rowdy and half-drunken young men, on their way to the theater, the gambling-house, the bowling-saloon, or the brothel—or most likely to all in turn," Foster decried. The very descriptions of oyster cellars evoked images of lasciviousness. Editor N. P. Willis, for example, described Florence's Oyster Saloon in sensual terms, from the huge stone turtles that flanked the entryway, "waving their huge paws perpetually with indolent and voluptuous invitation," to the "ambrosial air," "sumptuous structure[s]," "succulent fruits," and other "temptations," including, of course, the raw oysters themselves.[87] Like the ice cream parlors, some oyster restaurants, Florence's among them, were both lavishly appointed and borderline respectable.

Their fluid reputation stemmed in part from the fact that oyster cellars often catered to a bachelor clientele. These men partook of the sporting male culture that emerged in antebellum New York and that was intimately tied to the city's growing consumer culture. In the early nineteenth century, young, single men flooded into the city from abroad and from the local hinterlands. Seeking their fortunes in the commercial city, these bachelors lived on their own in boardinghouses, removed from parental and employer controls. Many of them participated in the sporting man's subculture, with its bawdy and sometimes bloody entertainments. These included various forms of gaming, such as cockfighting and prizefighting; consorting with prostitutes; and visiting theaters, concert saloons, and other salacious venues. The antebellum sporting man's culture was a very visible one on the streets of New York, with groups of rowdy youths (known as "sports") roaming its avenues and sometimes wreaking havoc with their boisterous and occasionally violent behavior. Along with bachelor visitors to the city, the young sports of New York laid claim to the city's oyster cellars and some other late-night restaurants. They especially enjoyed venues with private rooms where they could engage in various activities other than dining, in relative privacy.[88]

Considering these offerings, it is not surprising that contemporary accounts frequently drew a link between restaurants and commercial sex. Ministers and conduct advisers warned of scoundrel bachelors, schooled in the evils of the world in urban gambling dens and restaurants. Likewise, prescriptive stories in women's magazines like *Godey's Lady's Book* exhorted women to create a warm and welcoming home for their husbands lest they seek comfort in the city's vice-laden restaurants. In these cautionary tales, restaurants served as a shorthand for the lures and snares of the metropolis, not just closely tied to its burgeoning consumer culture but an actual symbol of it.[89]

Prescriptive writers did not conjure up this link. Prostitution did indeed occur at many of the new commercial entertainments in antebellum New York City. Historians have documented the notorious "third tiers" of the city's theaters—semiprivate balconies reserved for sex-seeking men and their female consorts that essentially served as a way station between the theater and the brothel. Prostitutes prowled the balcony in search of customers, as did men in search of willing partners. Such activities prevailed at all of New York's theaters. Even the Park, the most elite and respectable among them, had an active third tier. Once a match was made, prostitutes could take their customers back to their nearby brothels. A house of assignation directly behind the Park Theater, and linked to it by a rear alley, catered exclusively to actors. Other brothels were also conveniently located adjacent or near to theaters.[90]

But New York's theaters did not have a monopoly on salacious activity. Dance halls and drinking saloons, for example, served up commercial sex, as well as food and drink. And many late-night restaurants and oyster cellars also hosted illicit activities, part of the constellation of entertainment venues associated with prostitution and gambling in the growing metropolis. One typical establishment was the all-night house the Sailor's Home and All Nations' Retreat, on West Broadway. This restaurant was located in an entertainment zone around Lower Broadway that included hotels, theaters, brothels, gambling houses, saloons, and other late-night restaurants. There, the "lady boarders of questionable morals" ate, drank, and took advantage of unwitting male patrons, whether by seducing them or picking their pockets.[91]

Like the lady boarders at the Sailor's Home, "girls of the town and their lovers" frequented the many eating houses on and around Mercer and Greene Streets. The finest of these establishments had private boxes for the

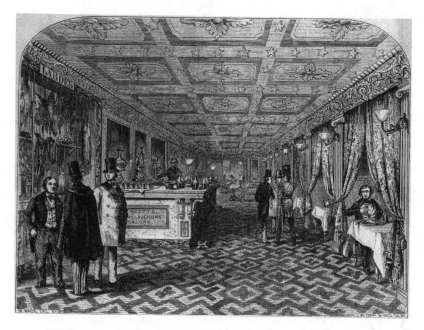

Interior image of a midcentury eating saloon. Note the private boxes along the sides of the room. (Collection of the New-York Historical Society)

comfort and privacy of their customers and offered dishes for double the price of Taylor's or Delmonico's. Restaurants with private boxes could be found "along the avenues . . . at most of the street corners above Sixteenth street." Even expensive restaurants might provide their customers with "private supper rooms," or boxes so that male diners could make assignations while eating their meals.[92]

Given these associations, women concerned about their reputations were careful about the restaurants they would frequent, and restaurateurs seeking their trade took pains to make their establishments comfortable for ladies. Even certain late-night restaurants aimed for respectability, distinguishing themselves from the more racy all-night venues. These businesses took a cue from Butter-Cake Dick's, a famous cake-and-coffee shop in 1840s and 1850s New York. Owned by Dick Marshall, a former newsman, and located on Spruce Street between Nassau and William, directly under the offices of the *New-York Tribune*, Butter-Cake Dick's served cakes and coffee to journalists and the newsboys who sold their copy. In 1850, a cup of coffee and the cake that gave the shop its name, described by George Foster as "a peculiar sort of heavy biscuit with a lump of butter in its belly," sold for three cents.

One of the many late-night coffee and cake shops found throughout the city, especially in and near the public markets. This one was located on Cortlandt Street, "along the docks of New York." (Picture Collection, The New York Public Library, Astor, Lenox, and Tilden Foundations)

Or a hungry newsboy could purchase a large slice of pie for four cents and huge doughnuts, "the size . . . of ebony walking-sticks," for a penny each.[93]

Butter-Cake Dick's cakes were essentially doughnuts or, as they were known at the time, "sinkers," thanks to their heft, which derived from a heavy dose of lard and butter. Like Downing's nearby oyster house, where patronage was served up alongside oyster pie, Butter-Cake Dick's served a political as well as a recreational function. By one account, "aldermen, and politicians of every grade" might "drop in at all hours of the night," especially during election time when the "custom from Tammany Hall alone has often amounted to ten dollars a night." George Foster too noted Butter-Cake Dick's association with New York politicos, some of them drawn from the ranks of the newsboys.[94]

Some coffee-and-cake saloons also served heartier fare such as pork and beans, corned beef, and mince pie which, along with the coffee and cake, supplied a hearty meal for fifteen cents. Thus, the coffee shops came to be full-fledged restaurants, offering hot, all-night food at low prices. While not glamorous, these restaurants had a reputation for being cheap, clean and respectable, unlike the cheap and nasty joints located nearby or some of the other all-night options in the city. The proprietors of the cake shops, noted one commentator, "wear a very tidy appearance, with clean white aprons and a rather professional air. All the utensils are as bright as silver," the pastry offerings tempting and the coffee very hot. These shops grew into "institutions that are peculiar to New York," with its round-the-clock culture. They could be found wherever people worked or played late, including Newspaper Row and Fulton Market, whose cake-and-coffee shops catered to late-night passengers on the nearby Brooklyn ferries, which ran twenty-four hours a day. Oyster saloons competed with the coffee shops for the late-night trade at Fulton Market. Dorlon's, the most famous of Fulton's oyster houses, did a brisk nighttime trade, catering to young New Yorkers out for the evening, and "solid business-like men" who lived in Brooklyn and worked late in the offices of Manhattan.[95]

The range of late-night eating houses reflects the importance of restaurants in nineteenth-century New York's growing consumer and public culture in several ways. First, the late-night restaurants were part of a growing constellation of commercial entertainment options in the expanding metropolis. New Yorkers out on the town might stop into all-night oyster cellars, dining saloons, and cake-and-coffee shops on their way to or from the theater, the billiard saloon, bowling saloon, or brothel. Just as daytime restaurants like Taylor's were intertwined with the department stores, hotels, and other commercial entertainments of "sunshine" New York, the all-night eating houses were related to the other entertainment options of the gaslight city. Furthermore, the nighttime market offerings were a part of the commuter city in much the same way the sixpenny houses were during the daytime.

Second, like the earliest downtown short-order houses, the late-night restaurants catered to a variety of New Yorkers, including commuters who sought a quick meal on their way to or from home. The only difference in their case was the hours of work, requiring a late-night, rather than a midday, dinner. Third, the all-night eating houses, like the daytime ones, labored under the effort to seek a respectable clientele though they faced a far more difficult challenge than their daylight counterparts, given the associations between nighttime and commercial sex, especially in the city's entertainment sector. Finally, the proliferation of late-night eating houses added another element to New York's restaurant culture—the city that never sleeps had emerged. New York's visitors and residents had commercial dining options around the clock, from the market cake shops that served coffee and cake to early risers, to the sixpenny houses and oyster cellars that offered up a cheap lunch, to the fine restaurants that served evening patrons, to the late-night restaurants that catered to revelers, commuters, and curiosity seekers.

Thus over the first half of the nineteenth century, New York developed a large, complex, and comprehensive restaurant culture. The commercial city relied on these institutions to feed businessmen, clerks, travelers, and others and to host business connections and transactions. And entrepreneurs found ways to capitalize on new markets by developing new restaurant types such as the ladies' lunchrooms and all-night coffee shops. Restaurants provided a space (several in fact) for New Yorkers of various backgrounds to share a common social experience, one firmly tied to new consumer patterns and behavior. At the same time, this space served as an important stage for conspicuous consumption and for social stratification. Restaurants thus served a central role in the public culture of the emerging metropolis.

# FIVE

# "No Place More Attractive than Home": Domesticity and Consumerism, 1830–1880

In 1855, the middle-class parlor magazine *New York Observer and Chronicle* included a short article entitled "Two Mothers." Jane Mason arrives at her friend Lucy Frost's New York townhouse to find her arranging her dining room. Jane attempts to lure her friend out on social visits in the city, but Lucy insists on preparing her home for the imminent return of her three children from college and boarding school. When Jane reminds her friend that she has plenty of servants to take care of the home, Lucy responds that it is her duty as a mother to create a warm, inviting home for her children, that "no child of mine should find any other place more attractive than home; that 'evenings and home' and even mother's pies and cakes, should seem better than any other." Her efforts have a specific end in mind, as she declares, "none can deny that their love of home is keeping them from the temptations of this wicked city." After "several busy hours, when the rooms had the inviting homelike appearance the mother desired," Lucy went to her well-appointed kitchen and prepared several pies and cakes. Mrs. Frost's efforts were rewarded the next day when her grateful and gracious children returned, delighted by their home and their doting mother.[1]

This story, like many of its kind in the mid-nineteenth-century middle-class periodical literature, illustrates some important themes regarding the middle-class home in general and its food spaces in particular. With industrialization, homes in New York and other cities grew more specialized in function. Once used for various work and domestic purposes, the rooms in these homes increasingly were given over almost entirely to domestic needs. As the middle-class home became less of a productive space and more of a reproductive one, it took on an important symbolic role. Overwhelmingly, ladies' magazines, cookbooks, architectural plan books, sentimental novels, and other popular literature celebrated the home as a haven from the harsh, competitive, and seductive world of the commercial city and its consumer culture. Paeans to the home were widespread in the nineteenth century: in novels, ministers' sermons, newspapers and magazines, and books of all kinds. More than merely a shelter or dwelling place, the ideal home, as represented in volumes of antebellum writing, was a place of refuge, comfort, and hospitality. As the world—particularly the urban world—came to be represented as unsafe and untrustworthy, the home was idealized as a moral haven.

But as "Two Mothers" shows, the route to domestic bliss was found in part through a careful embrace of consumer items, using them to make the home as comfortable a space as possible for the family that lived there. The arbiters of domesticity thus did not eschew women's participation in the public sphere. The situation was far more complicated than that. Rather, they encouraged middle-class women to use the tools provided by consumer culture to craft a domestic environment that was nurturing of family life and the replication of middle-class status. In so doing, they put the public sphere to service in creating the ideal private one.

The domestic sphere itself was not nearly as self-contained and isolated from the public world as the ideal would suggest. Middle-class men still transacted business in their homes as they greeted and entertained business associates. Their wives engaged in a world of work inside the home that bolstered their commercial interests as well as their domestic ones. And the home was a work space for the domestic servants who increasingly were relied upon to ensure that it was indeed a comfortable and refined environment for those who dwelled within. Furthermore, certain spaces within the home were semipublic in function. Historian Karen Halttunen, for example, argues that the middle-class parlor served as a third realm between the public and private spheres.[2] The parlor offered a setting for playing out status via its placement, decor, and uses.

Historians have paid less attention to the dining room as a similar setting. But as much as the parlor, the dining room served a semipublic role. Families held entertainments and invited guests to meals in their dining rooms. And the rooms incorporated display cases for consumer goods and offered a decorative slate for showing off a family's wealth and a homemaker's skills and taste. The dining room also became increasingly ritualized in the mid-nineteenth century as an important family gathering place. Daily dinners brought a now-scattered family together around the table, and the meal became more symbolically important.

Consumer goods also played an important role in shaping a new middle-class lifestyle in the nineteenth century. Members of the growing white-collar professions and their families enjoyed more disposable income and a rising standard of living in nineteenth-century New York. The people that sociologist Thorstein Veblen called "the leisure class" included not only the elite but also middle-class people who worked in nonproductive positions and could support the "conspicuous consumption" that was central to expressing status in an advancing industrial, urban society.[3]

At the same time, poor and laboring New Yorkers experienced a declining standard of living in the antebellum years. Relegated to tenant dwellings in overcrowded tenement districts, the impoverished and struggling "other half" paid little attention to kitchen conveniences or dining rooms, although they did experience some of the changes. At the other end of the economic spectrum, the wealthy continued on the course of luxury and refinement that they had traveled since the eighteenth century. They now built larger and more sumptuous homes and filled them with furnishings and accoutrements from farther afield. They enjoyed greater comforts and conveniences such as gas lighting and plumbing. But it was their servants who really gained the benefit of not having to empty chamber pots or tend fires.

The antebellum middle classes, however, saw a true improvement in their standard of living from that of their parents' generation. Piped water, gas lighting, and larger and more specialized homes were among the improvements. But so too was a lifestyle of greater comforts and greater luxuries, of embracing refinements that previously were the exclusive province of the wealthy. Thanks to industrial processes like mass production, and improved transportation networks, household goods from flatware to carpets to furniture became affordable to middle-class New Yorkers and Americans in general. The ownership, use, and display of these goods quickly became central to expressing and confirming middle-class status.

In the homes of New York—the center of the United States' burgeoning consumer culture and index to its changing foodways—these goods helped to create a consumer-based domesticity. Even as the middle-class home became idealized as a private, cloistered realm, a protected space from the commercial city, it provided an entrepreneurial opportunity for retailers to expand the market for their consumer goods. And for middle-class homemakers, the semipublic spaces of the home served as a bridge to the commercial city. The growing sophistication and cosmopolitanism of the city's public dining sector thus found a corollary in its domestic spaces as well.

The growth of the metropolis influenced not only what New Yorkers ate and where they procured it but also *how* they ate. Industrialization and the spatial growth and stratification of the city contributed to the separation of home and work space. Rather than work together in a household system of production as middling families had in the preindustrial era, family members separated during the day, going to work, school, shopping, and visiting. This was especially true in cities like New York where spatial stratification ensured that family members' daily activities took them to neighborhoods at a distance from their homes. While only 2 percent of the city's proprietors maintained a separate home in 1790, 75 percent claimed ownership of a home *and* shop by 1840.[4] Unlike their fathers and grandfathers, antebellum men ate "dinner" (now lunch) in commercial spaces. Their wives too dined away from home while paying social visits or shopping downtown. Dinner, now at the end of the workday, took on increasing symbolic importance as a family gathering time. Furthermore, with productive and commercial functions removed, middle-class homes now reserved more space for domestic purposes. The homes built during the first few decades of the century were larger, contained more rooms, and were more lavishly furnished than their predecessors. The rooms within these homes had specified functions—formal parlors for entertaining company, kitchens devoted solely to food preparation, and dining rooms which, by 1850, were de rigueur in middle-class homes.

Dedicated dining rooms were not a new idea in the nineteenth century, of course. Any visit to the extant mansions of the eighteenth century such as Washington's Mount Vernon, Jefferson's Monticello, or New York's Van Cortlandt House clearly demonstrates that the eighteenth-century American dining room existed and was appointed in fine style. But except for elite homes, domestic space was much more flexible in the eighteenth century. Typical colonial homes generally contained a "hall" where the family worked, ate, slept, and occasionally cooked. Families sometimes added a parlor or two, but these rooms were not specialized, as they became in the middle decades of the nineteenth century. Rather, they were used as sitting, eating, and sleeping rooms. Even the dining rooms of wealthy homes might contain a desk or a sitting area.[5]

But in the nineteenth century, domestic advisers singled out the dining room as an increasingly important space within the middle-class home, one where the family should enact rituals of cohesion and inculcate children with middle-class values. Architects like Calvert Vaux and Andrew Jackson Downing, household advisers like Catharine Beecher, and editors of ladies' magazines like Sarah Josepha Hale of *Godey's Lady's Book* engaged in a movement to elevate the dining room in importance. They urged middle-class homemakers to set aside a room specifically for dining. They stressed the need to make this room attractive, comfortable, and above all to use it daily for the family rather than reserving it for guests. Indeed, the dining room became an important space for enacting the ideology of domesticity that was at the heart of the idealized Victorian family. This creed saw the middle-class home as an important space of family unity in both the practical and spiritual sense.[6]

The dining room played an important role in this idealized domesticity because it was the locus of a daily family reunion—the family dinner. Families had always shared meals even in preindustrial times, but the ritual aspects of those meals gained emphasis as the middle-class home became more firmly a domestic space. The evening meal became a time for the family to come back together in the idealized domestic sphere. Daily dinners became both more ritualized and more symbolically important to conduct advisers. Historians, most notably Mary Ryan, have argued that the family became the "cradle of the middle class" in the nineteenth century—the crucible for inculcating children with middle-class values and for passing on middle-class status from one generation to the next.[7] Perhaps more than any other ritual, the family dinner played this role because of its daily regularity. Like the hearth, the dining table became a symbolic family adhesive and, ideally, a place of respite.

Journalists, architects, and authors of cookbooks and household manuals stressed the role of the family meal in bringing a scattered family together, for what architect Calvert Vaux, a major proponent of the ideology of domesticity, called "a constant and familiar reunion." Domestic advisers urged homemakers to recognize the symbolic importance of family mealtime by ensuring that it occur in a suitable environment. They lamented the common notion, as expressed by one editor, "that any room in a house, provided it is conveniently near the kitchen, will do to eat in." Vaux explained that "the art of eating and drinking wisely and well is so important to our social happiness" that it merited a space devoted solely to it.[8]

Likewise, *Appleton's Journal* explained that "breakfasting and dining are the two occasions that specially assemble all the members of the household together," so these meals and their setting should thus be afforded due consideration. The magazine advised bright, refined, and tasteful furniture and "an atmosphere of quiet joyousness" to lend breakfast and dinner a cheerful tone. And a *New-York Times* editorialist implored his readers to emulate the London middle-class fashion of making the dining room "*the* habitable chamber of the house . . . the centre around which all things revolve . . . the sun of English life."[9]

This issue took on a particular shape in New York City, where basement dining rooms were the norm. This Manhattan peculiarity was born both of space constraints and convenience. As one chronicler put it, "New York . . . had to pay the penalty . . . of its long-waisted site."[10] The narrowness of Manhattan Island and the constant eye to real estate concerns in planning the city led to narrow lots of twenty-five by one hundred with no space at all between homes. Builders did the best they could with these space constraints, placing two rooms per floor, front and back. New York builders also followed the style, carried over from Dutch influences, of constructing a stoop entrance to the first floor. Below the stoop was a basement-level floor with a separate cellar below. The basement housed the kitchen for obvious and practical reasons—proximity to the cellar where foodstuffs were stored, and adjacency to the backyard where kitchen gardens and exterior work-spaces were located. The dining room was placed on the same floor as the kitchen because of the impracticality of carrying food upstairs thrice daily.

Some crafty home owners customized their space to accommodate an upstairs dining room. For example, John Pintard built a dining room in the back of his home, taking up some of the backyard to make way for the ground-floor room. When his daughter Louise held an entertainment in the parlor rooms, Pintard found the back dining room "admirably accommodating for making the Tea, &ca." and was pleased to have the dining room on the first floor. "What climbing up & down stairs was my lot thro life. Modern buildings are wonderfully adapted for domestic convenience," Pintard exclaimed.[11] But Pintard's home was not typical. The more common arrangement was a basement dining room "where the family live, except when they have company," as several observers described it. Meanwhile, a more formal upstairs dining room was reserved for company and special occasions.[12] Even Pintard, who eschewed a basement dining room in his new home, had two separate dining spaces. As he explained to his daughter Eliza: "The Back building . . . contain[s] 2 Rooms . . . of 10 Feet by 15, the first for my closet, the latter a pretty breakfast room & when alone large eno[ugh] to dine in, thus keeping the principal dining [room] free from dust & daily use."[13]

The basement dining room was akin to a modern-day family room in serving multiple purposes. Families ate meals there but also used the room for recreation and informal entertaining of extended family and close friends. New Yorker Caroline Dustan illustrates the daily life of her basement dining room in the diary she kept in the 1850s. Dustan and her family dined most frequently in the basement room, keeping the upstairs dining room for entertaining. When she renovated her house to lay underground pipes, the basement floor became unusable. "All our meals [were taken] up stairs," Dustan noted in her diary, a departure from their usual practice of dining downstairs. When a friend visited during this same period, Dustan found it worthy of recording: "Miss Hyslop dined on pot pie in 2nd story," again indicating that under normal circumstances, this meal was conducted in the basement dining room. After the construction was completed, Dustan reported that, once again, they had resumed their practice of dining downstairs.[14]

These patterns were unique to New York. Town houses in other cities, such as Philadelphia, had ground-level kitchens and dining rooms and reserved basements for cellars. A journalist lamented that New York builders did not follow the example of their Philadelphia counterparts in constructing houses "for comfortable living," critiquing the continued New York folly of "devoting the best and most convenient floors of the house to large parlors and company use alone."[15] Fiction also reflected the New York peculiarity. In "Mr. and Mrs. Woodbridge," an 1841 story in *Godey's Lady's Book*, the protagonist Charlotte Woodbridge, a newlywed from New York who moved into her new Philadelphia home with her new husband, was shocked to find the basement dedicated to storage purposes. Charlotte desired a layout like the home she grew up in, whose basement housed the kitchen and a nearby sitting room, "where we sit when we have no company, and where we always eat." Mr. Woodbridge was perplexed that he never saw this sitting room while courting his wife, whom he met in the formal parlor. But Charlotte explained that fashionable young ladies did not receive male visitors in the basement room. However, she clarified, "beaux and husbands are different things."[16] Like many actual middle- and upper-class New Yorkers, Charlotte Woodbridge's childhood home contained both a formal dining room for company and a multipurpose "family room" for everyday purposes. Increasingly in the nineteenth century, domestic advisers sought to merge the two.

The custom of dining in the multipurpose basement room evinced little comment in the colonial and early national period. But after 1840, architects, domestic advisers, and even the New York press inveighed against the practice of basement dining. Calvert Vaux, who considered dining central to physical and spiritual well-being, concluded that "it deserves to be developed under somewhat more favorable circumstances than is possible in a basement dining-room."[17] Vaux's position is not surprising given his domestic environmentalist position, which saw the home as an important instrument of uplift and moral instruction.[18]

But Vaux was not alone in attacking the basement dining room. Others urged New Yorkers to choose better spaces for their meals. A *New-York*

*Times* writer decried the lack of attention to the furnishings and heating of the basement dining room. Home owners relegated the furniture and appliance rejects from the upper part of the house to the oft-used room, "where furtively and in guilty haste the American family assemble to worship with imperfect rites the goddess of dining."[19] Complaints about basement dining rooms as the New York standard continued well into the late nineteenth century. An 1871 article in *Appleton's Journal* identified "a great defect in our New-York households," namely "[to] select a room half underground for the purpose."[20]

These commentators did not shun the basement dining room simply because it was underground. Rather, they disliked the habit of keeping two rooms for dining and shutting off the most attractive spaces in the house for the exclusive use of company. Women's magazines, popular novelists, and sermonizers warned their audience not to sacrifice the family's comfort to impress strangers. These commentators feared that homemakers were neglecting the location, comfort, and decor of the dining room and focusing all of their money and attention on creating opulent, yet uncomfortable and uninviting spaces for receiving guests. Proponents of domesticity saw sacrificing family comfort for fashion as dangerous because it ran counter to the very ideal at the heart of the ideology of domesticity: that the home was a cloistered, family realm, a safe haven from the harsh competitiveness of the commercial world. Instead of making their homes domestic havens, advisers feared middle-class women were creating museum-like rooms, paeans not to domesticity but to consumerism and status.

Such critiques spanned the mid-nineteenth century. As early as the 1820s, James Fenimore Cooper had complained that the dining rooms of middle-class New Yorkers mimicked those of the elite, with their expensive furnishings, carpets, wall coverings, curtains, serving dishes, and utensils. Cooper urged those of modest means to "substitute taste for prodigality in their tables" and to furnish the dining room for the family rather than for company. Fifteen years later, Catharine Beecher warned that sacrificing the family's comfort in order to show off one or two elegant rooms to guests was "a weakness and folly, which it is hoped will every year become less common." Beecher's hopes remained unfulfilled. Writing in 1870, architect Sereno Todd complained that Americans everywhere made of their dining rooms "a sacred sanctorum," while "the family live in the wood-house."[21] The shrillness and longevity of the prescriptive advisers' concern that middle-class Americans were decorating dining rooms for the use of guests rather than for the family suggest the persistence of the practice. So does experience. Even today, many middle-class families reserve their dining rooms only for special occasions.

Domestic advisers did not limit their concern about fashion over comfort to the dining room. Commentators made a similar argument about the frivolity and excess of middle-class parlor furnishings, attacking homemakers' insistence on spending the family's fortune on furnishing a room that existed primarily for show rather than the family's enjoyment and ease.[22] Antebellum cookbook author Elizabeth Lea counseled readers to choose utility over fashion in selecting furniture, arguing that young homemakers too often overspent on the parlor and thus were forced to forgo useful articles for lack of means. "Be persuaded that happiness does not consist so much in having splendid furniture, as in attending to the every day comforts of those around you," Lea warned.[23]

Such messages made their way into fiction as well. Novels and stories in popular magazines offered admonitions against eschewing comfort for showiness. Historian Katherine Grier labels them the "moral tales of furnishing."[24] The stories followed a common formula. A young wife furnishing her home emphasized display over comfort. These topsy-turvy priorities threatened domestic bliss and the family's finances. But in the end the young housekeeper saw the error of her ways and used her best rooms and accessories daily, rather than saving them for company. For example, in "Mr. and Mrs. Woodbridge," Charlotte Woodbridge, the young New York bride transplanted to Philadelphia, is a consummate household consumer. She decorates herself in the most fashionable clothing available and furnishes the parlors of her new home in the finest and most fragile of materials. But she drives her husband close to madness by insisting that these rooms are off-limits, lest they be soiled. Worse yet, she sets aside one "vile little room" to serve no other purpose than as an "eating-room, or a dining-room, or a sitting-room, or whatever you please to call it—to take our meals in without danger of being caught at them, and to stay in when I am not drest and do not wish to be seen."[25]

Charlotte threatens not only her marriage but also her hospitality by refusing to make her home more comfortable. She drives away all of her servants for they cannot bear to work in so ungracious a home. When her brothers visit Philadelphia, they choose to stay in a hotel rather than suffer her miserable hostessing. Her husband Harvey is himself forced to dine at a hotel, so repelled is he by the stingy, unpalatable meals his wife provides. Finally, a visit from Charlotte's father serves to reform his daughter. When she sees how unhappy and bitter her father has become as a result of her mother's failure to create a proper, inviting home (replete with a suitable dining room), she converts the vile little room into a library and henceforth serves inviting meals in their beautiful *and* welcoming ground-floor dining room.[26]

Prescriptive writers did not eschew consumer goods or the commercial sphere that produced them. They saw furnishings, decorative items, and housewares as a means to create the comfort that was so central to domestic ideology. They urged their readers to practice restraint in household decor, arguing that too much attention to the dictates of fashion was frivolous and extravagant and the ruin of countless middle-class families (and bank accounts). But they encouraged middle-class women to see the decor and furnishing of their homes as an extension of themselves and to carefully choose and use consumer goods to best reflect both their taste and economy. Furnishing and decorating a home comfortably and tastefully became a mark of achievement and even of civilization for middle-class women, at least in the ideal.[27]

In fact, domestic advisers leaned on consumer goods—on furnishing the dining room in as comfortable a style as possible and filling it with pleasing decorations—to create the idealized domestic sphere, in effect placing consumer goods at the very heart of the ideology of domesticity. "There can be no question that elegance, comfort, social enjoyment, and, it may be added, health, materially depend upon attention to the table," *Godey's* explained. *Godey's* instructed its readers that if they were attentive to offering good food, served on a neat, clean, well-appointed table, they would ensure "the comfort of both husband and friend."[28]

Both consumerism and domesticity thus shaped middle-class status and identity. These two impulses—what Katherine Grier calls "culture" (consumerism) and "comfort" (domesticity)—seemed to be at odds with each other.[29] But in fact they worked together to create an idealized domestic space that was *made* comfortable and welcoming through the use of manufactured consumer goods. This seemingly paradoxical development makes perfect sense to modern readers. Still today, American homes are idealized spaces of comfort, made so through consumer goods and design.

The relationship between the home and consumerism did not go unnoticed by nineteenth-century commentators. While he wrote at the tail end of the nineteenth century, sociologist and economist Thorstein Veblen offered an analysis of the burgeoning consumer economy that had begun to take root a few decades earlier. Veblen posited an explicit place for the home in the twin processes of "conspicuous leisure" and "conspicuous consumption" that were central to his "theory of the leisure class." According to Veblen, by filling the home with consumer goods, including furniture and "bric-a-brac," families showed their wealth and status.[30] Since they were responsible for the domestic sphere, women had a particular role to play in showcasing the family's status, according to Veblen. Indeed, it was through their wives and children as vehicles for display (through dress and home goods) that men advertised their wealth and status in an advancing consumer society. The wife who once effectively served as her husband's chattel now performed "vicarious consumption" on her husband's behalf, becoming "the ceremonial consumer of goods which he produces."[31]

The links between domesticity and consumerism were found not only in the theoretical and prescriptive literature but in the marketing and retailing of household goods. Manufacturers, retailers, domestic advisers, and homemakers themselves worked together to create specialized spaces within the home that reflected an emphasis both on domesticity and consumerism. First, manufacturers created increasingly specialized furniture for the middle-class dining room. These dedicated furniture pieces were intended to anchor a particular room rather than be moved around to suit a flexible space, as was the case with middle-class dining furniture in the colonial and early national periods. Federal-era dining tables incorporated drop leaves and spindly legs for flexibility and mobility. And federal sideboards were primarily surface—up to seven feet wide—with small drawers and cabinets underneath. Mid-nineteenth-century dining furniture on the other hand was heavy and cumbersome and more specialized than ever before, necessitating extra expenditures on furniture for particular rooms.[32]

Furniture patents reflected the propensity toward permanent dining furnishings over the course of the mid-nineteenth century. For example, an 1858 issue of *Scientific American* featured an article on "Gross's Patent Extension Table," a table that could be extended by four times. The piece did double duty; it could serve as a two-foot-wide sideboard or be expanded to an eight-foot-long dining table. But in both cases its purpose was to sit in the dining room and serve as a decorative, storage, and serving piece for that particular room. A decade later, the magazine announced another extension-dining-table patent, this one far more streamlined than the earlier version and an indicator of both changing fashion and improvements to the patent. The more modern extension table obviated the need to remove heavy leaves and instead allowed for three leaves to be folded into the table frame. This table thus assumed a fixed position rather than a flexible orientation. The article also suggested the growing commonality of specialized dining furniture, opening with the claim that a dining table that could seat up to twelve people is "now in almost universal use." New Yorker Abram

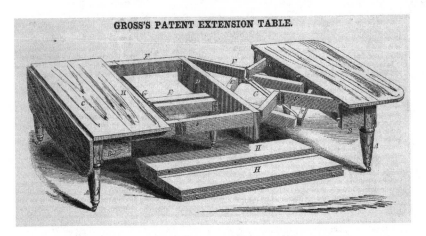

GROSS'S PATENT EXTENSION TABLE.

One of many patent extension tables produced in the United States at midcentury. It shows the development of furniture that was meant to be anchored in the dining room but used flexibly, for both the family and company. (Courtesy, American Antiquarian Society)

Dayton concurred. Recollecting daily life in the New York of his youth in the 1830s, Dayton remembered the one-course meals being set on crowded tables, "as extension tables had not then been introduced."[33]

Likewise, the sleek, table-like sideboards of the early republic yielded to the large and heavy sideboard closets of the antebellum period. These pieces clearly were designed to anchor a room, rather than to be moved around. Victorian sideboards had far more storage space than their earlier counterparts. And unlike the low, long federal-era sideboards, the newer ones reached to the ceiling, filling the room. Their multiple display and storage spaces were meant to accommodate the family's growing stocks of silverware, dishes, and other dining utensils. Another indication that sideboards were growing fixed and requisite was the availability of sideboard accessories including stoves and refrigerators. For example, an 1875 item in *Scientific American* announced the introduction of a "sideboard refrigerator," by New York refrigerator manufacturer Alex M. Lesley. The magazine suggested the permanence both of the sideboard and the dining room itself in the middle-class home. Lesley's invention, explained the article, finally achieved the longtime "desire of many housewives to have a refrigerator that would not disgrace a dining room." His sideboard refrigerator was built of solid oak and black walnut and ornamentally carved to make it suitable "for even the most stylish dining room."[34]

In another sign of its increased permanence, architects increasingly designed the middle-class dining room itself as a specialized room with built-in recesses for sideboards, low-slung lighting fixtures to illuminate dining tables, and built-in china cabinets. Eliza Leslie referred to these architectural features as early as 1844, in her domestic manual, *The House Book*. Leslie recommended that homemakers install two small sideboards into recesses built for that purpose rather than taking up space with a larger, stand-alone cabinet. In some cases, sideboards were actually built into the dining room walls.[35]

Henry Ward Beecher also alluded to the permanency of the furniture and storage space in his description of his own dining room. It included a sideboard with multiple drawers intended for spoons, napkins, and other small items. Beecher's house itself was constructed to accommodate more utensils, serving dishes, and dining accoutrements. In addition to kitchen pantries and storerooms, his home included a china closet, hall closet, and

The heavy dimensions of this midcentury sideboard suggest a fixed position in the dining room, as opposed to the more flexible sideboard tables of the early national period.
(Courtesy, American Antiquarian Society)

kitchen closet as well as a closet between the dining room and kitchen, all full of drawers bearing various eating utensils.[36]

Indeed, along with the sideboard came a host of consumer items to fill it. Manufacturers, retailers, and domestic advisers worked together to expand the idea of what was necessary for outfitting a proper dining room and kitchen. Mass production and technological advances made flatware, ceramics, furniture, and other housewares more accessible to those with middle-class incomes. Machine-pressed glass, transfer-printed earthenware, bone china, and Britannia metal or silver-plated tableware were all made affordable by mass-production techniques by the mid-nineteenth century.[37] Despite the relative affordability of manufactured silver plate, sellers and purchasers alike saw silverware sets as a once-in-a-lifetime purchase. Manufacturers thus sought ways to encourage purchases, through fashion (creating distinctive designs that came in and out of style), improved design (a more efficient cutting fork, for example), and most important, specialization. Midcentury dinner sets contained up to five hundred pieces, including dinner plates, soup plates, side plates in various sizes, hot-water plates, serving bowls, platters, soup tureens, sauce tureens, and gravy boats. In addition to dishes for the main meal, tea sets, dessert sets, and display items were also available to grace the sideboard. Flatware sets included specialized utensils, such as fish forks, oyster forks, grapefruit spoons, and asparagus forks.[38] While few middle-class families needed such a large tableware collection, those who hoped to serve proper dinners in several courses could avail themselves of a greater variety of accoutrements than ever before.[39] And by bothering to create and produce a range of pieces over time, manufacturers expressed an expectation of a market for these goods.

Cookbook and household advice authors also expanded the list of requisite dining accoutrements. For example, Catharine Beecher, perhaps the nation's foremost mid-nineteenth-century proponent of domesticity, instructed her readers to fill their sideboards and china closets with specialized dishes, utensils, serving pieces, and table linens. In setting up a dining room, Beecher recommended having on hand service for twelve, including one dozen each of forks, tumblers, soup plates, and silver spoons; two dozen each of wineglasses and large knives; and four dozen plates. This number, Beecher explained, would "allow one plate for fish, and two for changes of meat for each guest." For those who wanted more specialized dishes, she added three dozen dessert plates, two dozen dessert forks and knives, one dozen saucers, and a dozen dessert spoons.[40] Beecher's contemporary Eliza Leslie also included knife rests, butter knives, finger glasses, crumb-cloths, and salt-cellars in her list of requisite dining paraphernalia.[41]

Beecher and Leslie's advice was representative of cookbook authors of the period. In her 1861 *Housekeeper's Encyclopedia*, Mrs. E. F. Haskell filled two pages with "convenient kitchen furniture," including such conveniences (but hardly necessities) as apple corers, egg scalders, several specialized graters—for bread, cheese, chocolate, nutmeg, dried beef, and horseradish—a chocolate mill, coffee roaster, coffee boiler, bread toaster, and cheese toaster. Haskell's list was typical. Other cookbook authors and advisers included a similar group of "small articles" in their manuals.[42]

Many of these consumer goods served a largely ornamental purpose. No one individual actually *needed* more than one fork, let alone various specialized ones. Indeed, the fork itself was a relatively modern utensil. Until the mid-seventeenth century, most Americans eschewed utensils altogether, except when serving themselves from communal dishes. While sharp-pointed knives and large spoons were used to spear meats and serve stews, even the most refined colonists ate with their hands.[43] The codes of nineteenth-century refinement combined with industrial processes and savvy marketing to increase the expectations of the tools that were *necessary* to eating and dining.

This process occurred not only with dining utensils and furnishings but also with kitchen appliances such as the refrigerator and the cookstove. Over the course of the nineteenth century, these appliances traveled from unheard-of to required devices in middle-class homes. This was especially true of the cookstove, which, thanks to the increasing expense of fuel, truly did become a necessity. By the 1830s, wood was such an expensive form of fuel that cookstoves became a cheaper alternative than hearth cooking. In New York and other cities, the poorest households were the first to adopt and incorporate the cookstove; indeed the stove initially was associated with poverty and want rather than convenience and plenty. In the lean times of the early 1830s, John Pintard explained that the high cost of cooking fuel forced poor people to utilize small cooking stoves. Pintard also pointed out that high fuel prices encouraged manufacturers to improve the stove in anticipation of a market for the devices. Pintard himself installed one in his home as early as 1827.[44]

Pintard was in the vanguard for his class but by the mid-nineteenth century, the cookstove was a common item in the homes of both poor and wealthy New Yorkers. A "Manual Laborer" writing in the magazine *The Cultivator* in 1848 estimated conservatively that one hundred thousand homes in New York State had a cookstove.[45] Caroline Dustan indicated that the poor New Yorkers she visited on her charity runs had cookstoves in their homes. And Dustan referenced her own cookstove in her diary, noting in

April 1856, that "Mr. Hardick began to take down the oven in the kitchen," in preparation for summer and recording the arrival of "six tons of Lehigh coal for range" the following year. Architects included cookstoves and ranges in their plans for town houses. Some wealthier families even had two cookstoves—a large one for the kitchen and a small "parlor" stove for the family room.[46]

Housewares companies and exclusive cookstove retailers filled the back pages of mid-nineteenth-century newspapers and magazines with advertisements for stoves and their attachments.[47] Cookbook authors also began to include instructions for cookstoves in their volumes. Their instructions and commentary indicated their expectation that most of their readers had completed the switch from open hearth to cookstove. This is especially evident in cookbooks that underwent several editions over the mid-nineteenth century. For example, in *The Young Housekeeper's Friend*, originally published in 1841, Mrs. Cornelius devoted a large section of her first chapter to "Ovens—and How to Heat Them," explaining that each family should have a brick oven (attached to a hearth) with room for ten to twelve plates. In the completely revised 1875 edition of the book, Cornelius included the same instructions but prefaced them with the claim that cookstoves had come into such common use that open-hearth instructions were of little use for modern cooks. Their inclusion thus seems to have owed more to nostalgia than necessity. Likewise, in her 1861 *Housekeeper's Encyclopedia*, Mrs. E. F. Haskell placed a cookstove or range as the first item in her list of "Necessary Kitchen Furniture."[48]

Household manuals and cookbooks also incorporated the refrigerator into their advice. The 1854 *American Home Cook Book* included a "Closet or Upright Refrigerator" in its list of requisite articles for the home. And Mrs. Jenny C. Croley included care of the refrigerator in her 1866 household manual. Refrigerators made their way into recipes as well. A recipe for baked fish in the *New York Evangelist* recommended putting the filleted fish in a refrigerator while preparing the stuffing. And an 1875 item in *Harper's Bazaar* suggested optimizing the flavor of a melon by putting it "in the refrigerator until the next day."[49] Even the article "the" instead of "a" is suggestive of the commonality of refrigerator ownership for the readers of these recipes.

One can imagine the difference in the texture of daily life that a refrigerator provided. Daily marketing became less necessary as refrigerators became more reliable and widespread. The arduous process of food preparation and laying up supplies for winter was eased a bit by refrigerators as well, both the home variety and the refrigeration that kept food fresh on railcars and steamboats. An 1882 letter to the *New York Evangelist* defending the practice of apartment living argued against *Harper's Bazaar's* claim that apartments were not true homes because they did not have cellars or storerooms. "What need of a cellar," the writer inquired, "with a good refrigerator, and a grocery within a stone-throw?"[50] But even as these appliances became more entrenched in the middle-class home and lauded as conveniences, they in fact "made more work for mother," as historian Ruth Schwartz Cowan put it. In this way, they played a part in the consumerist aspects of domesticity by both incorporating consumer appliances into the home and contributing to the "conspicuous leisure" of the homemaker and her servants. The refrigerator added work to the chores of the middle-class housewife and her servants who had another appliance to clean and maintain.

The cookstove also simultaneously made some household tasks easier and others more difficult. On the one hand, cookstoves opened up cooking opportunities. Modern cookstoves were elaborate appliances with up to ten burners, ovens, tea kettle, steamers, broilers, flatirons, and other attachments. Unlike the one-dish cooking that the open hearth necessitated, the cookstove allowed for different kinds of cooking—boiling, roasting, and baking, for example—with the same fire. With the cookstove at her disposal (and much labor expended), the home cook could provide her family with a variety of dishes at one meal, including a roasted entrée, boiled vegetables, and a sweet *and* savory pie. And the entire meal could come out of the oven at once.[51]

But while using a modern stove was less arduous and dangerous than cooking in an open fire, the cookstove inadvertently created novel stresses for the new housekeeper and new challenges to cooks. In the "Chapter to Husbands," in her *Housekeeper's Encyclopedia*, Mrs. E. F. Haskell urged readers to understand that cooking mistakes were sometimes not the fault of the cook. A new, untested cookstove or one that "may prove a poor baker, either drying or burning every thing that goes into the oven," could ruin a meal. Cooking on a stove required practice and experience. Roasting, for example, was very difficult in a cookstove since the fire did not surround the meat as it did in an open hearth. Cookbooks recommended boiling meat instead of roasting, to accommodate the cookstove. For the cook who insisted on roasting (or for the recipes that necessitated it), they offered advice for keeping the meat moist, such as setting the fire to low, surrounding the meat with water, rotating the pan, and basting frequently.[52]

Baking in a stove also required more attention than in a brick oven. Cookbook author Elizabeth Lea explained to her readers that "to bake [bread] in a stove requires care to turn it frequently." She suggested leaving the stove door open at first to prevent the bread from browning too quickly.

Lea also offered instructions for testing the heat on a stove by dripping water on the top and waiting for it to boil. She recommended keeping the heat consistent at this level, another expenditure of time and attention for the home cook. The cookstove even affected the arrangement of the domestic space. Architects and authors of household manuals instructed homemakers to organize new kitchens around the appliance, placing the range away from windows and doors.[53]

Some cooks adjusted easily to the new technology. But popular literature was replete with stories of failure at the stove.[54] Henry Ward Beecher relayed the adventure of cooking on a gas stove and a separate gas broiler (since effective broiling was difficult in the stove) while his wife and family remained in the country. First, Beecher had to hook the stove up to the central gas line by means of "a long flexible tube." Then onto the broiler: an enclosed pan with a flame on one side, powered by gas.[55] Beecher declared the broiler "a capital contrivance!" but soon discovered the dangers of the modern convenience. The pressure in the broiler sent the meat juices out of the broiler plate and all over the dining room carpet. Then, just as the meat was starting to cook, the gas tube detached and the fire abruptly extinguished, but not before shooting out flames that burned Beecher's hand, leading him to drop the broiler on the ground. Beecher eventually was able to finish broiling the steak, but only after several repeats of the mishap, finally holding the tube to the broiler with one hand while seasoning and flipping the steak with the other. In the end, the meat was "serviceable" but tough: "We could hardly cut it and could not chew it," Beecher reported. But rather than getting rid of the gas stove, Beecher resolved to gain an appreciation of his wife's skills at housekeeping, which he determined to avail himself of thenceforth.[56]

Cookstove horror stories expressed a common theme—the cookstove required a host of skills and training. The proper use of the new consumer technology made life more complicated in requiring an extensive new knowledge set of the user. Despite these difficulties, consumers treated these new appliances and technologies as a fait accompli. Users might complain about their conveniences, but they never considered returning to the old ways. Rather they accommodated and improved the new. Most nineteenth-century homemakers took the time to master the new devices. But the time and energy called into question the title of "conveniences" and highlights the changes to daily life that the cookstove and other consumer appliances wrought.

In fact, these household consumer goods, from cookstoves and refrigerators to dining furniture, utensils, and dishes, added to the ornamental household chores that made the middle-class home a display space, reproductive of middle-class status rather than a production system. Furniture and silverware required polishing; porcelain dishes needed to be cared for; stoves and refrigerators needed to be maintained. The refrigerator for example, required draining, cleaning, and organizing, and a regular ice delivery and the maintenance that went along with it. Mrs. Jenny C. Croley instructed her readers to be sure their refrigerators were "thoroughly scrubbed out every week, and . . . aired every day," and checked weekly for spoiled food. As for the stove, the ashes needed to be cleaned out completely once or twice a month. And "blacking the stove"—scrubbing it with a solution to prevent rust—was an arduous and necessary process to be performed twice a year, as was patching the occasional crack.[57]

In terms of cooking too, the cookstove made possible more complex dishes, opening up opportunities but also raising the expectations of the kinds of meals that home cooks would put on the table. Increasingly, cookbook authors argued that the more variety in a meal the better, urging the home cook to incorporate a range of dishes in a given meal. In her 1852 *New Book of Cookery*, for example, Sarah Josepha Hale urged her readers to eschew the old wives' advice to cook plain meals for their families. Hale cited the famous nineteenth-century cooking authority Dr. William Kitchiner who advised that "elaborate culinary processes are frequently necessary in order to prepare food for the digestive organs." Rather than cooking one "family joint," Hale advised cooking the same cut of meat as two or three distinct dishes. Likewise, Mrs. Cornelius emphasized variety at the table, arguing that a diverse diet was both more enjoyable and healthier.[58] In insisting on varied meals and complex dishes, the cookbook writers perpetuated the need for their services. In earlier periods, women had learned simple, one-pot preparations from their mothers and other female relatives. But the more complicated, composed dishes made possible by the cookstove—and desirable by the prescriptive literature—required detailed instruction that, initially, only cookbooks could provide.

Indeed, with the new appliances came an industry of advice for using them. Technological innovations in printing, such as the invention of the steam press, and improvements in typesetting, bookbinding, and papermaking, combined with better methods of distribution to produce an unprecedented volume of literature aimed at a popular audience, particularly after 1830.[59] Advice books of all kinds made their way onto the popular scene, and cookbooks and other household manuals led the pack.

While cookbooks were imported from Europe throughout the colonial period, and produced in the United States from 1796 forward, the production and demand for these texts exploded during the first half of the nineteenth century, when at least 160 new titles were released.[60] Cookbooks became a crucial component of middle-class libraries not only because they were so abundant during the nineteenth century but also because technological innovations such as the cookstove made them necessary. Cookbooks thus contributed to the links between the consumer and domestic worlds.

Since domestic ideology placed such emphasis on the home as an index to the taste and skills of the homemaker, the most successful home was not only tastefully and beautifully decorated but also neat and orderly. Victorian housekeeping standards were a far cry from expectations of eighteenth-century goodwives, for whom household production tasks, not cleanliness, were the markers of stature and success.[61] But in the nineteenth century, middle-class homemakers often relied upon servants rather than doing the tasks themselves. Thus, neatness and tidiness became marks of a competent household manager and—in the ideological realm—a caring and devoted wife and mother. In describing a proper kitchen, one midcentury ladies' magazine explained that above all, "the room shall be clean; . . . the windows shall be transparent, the paint thoroughly washed, the plain furniture and the corners of the room well dusted, and the floor scoured till it is white as polished marble." Cleanliness thus achieved, the ideal homemaker also wanted everything organized and put away, obliging "every good dame who enters . . . to say, 'How handy every thing is here!'"[62]

Domestic advisers stressed the importance of neatness and cleanliness in the dining room as well, arguing that an orderly, well-laid table was at the heart of family happiness, one going so far as to argue that "economy in cooking" was defined by a neat table. The very act of proper digestion depended on the eating environment, no small matter in an era when dyspepsia (or indigestion) was virtually a national ailment. "The clean floor, well-dusted furniture . . . and vases of flowers in summer, wonderfully assist the appetite, and add greatly to the enjoyment of the *plain* but *excellent* fare," explained one cookbook author.[63] The onus of maintaining family happiness thus fell to the woman of the house, and that happiness depended on her keeping a tidy home, a task that required a good deal of time and attention—and, of course, the requisite goods to keep the space welcoming and well appointed.

These ideological developments were national in scope. But New York City played an important role as tastemaker and provisioner of the consumer goods that fed consumer-based domesticity. New York led the nation in dining room fashions and housewares, and New York retailers participated in bridging the gap between home and commerce. By the 1850s,

Lower Broadway housed a concentration of dry goods and furnishings stores, including nationally known firms such as Warren, Ward & Co., Berrian's, and E. V. Haughwout's, which supplied the formal china to the Lincoln White House. The New York firms set the pace for design and fashion as these trends became both accessible to and markers of status for middle-class families. They placed ads in New York newspapers and magazines for specialized household goods such as tea sets, coffee urns, ice pitchers and chocolate pots, silver-plated utensils, cutlery and carving knives, napkin rings, refrigerators, ice cream freezers, and meat safes. New York retailers did not merely advertise housewares. In many cases they took on the role of domestic advisers themselves. For example, Dailey and Haughwout's (a firm co-owned by E. V. Haughwout before he struck out on his own) printed a list of "articles . . . which are all requisite in going to housekeeping." The list was thirty-two lines long in two columns.[64]

New York designers and furniture suppliers advertised to a local and national clientele, offering to send New York fashions and design ideas around the nation and beyond. In 1867, for example, Hadley's advertised an assortment of French china, cutlery, plated ware, pressed glassware, and fancy goods "packed to go all over the world, by express or other wise." And William H. Lee Furniture advertised both a variety of wood furniture and the great care the firm took in packing its inventory for shipping.[65]

In marketing and selling these goods, New York retailers established a bridge between the commercial city and the private home. And they introduced some novel marketing tactics to ease their customers into the burgeoning consumer culture. Many of these techniques look familiar to the modern consumer. One such approach parallels the demonstration kitchens in contemporary department stores and housewares stores like Williams-Sonoma, set up to introduce customers to cooking techniques and the products that support them. In this vein, Stephen Smith's housewares store on Broadway offered a series of lectures on science in the kitchen, delivered by Professor Hume, a specialist in chemistry. Hume offered demonstrations on steam, refrigeration, and other topics. Not merely edifying, Hume's talks were also marketing devices. The professor used them as an opportunity to show off such household gadgets and appliances as pressure coffee pots, tea steepers, julienne mills, water coolers and filters, ice cream freezers, and refrigerators, all of which were available for purchase at Smith's.[66]

The marketing and product placement extended to the periodical literature as well. As they do today, women's magazines like *Godey's*, *Ladies' Home Journal*, and *Harper's Bazaar* included references to specific stores and manufacturers in their reviews of home fashions. New York retailers like can easily turn for pastime, a large quantity can be cut into beautiful forms in a very few moments, and make handsome ornaments for meat, after having assisted to flavor the soup.

The second lecture was on the subject of "Refrigerants," and the beneficial uses of ice and cooling drinks in warm weather; also, the best methods of preserving food in ice, and the various means by which substances can be preserved by exhausting atmospheric air. These subjects were illustrated by numerous experiments, in the course of which the lecturer said that ice and the effects of cold appliances were not half appreciated by people generally. He stated that a small quantity of ice, broken up and eaten in warm weather, would act with a stimulating effect equal to that produced by a glass of wine, especially on a person not accustomed to stimulating liquor. He greatly objected to the use of hot and cold drinks at the same time, said that was the cause of the early decay of teeth common to the American people. His remarks under this head were exceedingly interesting; but as our object is to give as much information as possible to housekeepers, we submit the following figure (10) as a specimen of *refrigerator* which Mr. Hume pronounced exactly adapted to its purpose.

In this it is seen the closet part is distinct from the ice-box, which is at the top, and therefore the food which is put in for preservation does not come in direct contact with the ice, and there is therefore none of that disagreeable mixture of flavors which arise from putting a variety of food in a common refrigerator, besides other annoyances which experienced housekeepers understand. It is also more economical, while its principle of refrigeration is perfect, the current of cold air penetrating to every part through the perforated shelves, and meeting no opposing current of warm air, because by an ingenious little contrivance the water passes off, so that there is no aperture through which warm air could ascend.

FIG. 10.

Numerous articles designed by Mr. Smith for family use, all having a bearing on this subject, were introduced as illustrations, from which we select the

PATENT DOUBLE ICE-PITCHER,

as particularly interesting for the approaching season. The principle is not new, most of our readers having seen it in operation in the large coolers which are used by hotel keepers in saloons, restaurants, etc.

But the ice-pitcher is adapted to the wants of families, many of whom would consider it an inestimable acquisition to be possessed of a water-pitcher which will keep ice six hours;

is a handsome addition to the table or sideboard, and which there is at the same time no possibility of breaking. Very recently Mr. Smith has constructed another, to supply a demand for a less expensive article, and also intended for nursery use. This will keep ice all night, and has also a porcelain cup fitted into the top, which will preserve milk for the "baby," or for "papa," if he wants to start off on a journey early, and have his coffee prepared before the milkman comes round

FIG. 11.

Figure 12 is another.

WATER-COOLER,

which will preserve ice-water twenty-four hours, and is suitable for hotels or private families. These are, indeed, in very general use now, and it would hardly be worth while to introduce it here, except from its connection with the subject, and the fact that having devoted so much attention and scientific research to the *principle*. Every article of this description is prepared by Mr. Smith in the *best* possible manner.

FIG. 12.

Figure 13 is a

WATER-FILTER,

intended for family use, and which will filter from five to fifteen gallons per day. Of the advantage of these it is not necessary to speak. The bad consequences of drinking impure water, to which so many are subject, are too well and universally known; but it is not so generally known that all water is polluted, full of animalculi, which, if we could see when we eagerly grasp the apparently clear and crystalline liquid, we should start back in horror.

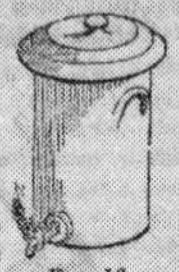

FIG. 13.

The principle of preservation, by the expulsion of atmospheric air, was finally illustrated by figure 14, which is,

ARTHUR'S PATENT SELF-SEALING PRESERVE CANS AND JARS.

These were shown in glass, white queensware, earthenware and tin. The lecturer, however, said he should prefer, for his own use, the glass or earthenware. The waste and loss of fruit by evaporation and otherwise, experienced in the ordinary

This 1857 article from *Ladies' Home Magazine* relays scientific lectures by Professor Hume demonstrating novel household products sold at Stephen Smith's Broadway housewares store. Among the items demonstrated were a "super-refrigerator," an ice pitcher, a water cooler, and a water filter. (Courtesy, American Antiquarian Society)

Warren Ward & Co., Lord & Taylor, DeGraaf & Taylor, A. T. Stewart, and Herter Brothers paired with magazines like *Harper's Bazaar,* sending the editors free samples of their goods. In exchange, they hoped—and often were satisfied to find—that the magazine would mention them by name when announcing new household fashions.[67]

In making design choices for their dining rooms, New York's homemakers also incorporated elements of New York's public dining culture. New York's restaurants served as a model of design and taste for private dining rooms in the city and beyond. Historian Katherine Grier has shown the several ways that "commercial parlors"—in hotels and photography studios, on steamboats and railroad cars—provided a model for women of means in designing and decorating the parlors in their private homes.[68] New York hotels like the Astor House, the St. Nicholas, and the Fifth Avenue Hotel enjoyed influence far beyond their guest rosters. Their barrooms and dining rooms were open to the public, and they hosted public events and exhibitions. Furthermore, their lobbies, lounges, and parlors were accessible to nonguests, and if someone looked like he or she belonged there, the person's presence probably would not be questioned.[69]

Restaurants and other public dining rooms served a similar function for the home dining room. The choices of flatware, china, furniture, chandeliers, wallpaper, and other design elements displayed in fine New York hotels and restaurants stood as a decorative model for homemakers. For example, in its October 1882 issue, the *Art Amateur Magazine* demonstrated its advice on choosing wallpaper for the dining room by pointing to the dining rooms of some of New York's fine restaurants, including the cafés at the Brunswick House and the Gilsey House.[70]

The restaurant as decorative model extended to the table as well as the decor. The *Ladies' Home Journal* included a feature entitled "How Delmonico Sets a Table," which encouraged its readers to follow the restaurant's model in their own homes, noting that Delmonico's "has stood for generations for all that is good in a gastronomical way." Charles Delmonico offered the reader such tricks of the trade as choosing a round over a square dining table, since it gave an impression of King Arthur's court; including flowers in the centerpiece; and keeping the temperature of the room "a trifle cool." He then offered advice on setting the table, including linens "bearing the family crest or coat of arms," dishes from the family's best set, and flatware and serving pieces including the basics, plus oyster forks, soup spoons, candelabra, compotiers (small dishes for holding compotes), fruit dishes, saltcellars, and finger bowls.[71]

Clearly, the dinner that Delmonico, and the author of the article, Foster Coates, had in mind was not one that the average New York homemaker would host. The tablecloth bearing the family coat of arms, the silver and gold dishes and ware, the corsage at every lady's place, would mark the hostess of this meal as a member of the elite. But it was not only the elite who read *Ladies' Home Journal*, a magazine that catered largely to women of the middle classes. These women were unlikely to set a table like the one that Delmonico recommended. But they *were* aware of the model of Delmonico's as an aspirational one, one that set the standard even if it was not adhered to in full in practice. As homemakers do today, nineteenth-century homemakers probably picked a few elements from the advice literature and the public models to incorporate into their own furnishings and home decor.

The restaurant offered an aspirational model for cookery instruction as well. Like today's celebrity chefs, restaurant cooks, caterers, and even waiters authored instructional manuals for the home. Among the most famous cookbooks of the late nineteenth century was *The Epicurean*, authored by Charles Ranhofer, the head chef at Delmonico's. In the enormous tome (over one thousand pages in total), Ranhofer offered advice for marketing, cooking, and setting a table and famous recipes associated with Delmonico's like chicken à la king and lobster Newburg.[72] Several years before Ranhofer's book came out, Astor House chef Thomas Jefferson Murrey authored the 1880 edition (and subsequent editions) of *Valuable Cooking Receipts*. Murrey recognized the value of his association with the Astor and other hotels. He placed his credentials on the book's title page: "Formerly Professional Caterer at the Astor House, etc." And in his preface, the publisher distinguished Murrey's work from the volumes of cookbooks on the market by proclaiming the author's experience in famous hotels and restaurants around the country. The publisher saw this experience as proof positive of Murrey's culinary superiority, asserting that the reputation of these establishments "would of itself form testimony conclusive of his culinary ability."[73]

Murrey's book featured recipes from restaurants, hotels, and caterers including Astor House Pudding and corn bread and muffins from the Continental Hotel, as well as one for oysters in cream sauce celebrated as "a favorite dish of Hotel Brunswick *habitués* in New York."[74] Hotels and restaurants thus held a certain cachet in cookery and household advice, again bridging the commercial and domestic spaces of the city. Even Mrs. Henry Ward Beecher, a celebrant of home and domesticity and of home-prepared foods as a paragon, was impressed by the efficiency and organization of the kitchen at Boston's Parker House Hotel and advised her readers to emulate it in theory if not in scale.[75]

Manufacturers of housewares and home furnishings also sought to capitalize on the notion of restaurants as models. They offered deep discounts and incentives to hotels and restaurants to use their brand, recognizing the marketing potential of being chosen by Delmonico's or the Brevoort Hotel. A representative of the silverware company Reed & Barton made this point explicit in 1877 when he instructed his branch manager in New York to offer Delmonico's some silverware at a very low cost. "There would be no money in them at this price but we would like to have them in Delmonico's as an advertisement," he explained.[76] Silverware firms like Reed & Barton kept track of new public institutions in cities such as New York and sought their commissions, recognizing that consumers could see novel designs in hotels, restaurants, and other public dining rooms, and hope to emulate these standards in their own homes.[77]

Most homemakers, however, could afford neither to eat in such restaurants on a regular basis, nor to replicate their furnishings in their homes. The prescriptive literature itself acknowledged the difficulty, if not impossibility, of importing the restaurant environment into one's home. An 1874 article in the *New-York Tribune* pointed out the challenge, noting that the average housekeeper "has no French cook in her kitchen, nor skillful waiters in her dining-room with whom serving is a high art. She cannot even afford, except upon the rarest occasion, to order from a caterer both dinner and waiters. She has a cook from Cork, a chambermaid from Tipperary."[78] As is the case today, it was very difficult to actually replicate a restaurant meal or experience in the home.

But homemakers borrowed ideas and elements from New York restaurants when decorating their dining rooms, choosing their furnishings and dishes, and preparing their meals. One indication that restaurants influenced actual homemakers comes from the cooking columns of New York's newspapers. The *New-York Times'* "Household Column" published readers' queries on recipes and household tips, soliciting the advice of other readers. Frequently, a reader wrote in asking for a recipe that she had tasted in a restaurant. For example, H. A. P. asked for instructions "to fry saddlerock oysters as they do in Fulton Market or in the restaurants." Likewise, a reader calling herself "Cuisine" wrote to the column asking "how to make those delicious little butter-cakes sold in first-class restaurants."[79] "Cuisine" and the other letter writers demonstrate prescription in action. Of course, we do not know how "Cuisine" furnished her dining room. Perhaps she did follow Delmonico's advice to the letter. But more likely, she compromised, replicating a small, accessible piece of the restaurant experience by making delicious butter cakes in her home.

Household inventories and other data also show the prescriptive advice at play, providing clear indications that middle-class homemakers adorned their tables with more and more specialized dishes, utensils, and linens, dividing their dinners into a series of courses, and engaging in more ritualized conduct around food. Archaeological evidence suggests a far greater range and specialization of ceramics and plate ware even in Gotham's working-class homes.[80] Prescriptive advisers thus had some influence on the ground as middle-class and even working-class New Yorkers placed a greater emphasis on the rituals and accoutrements of dining. The press confirmed this point. The New-York Times wrote approvingly in 1876 of "the growing taste for something better in the way of cookery than what is in common use." And a few years later, a British visitor argued that "Americans have entered upon their epicurean era." He went on to declare that "for beauty . . . and taste the homes of America challenge competition with the world."[81]

These assessments surely pleased domestic advisers. After all, they had worked hard to convince their readers that the dining room and the family meal should be given a privileged place in the home and daily life of the family. But their concern was not solely aesthetic. They had high expectations for the dining room as a space for family education and cohesion. These roles, although rooted in the ideology of domesticity, were also strongly linked to commercial imperatives.

For example, because of the symbolic importance of the family meal for family bonding, domestic advisers suggested that servants should not eat with their employers, a departure from the preindustrial household system of labor whereby masters, laborers, servants, apprentices, and slaves ate meals together. In the new domestic sphere, mealtime was family time. And servants were decidedly *not* members of the family. As Catharine Beecher explained in her *Letters to Persons Engaged in Domestic Service*, the male head of household, separated from his wife and children all day, reunited with them only at mealtimes. As such Beecher explained, "he wishes to be at liberty to talk freely, as he could not do, if every stranger he hires must come to his family meal."[82]

This portrayal of servants as strangers, rather than as members of the family, reflected a new understanding of the role of domestics in the nineteenth century, itself rooted in increasing consumerism. The old paternalistic model that guided the preindustrial household system of production included servants and slaves as part of the master's extended family. As remunerative work left the home and as slavery was phased out in the North (and eventually in the South), servants became employees. Furthermore, middle-class women purchased more of the items that their mothers and grandmothers would have produced themselves. Servants remained—and in some cases proliferated—in the middle-class home but were concerned more with the upkeep of the household than with its productive capacities.

In addition, in New York City, servants increasingly came from the growing ranks of European immigrants, separating them further from their native-born, middle-class employers. Servants were seen as apart from, rather than a part of, the family, and their status within the home declined accordingly. A major indicator of the formalization of servitude was the growing general custom of servants eating separately from the families they served. "The old New England notion that the word servant was degrading, and that a separate servant's table was a thing not to be thought of, has died out in this meridian long since, and it is well so," claimed *Harper's Weekly* in 1857.[83]

Servants did not see it this way. Historian Faye Dudden points out that "hired girls" understood the symbolic importance of eating with the family they served. They thus resisted the trend toward a servant's table, especially as it became the norm in US cities.[84] Conversely, domestic arbiters urged employers to keep servants apart to further emphasize the mealtime as family time.

The very structure of Victorian homes incorporated the separation of servants and employers during meals. Newer homes included a butler's pantry between the dining room and kitchen, where servants were to stay until called to deliver and clear dishes. And dumbwaiters were installed to ease the carriage of heavy dishes from kitchens—servants' quarters located out of sight in the basement—to the more public, upstairs regions of the home.[85] Just like the bursting sideboard, the presence and incorporation of servants into the dining room further demonstrated the family's status even if company was not present. Servants performed tasks that were not productive but rather ceremonial, thus demonstrating Veblen's "conspicuous leisure." The dining ritual served as a particularly clear example. Servants did jobs that the family members easily could have done themselves. Performed by paid employees, however, these activities added to the ritual aspects of the meal and allowed the family to concentrate on cohesion and socializing rather than the mundane chores of cooking, serving, and clearing dishes.

The presence of servants also allowed middle-class parents uninterrupted time around the table to socialize their children in the etiquette and

manners that were an important part of middle-class norms. Popular nov-
elist Catharine Sedgwick described family meals as "opportunities of improvement and social happiness," a thrice-daily chance to teach children
such values as punctuality, order, neatness, self-denial, generosity, and hospitality.[86] Parents did not bear their educational burden alone. They could
lean on a host of etiquette manuals that flooded the market as cookbooks
did in the first half of the nineteenth century.[87] Etiquette advisers and those
who accepted their advice recognized the links between private and public
behaviors, again interweaving domesticity and commerce.[88] Manners were
evidence of good breeding—of the success of the parents and, by extension, domesticity itself. In addition, manners played an important role in
conspicuous leisure since one needed the free time (away from work) to
learn good breeding. Manners thus served as "vouchers of a life of leisure,"
helping to display and sustain an individual's social class both within and
outside of the home.[89]

Children had to learn how to behave at table, even if only the family was
present, because at any given time, guests could arrive. Furthermore, the
children eventually would be partaking of meals in others' homes, and in
the hotels and restaurants of the city. An individual and family's reputation
in the outside world could only be assured if children were taught early and
often not to eat off of their knives, or blow their noses on the tablecloth,
or speak with a mouthful of food. Catharine Sedgwick nodded to this issue when she wrote of a family where mealtimes were not seen as sacred.
"Would there not be some danger," she implored, "that young persons,
bred in such utter disregard of . . . *les petites morales* would prove, as men and
women, sadly deficient in the social virtues?"[90]

Learning proper comportment thus was crucial in an advancing consumer society. Behaviors and mores marked one as refined and middle-
class whereas poor behaviors around the table indicated a fish out of water
in society. Furthermore, behaving properly in consumer society and commercial transactions was crucial to replicating middle-class status. Manners
also showed that parents, especially mothers, were successful in creating
a nurturing domestic environment. Here again, at its heart, the domestic
ideal was the counterpart of the commercial sphere, not the opposite of it.
In serving as a haven from the world of commerce, the ideal home served
not to separate the members of the family from the public sphere but to
fortify them for it.

New York's nineteenth-century homes thus interacted with and corre-
lated to its increasingly cosmopolitan consumer culture in a host of ways.
Middle-class homes served as showcases to display a family's collection of

consumer goods and status as well as the requisite behaviors and rituals that marked them as middle-class. Most middle-class New Yorkers probably did not set aside and furnish dining rooms and fill their kitchens with consumer goods and the latest technologies *only* in order to display status. The rituals of consumption are far more complex. As they do today, many homes likely offered a sentimental haven to their denizens while simultaneously showcasing the family's status. Hominess and consumerism are not mutually exclusive. Likewise, the dining room could serve both as a venue for conspicuous consumption and leisure and a space of family tradition, fortification, and education. The rhetoric and use of the dining room highlight the strong links between public and private—the not-so-separate spheres of the nineteenth-century "cult of domesticity." Consumerism and domesticity were not at odds in the nineteenth century. Rather they worked together to link both the home and the family meal to the growing public culture of New York City.

*The Empire of Gastronomy, 1850–1890.* This map shows the
food wholesalers, restaurants, and markets referenced in
the chapter. (Map by Ben Benjamin)

# SIX

# "The Empire of Gastronomy":
# New York and the World, 1850–1890

By the 1890s, cookbook authors, food writers, restaurateurs, and observers of all sorts identified New York as the paragon and center of American food culture. The city gathered, processed, and sold more foodstuffs, had more restaurants (and a greater diversity of them), and marketed more food-related household goods than any other place in the country. Gotham had developed a food supply and distribution system that amazed and bewildered observers. To some, it seemed, all the peoples of the world were at the service of Manhattan's food needs. *Harper's Weekly* writer G. T. Ferris marveled that ships crossed oceans, trains traversed the continent, and the farmers, hunters, and ranchers of the nation offered delicacies from "thousands of miles away" to even the "greasy mechanic . . . ditch-digger," and "day-laborer toiling in the streets" of New York. In short, New York had clearly evolved into the "empire of gastronomy" that James Fenimore Cooper had predicted it would become more than sixty years before.[1]

New York City had traveled a long way since the opening of the nineteenth century, from a colonial seaport led by a patrician government, its food supply local and preindustrial. The city's central position in the production and distribution of food placed it at the center of the country's gastronomic culture, a role that only intensified with time as Gotham's economy grew more global and its population more diverse. By the 1890s, New York led the nation in manufacturing and agricultural exports and imported goods from all points of the globe. In addition to goods, New York drew people from within the United States and abroad both as residents and tourists, who came to see the American metropolis. American mass media and mass consumer culture began to take root in the final decades of the nineteenth century, and New York served as the center of these industries and businesses as well. And of course, New York had by far the most diverse population of any city in the country and arguably in the world.[2] As its population diversified and New York became a majority immigrant city by the end of the nineteenth century, New York flavor became evermore international. All the cuisines of the world were on offer in New York. One could "visit" the various nations and regions of the world without leaving Manhattan Island, as observers commonly pointed out.

Gotham's rise as the gastronomic capital thus was linked to its emergence as a global city by the end of the nineteenth century. But New York still wore its mantle of cosmopolitanism uncomfortably. Guidebooks, newspapers, and periodicals representing New York celebrated the metropolis's diverse population, frenetic pace, vibrant culture, and financial and commercial prowess. They enjoyed their town's reputation as a world-class city on par with the capitals of Europe. But at the same time that they celebrated New York's cosmopolitanism, many native-born New Yorkers held their immigrant neighbors and their customs at arm's length.

This conflict was not unique to New York City but rather part of a larger American ambivalence about race, civilization, and power as the United States became a player on the world stage. The Anglo-American engagement with various cultures served in part to confirm American superiority. The world's expositions that took place in the United States in the final decades of the nineteenth century illustrate this process most fully. These expositions—in Philadelphia in 1876 and Chicago in 1893—celebrated and displayed the progress of civilizations around the globe.

Ethnic diversity was part of the attraction of the world's expositions. But, as historian Robert Rydell argues, the fairs and their organizers assumed the racial superiority of Anglo-American culture over non-Western and even many European civilizations. These assumptions influenced the organization of the fairs and the content of their exhibits, which emphasized the primitiveness of non-Western cultures. The ideas at the center of the fairs also served a purpose for white, native-born fairgoers who, in attending the expos, could see their own imagined cultural and racial superiority confirmed.[3] Not only at the midways and main exhibits of the world's fairs but also at amusement parks like Coney Island's Luna Park and Dreamland, in the representations offered onstage in American theaters, and even in the design choices that middle-class and elite Americans made in their homes, Anglo-American progress and achievement was measured in part by American superiority to the allegedly barbaric and savage cultures of Asia, Africa, and southern Europe.[4]

This larger zeitgeist carried over into New York's food culture. Observers and commentators of various stripes celebrated New York as a gastronomic empire incorporating the complex meaning of the term "empire." The press celebrated the importation of foodstuffs from foreign parts as a sign of New York's commercial and cultural prowess. The swarthy peoples of the world, these accounts suggested, lived to serve the needs of the civilized metropolis. And as the foods of Italy, China, and eastern Europe made their way into food shops and restaurants in New York's uptown middle-class and wealthy neighborhoods, native-born, middle-class New Yorkers colonized these cuisines. New York gastronomes bragged that their city housed restaurants of every nation. But their assessments of those restaurants were often laced with arrogance. And the representations they offered of their foreign hosts were usually romanticized and exoticized at best and outright xenophobic at worst.

Rather than celebrate the quality of the cuisine, native accounts of foreign restaurants lauded the "American" diner for his willingness to experience strange and novel cultures. Gastronomic adventurers in late nineteenth-century New York found their cultural superiority confirmed in visiting foreign restaurants. In this way, their excursions were similar to the native-born visitors to world's fair midways who perceived their own cultural supremacy in the exhibits of the "exotic" peoples of Asia and Africa. In neither case did the visitors gain much of an appreciation for foreign cultures.[5]

At the same time, New York's food sector offered economic, social, and cultural opportunities to newly arrived immigrants. Immigrant entrepreneurs opened groceries, food shops, peddlers' carts, and restaurants in ethnic enclaves throughout the city. These businesses provided an economic foothold to their owners and cultural and social outlets to their patrons. Overall, they contributed to the growing ethnicization of New York's food and public culture in the late nineteenth century.

Thus, New York's cosmopolitanism was simultaneously global and provincial—celebratory and fostering of its pluralistic and diverse population *and* proud of its Americanness. In the second half of the nineteenth century, New York's markets, processing plants, warehouses, food shops, and restaurants collected, distributed, and offered the foods of the nation and world *to* the nation and the world. In short, New York had managed to model a food culture that was as dynamic as the city itself. Celebrated for its commerce, diversity, and cosmopolitanism, Gotham had truly become an empire of gastronomy, with all that the term entails. By the late nineteenth century, provincialism and cosmopolitanism interacted to propel New York to the apex of American food culture, a position it holds to this day.

New York's role as the nation's food capital began with its wholesale markets and processing plants. Just as restaurants and markets served as an index to the larger economic changes of the early and mid-nineteenth century, in many ways the shape and tenor of New York's food manufacturing, processing, and distribution industries indicated the economic and industrial developments of the late nineteenth century. Like many Gilded Age concerns, New York's food industries were vertically and horizontally integrated businesses that drew from and linked to the metropolitan region and beyond. Food processors with headquarters in New York City had processing plants in New Jersey, Long Island, and Upstate New York. These locales contributed raw materials and customers as well. Food wholesaler Frances H. Leggett had a factory in Riverside, New Jersey, that processed and packed private-label jams, canned goods, and specialty items. The processing plant for Borden's condensed milk was located in Brewster, New York. And H. J. Heinz opened a sauerkraut plant in Long Island in the 1890s. *Harper's Weekly* went so far as to claim that due to their manufacturing connections to the metropolis, "Brooklyn, Long Island City, Jersey City, and Hoboken are essentially a part of the great city of Manhattan Island."[6]

While food processing was not as important a sector of New York's economy as the behemoth garment industry, food manufacturing did make up a significant portion of the local and national economy. As historian Donna Gabaccia points out, food industries formed the leading manufacturing sector in the nineteenth-century United States, expanding fifteenfold between 1859 and 1889. General manufacturing, on the other hand, increased only six times in that same period. By the end of the century, food processing composed 20 percent of the nation's manufacturing output.[7] Fourteen percent of the nation's food canning and preserving took place in New York City and Brooklyn. This percentage placed New York well ahead of any other city in the United States as a food processor. Its closest competitor was Chicago whose canning and preserving industry was less than half that of Gotham. These figures do not include the baking, sugar-refining, or bottling industries which New York City also dominated. Although Chicago blew New York City away in meatpacking, New York actually led Chicago in wholesale slaughtering without meatpacking (probably owing to New York's dominance of the kosher-meat trade).[8] In addition, by the 1890s, the city handled two-thirds of the nation's exports and two-thirds of its imports. These cargoes included a significant amount of foodstuffs.[9]

New York's position at the center of food wholesaling and processing makes sense since the city had laid the roots for a national and international commerce in food during the early and mid-nineteenth century. Some of the relatively modest mercantile groceries of the early nineteenth century mushroomed into horizontally and vertically integrated businesses in the late nineteenth century. Grocers expanded and modernized their inventories, adding canned goods and imported groceries and using such technologies as steam-powered coffee roasters and millers. As these businesses grew, they extended and consolidated the national and international networks they had established in the early nineteenth century for purchasing and selling foodstuffs. Gotham continued to serve as their base and thus the nexus of food distribution for the nation and much of the world.[10]

New York's wholesalers also drew on networks and institutions with deep roots such as Washington Market and its western annex. On the docks of Manhattan's west side stood "the termini of scores of inland transportation lines and the landings of hundreds of vessels engaged in the foreign and domestic fruit and produce trade," explained an 1880 guide to the city. Most of the four-hundred-plus produce, meat, and fish dealers at West Washington Market were commission merchants who handled small lots. They dealt almost exclusively in wholesaling foodstuffs and funneled much of their inventory through New York's port to places throughout the country and the world, barely touching the local market. In 1889, the city opened a new West Washington Market on the Hudson River between Gansevoort and Little West Twelfth Street to coordinate the wholesale food trade. These wholesalers handled American grains and breadstuffs for the domestic and European market, and imported delicacies like olive oils, teas, spices, and tropical fruit for the United States and foreign markets.[11]

In fact, New York was the preeminent tropical fruit market in the world, drawing ships from the Caribbean, Central and South America, the Mediterranean, and Asia. The tropical fruit trade suggests some of the international ties forged by New York concerns through food sales and distribution. By the 1880s, New York received almost three million boxes every year of lemons and oranges from Italy and Spain. "The fruit schooners constantly arriving and departing from this port, with their crews of quaint-looking swarthy sailors, make one of the most picturesque minor spectacles on the New York water-front," exclaimed a writer for *Harper's Weekly*.[12] The importing trade in lemons, oranges, and grapes was dominated by Italian agents who were connected with the European growers. They met the ships at the docks and unloaded their cargo. Once the fruit was in New York, it likely found its way to the auction house of Brown & Seccomb, which almost completely dominated the trade in Mediterranean fruits. From their building on State and Bridge Streets, Brown & Seccomb auctioned off lots of twenty crates minimum to large wholesale dealers and small fruit peddlers alike. Like

These trade cards—for H. K. & F. B Thurber & Co.; Austin, Nicholas, & Co.; and Bennett & Hall, wholesale grocers—show the national and global reach of New York's food manufacturers. Trains and boats bring produce from the metropolitan regions, the rural areas of the United States, and the tropical areas of the world to the wholesalers of New York City. (Collection of the New-York Historical Society)

other food-related businesses in late nineteenth-century New York, Brown & Seccomb was a horizontally integrated concern. The firm's headquarters housed auction rooms, offices, and warehouses.[13]

Produce arrived via rail as well from the southern states where truck farming concerns developed in Florida, Georgia, Alabama, and South Carolina to service the New York wholesale and retail trade. Commission agents met these boats and trains at the docks and depots and made arrangements to distribute produce to distant markets. During the summer and fall, local farmers from within a dozen miles of New York brought their wagons and carts to West Washington Market, contributing traffic of a thousand carts a day during high season. These country people stocked the retail grocers of the city and did a business of $5 million per year.[14] West Washington Market also concentrated the city's poultry trade, which spilled out to the old Washington Market and Fulton Market. Special commission brokers contracted with agencies that represented farmers and hunters in New York's near and far hinterlands. These brokers gathered live and dressed poultry and wild game as well as eggs and distributed the inventory within New York City and to wholesale dealers around the country.[15]

Meanwhile, across from Fulton Market on Manhattan's east side, fishermen dropped their catches for processing and shipping around the country. Fulton Fish Market's eighteen fish concerns formed a stock company that owned the building. As a group they supplied the needs of the city and much of the country, handling 150 tons of fish per day, half of which served the direct New York market. Each Fulton dealer owned several smacks (up to one hundred) operated by a host of intrepid fisherman who plied the local waters. In addition, Fulton Fish Market received shipments from up and down the East Coast and the Great Lakes, sometimes delivered alive, other times packed on ice in refrigerated cars. Among the variety the market offered was "the gorgeous redsnapper from the Georgia and South Carolina coast, the pearl-colored and toothsome pompano from Florida, the beautiful and shapely sea-bass and shad from North Carolina, the brilliant groups of lobsters from Maine, the monster and sharklike halibut from our own coast, the ciscoes from Lake Erie, frozen in strips four fishes broad and from six to eight fishes long," Harper's salivated. A "monster fish" from as far away as Oregon might even make an appearance.[16]

The fish market was alive with activity in the early morning hours, and its activity extended onto the streets around it for a quarter of a mile. Fisherman carried their loads of fresh and frozen fish over temporary bridges erected between the ships' decks, to the piers and thence to the market stalls and express wagons that transported the fish to retailers throughout the city and beyond. After the express wagons came the retail grocers, and by daybreak "the fishes are found lying in retail stores and markets in a thousand places in the great city and its dependent cities and towns, and traffic begins there," explained *Harper's*. Restaurateurs and boardinghouse and hotel keepers came next but for the most part, householders stayed away from the wholesale markets, opting instead for retail options near their homes.[17]

As for meat, by the 1890s, New York had ceded meatpacking to Chicago, which processed ten times the amount of meat that Gotham did. But New York was the second-largest meat processing center in the country. Livestock drovers brought live cattle to the New York stockyards from the Northeast, Midwest, and beyond, even from Texas and New Mexico. Large New York firms like the Eastman Company in the West Sixties and Schwartzchild & Sulzberger on East Forty-Seventh Street slaughtered and packed beef and pork for the local and distant markets. The large meatpacking concerns also had branch offices in New York, which served as the central distribution point for dressed meat for the eastern states and even Europe. Refrigerated railcars from Chicago brought fresh cuts of meat, which were unloaded to large warehouses on the west side of Manhattan and then repacked onto trains and special refrigerated compartments of steamships bound across the Atlantic.[18]

In the second half of the century, Washington Market spread far beyond its original structure, becoming "a locality rather than . . . a place," thanks to the "magnitude of the interests which have grown up around it," according to *Appleton's* guidebook to the city. Food importers, commission merchants, and food processors set up their offices in multistory factory buildings near the wholesale markets. New York's large grocery wholesalers handled huge inventories of goods, collecting the "food products of the whole world" at their headquarters. Austin, Nichols, & Co., one of the most successful, operated out of a ten-story purpose-built building on Hudson and Jay Streets from 1879 forward. Its main competitor, Frances H. Leggett & Co., had a similar operation on nearby Murray Street. According to one account, Austin, Nichols's building was "one of the busiest sites in the commercial metropolis." In addition to carrying "the fullest line of fancy and staple goods," such as sugars, oils, coffees, teas, olives, extracts, syrups, and spices, these large grocer wholesalers also processed and wholesaled food under their own private label.[19]

Other New York food processors expanded their operations as the food industry became more corporatized, including Durkee Spices, Horton's Ice Cream, Borden's Milk, and the New York Biscuit Company (precursor to

Nabisco.)[20] In fact, the New York Biscuit Company, founded in 1890, was the first food corporation in the United States, an example of New York's reach in terms of national and international food systems. A combination of over thirty East Coast cracker manufacturers, the New York Biscuit Company was completely centered in New York City. While two other cracker giants competed with it—the Chicago-based American Biscuit Company and the United States Biscuit Company, located on the West Coast—New York cornered a huge share of the nation's consumer cracker industry at a time when New Yorkers and Americans in general were becoming more reliant on manufactured and trademarked food products. All across the country and the world, consumers purchased and ate crackers and biscuits with the name "New York Biscuit Company" on the box. Nabisco's products, King's Handbook to New York City explained, "reach all civilized parts of the world."[21]

The formation of the New York Biscuit Company was part of a move toward consolidation in American industry in general and food industries in particular. The Sugar Trust, formed in 1887, was a prime example of these monopolies, eventually controlling 98 percent of the American sugar industry. The president and founding member of the trust, Edward Havemeyer, got his start in his family's Brooklyn sugar refinery on the East River. And like the National Biscuit Company, the Sugar Trust—along with its sugar brand Domino's—was headquartered in New York City, a major sugar-refining center dating back to the eighteenth century.[22]

The food industry most associated with nineteenth-century New York, however, was oyster processing whose evolution, again, shows New York's development as a food business center.[23] Gotham was the nation's oyster wholesaler and processor, collecting oysters at its markets and slips and packing and shipping them around the United States and to Europe. Before refrigeration and steam transportation, most of the oysters sent abroad or out west were preserved by pickling or canning. The wholesale market for fresh oysters increased in the 1850s. The same new technologies that expanded the city's food supply did so for its wholesale trade as well—ice harvesting and storage, refrigerated railcars, and packing techniques allowed oystermen to ship fresh oysters all the way to California. In the 1850s, about fifteen hundred boats were engaged in bringing oysters to the New York market, and over fifty thousand individuals were employed in one way or another—planting, harvesting, transporting, exporting, or selling oysters. The city's oyster industry yielded between $5 and $6 million a year. By mid-century, the industry began to undergo vertical and horizontal integration, a few firms controlling all aspects of the oyster business including cultivation, processing, and sale. Like the fish dealers at Fulton Fish Market, Manhattan's oyster dealers owned a fleet of smacks and, in many cases, the beds from which the oysters were harvested.[24]

The city's oyster firms concentrated at two wholesale markets, one on the Hudson River just north of Washington Market and the other on the East River near Catharine Market. The oyster concerns operated out of wooden barges that they parked at the markets, each barge owned by a different dealer. In season, two hundred oystermen would arrive daily in sloops and schooners, pull up to the barges, and unload thousands of bushels. Oysters came to New York from local beds on Long Island, New Jersey, Staten Island, and Connecticut and, in smaller numbers, from New England and the Chesapeake, the source of the seed oysters planted in many of New York's waters. Oysters also arrived by rail and by steamboat from Virginia and Connecticut. Meanwhile, purchasers who arrived on wagons usually entered the barges from the street side. The barges housed offices on a second story.

By the 1880s, thirty barges were parked permanently at the wholesale oyster markets, giving the look of a row of storefronts along the waterfront. The barges were a hub of activity as packers, cullers, and shuckers gathered and prepared the bivalves for market. By this point, according to an estimate in *Harper's Weekly*, New Yorkers consumed "over a million dozen oysters every day." Over time the barges moved northward, especially on the west side where they migrated from Vesey Street to Spring Street to Christopher

This stereograph shows the oyster barges at the foot of West Tenth Street, one of the centers of oyster wholesaling in late nineteenth-century New York.
(Collection of the New-York Historical Society)

Street. Toward the end of the century, they settled at West Tenth Street, near West Washington Market. At this point, the industry was also concentrated in the hands of a few firms.[25]

Like other New York food concerns, oystering was an international industry, reflecting New York's position at the center of a global food trade. But the food culture was also growing increasingly cosmopolitan within the city itself. Thus, New York led the nation in the size and diversity of its immigrant groups, who emerged both as consumers and suppliers. This development was to be expected since, in the second half of the nineteenth century, New York was rapidly becoming an immigrant city. The factors that drew imports of produce also encouraged large-scale immigration. Between 1865 and 1890, even before the major wave of immigration that passed through Ellis Island, thousands of immigrants settled in New York City.

Immigrant groups created a manufacturing subsector, opening factories to cater to the diverse population of the city and immigrant pockets throughout the United States. For example, as the center of American Jewish life, New York dominated kosher-meat preparation in the United States even as Chicago supplanted Gotham as the center of the nation's main meatpacking industry. In the first decades of the twentieth century, nine thousand of the ten thousand kosher butcher shops in the United States were in New York City.

Jewish New Yorkers also invented the matzoh business in the United States. As early as 1859, nine New York Jewish bakeries were preparing matzoh for Passover and shipping it to Jewish communities around the country. Like crackers, matzoh-making became a corporate affair when Hungarian-born Jacob Horowitz founded Horowitz Brothers and Margareten in 1883. Competitors such as Strumpf soon followed. Most immigrant processing, though, was considerably more local. Engaging in what today we would call small-batch production, immigrant women turned part of their kitchens into tiny factories creating domestic versions of imported foods like pasta. In some cases, immigrant women offered rudimentary catering services in their homes, selling meals, baked goods, and other specialties from their tenement kitchens.[26]

Some immigrant entrepreneurs took these activities a step further, opening restaurants, cafés, and other food businesses in their neighborhoods. In the second half of the nineteenth century, immigrant-owned food businesses were linchpins in the city's many ethnic neighborhoods. In the 1890s, the Jewish Lower East Side alone had hundreds of food businesses catering to local customers including 140 groceries, 131 kosher butchers, 36 bakeries, 10 delicatessens, and countless peddlers who sold foodstuffs from pushcarts. Immigrant-owned groceries, restaurants, cafés, and food services served multiple purposes in the lives of the immigrant communities and the larger city.

First and most obviously, food shops, pushcarts, peddlers, and restaurants sold necessary foodstuffs to the householders of the ethnic enclaves that began to dot the city in the 1840s and 1850s: Little Germany, or Kleindeutschland (which stretched from Houston Street to Fourteenth Street on the Lower East Side); the French Quarter around Wooster Street in today's SoHo; the Italian Quarter radiating out from Mulberry Street; the Jewish Lower East Side; and Chinatown, centering on Mott Street, among them. They offered local produce and goods as well as foods from home like German brown bread and sausages; Italian macaroni and bologna; Chinese teas, herbs, and shark's fin soup. Itinerant immigrant vendors also traveled door-to-door in immigrant enclaves, offering specialized services to their neighbors. The *Krauthobler*, for example, visited the homes of Kleindeutschland, shaving cabbage for the German housewives who turned it into sauerkraut.[27]

Second, ethnic businesses offered rare economic opportunities to immigrant proprietors. Food businesses—especially the peddlers' carts that sometimes turned into brick-and-mortar businesses—required relatively little capital and could find a ready market. They thus enabled entrepreneurship for a disproportionate number of New York's immigrants. Of course, as is the case today, establishing a major business was difficult in nineteenth-century New York. And except in rare cases, immigrant entrepreneurship did not yield great fortunes or entry into the larger corporate economy of the late nineteenth century. But food did provide a foothold in New York for many immigrant proprietors. German immigrants in particular found a niche in New York's economy selling food. In the mid-nineteenth century, almost 7 percent of working German immigrants were involved in food-based trades. These included the dairy business, butchering, and baking, which Germans dominated by the 1860s. German bakers ran two-thirds of the city's bakeries by the late nineteenth century, selling bread both to their compatriots in New York and to native-born New Yorkers. For the latter, they baked the Wonder Bread–like "Vienna bread," more suited to native-born tastes than the coarse, dark breads that German immigrants preferred at home.[28]

German predominance extended to retailing as well. By the 1850s, Germans began to supplant their Irish counterparts as New York's primary grocers. If they sold fresh fruits and vegetables in their groceries, these German proprietors were likely vending goods grown by their compatriots since, by the middle of the century, "the Market Gardens are cultivated by Germans," as a census marshal explained. The many petitions filed by the market gardeners over regulation (or lack thereof) in Washington Market also reflected the German dominance of the trade in midcentury New York City. German grocers viewed their shops as a stepping-stone toward opening a larger and more respectable business such as a beer hall or formal saloon, and within a generation, many of the antebellum grocers followed this route out of the grocery trade.[29] Thanks in part to their high levels of entrepreneurship, Germans were viewed as a model immigrant community by many native-born New Yorkers. *Harper's Weekly*, for example, declared that "a large proportion of the most industrious, thrifty, energetic, enlightened, and successful men are Germans by birth."[30]

Food businesses, among others, thus served to ease the process of adjustment (at least economic adjustment) to the United States for many German immigrant proprietors. In some cases, food businesses like groceries were one of the only options available to immigrant entrepreneurs. This was more true of the Chinese who began to settle in New York in small numbers in the 1860s. With the completion of the transcontinental railroad and the rise of anti-Chinese laws in the West, Chinese migrants made their way eastward seeking opportunity in New York and other eastern cities and towns. Still, discriminatory laws limited opportunities for Chinese entrepreneurs, leaving them with just a few choices—laundries, restaurants, and groceries among them. Even banks refused to accept Chinese deposits.[31] So most Chinese immigrants did not have the capital necessary to start a grocery business. Grocer Wo Kee was a notable exception. He raised enough money to open a shop on Mott Street in Chinatown in 1872. Catering to the various needs of his customers, Wo Kee parlayed his initial modest investment into a $150,000 business by 1885 (over $3 million today).[32]

A third, important function of immigrant food shops and restaurants involved catering to the emotional, social, and economic needs of immigrant New Yorkers. This role went well beyond inventory and even beyond food. For example, in 1888, Chinatown's thirty-plus grocery stores, including Wo Kee's, sold Chinese provisions such as wines and spirits, duck cakes, dried cuttlefish, dried salt fish, bean extracts, mushrooms, and canned bamboo shoots to local residents. But they also served as assimilation points for new arrivals, post offices, information centers, and banks (loaning money to Chinese immigrants who couldn't borrow from American banks). Chinatown grocery stores acted as regional aid societies, each grocery representing a particular county or region in China and serving the needs of immigrants from that region.[33]

Italian cafés served a similar function. By 1890, New York housed over one hundred thousand Italian residents and one hundred cafés to serve their needs. Akin to the old corner groceries, the Italian cafés sold provisions but also set aside some space for meal service. In addition to coffee, they offered macaroni, beef stew, omelets, and other dishes. Like the Chinese groceries, Italian cafés were organized along regional lines: Florentine, Sicilian, Neopolitan, and Genovese. In addition to selling boxes of pasta, bundles of onions, garlic, and peppers, and a variety of Italian sausages, the cafés gathered Italian immigrants in a social and cultural space. Alive with activity, these establishments hosted men drinking coffee, smoking, and sometimes gambling, and women shoppers, haggling over the price of provisions.[34] Groceries and cafés thus contributed to the ethnicization of New York's food and business culture and to the life of the immigrant enclave.

While ethnic grocery stores largely served a local population, they also linked commercial New York City to the world by importing goods such as Italian olive oils, spaghetti, Chinese teas, dried fish, and herbs. In some cases, they also exported to foreign parts. For example, Wo Kee sent to China ginseng, decorative items, cutlery, firearms, and other American manufactured products. He also imported Chinese goods, which he reexported to Cuba and the West Indies, as well as cured meats, prepared vegetables, and Chinese American delicacies.[35]

Many immigrant businesses were far more mobile than the brick-and-mortar groceries and cafés yet no less important to the ethnic neighborhood and the immigrant entrepreneur. In fact, the street and pushcart vendors that had dotted the city since the seventeenth century increasingly came to be seen as particular to and characteristic of immigrant neighborhoods. Earlier in the century New Yorkers of various class and ethnic backgrounds might buy foods from street peddlers or carts on the street. But as the nineteenth century progressed, buying food outdoors became a mark of lower-class status and middle- and upper-class New Yorkers pursued indoor food options at their local grocers and food purveyors. Meanwhile, huge pushcart markets formed in immigrant neighborhoods. Peddlers defied a law that required pushcarts to move every thirty minutes and, by the 1880s, began to set up stationary markets around the city. The market that lined Ninth Avenue between Twenty-Eighth and Thirty-Fourth Streets became known as "Paddy's Market" since "sellers and buyers alike, have at least a touch of brogue in their voices." Farther downtown, Hester Street was thronged daily with carts and baskets selling goods to the residents of the growing Lower East Side, where "the Russian, Polish, and German Jews . . . are establishing something like a Ghetto," explained an 1892 guidebook to the city.[36]

Like the immigrant groceries, pushcarts and pushcart markets played a social and emotional role for the immigrants they served. First, these un-official markets replaced the public markets as gathering points for working-class New Yorkers, the cart-lined streets offering "picturesque sights," by one account. Paddy's Market and the huckster's market on First Avenue, between Seventy-Ninth and Eighty-Fourth Streets did most of their business in the evenings, especially Saturday nights when the working-class patrons were free from their labors. The "Jews Market" offered a similar scene. Hester Street was bustling with activity on Thursday nights and Friday mornings as local residents prepared for the Jewish Sabbath. "Everything that man needs is to be found there," explained one observer. "Fish of all kinds, mountains of black bread, choicest meats, are all on sale."[37]

Journalist and reformer Jacob Riis described Hester Street as the "pig-market," explaining that "the name was given to it probably in derision, for pork is the one ware that is not on sale in the Pig-market." Everything else was available on the carts and stands of Hester Street, at "ridiculously low prices." In addition to the dry goods, "damaged" eggs, live fowl, and half-plucked geese were found specialty services like the "woman churning horse-radish on a machine she has chained and padlocked to a tree on the sidewalk." In all, the market was bustling with business and activity and recalled the scenes of social and economic activity described at the city's public markets more than a half century prior.[38]

Colorful, vibrant, and cheap, the food offered by pushcarts and peddlers ensured that New York's Lower East Side could provide its residents with the cheapest groceries in the city and even the country.[39] And they offered foods from home to both newly arrived and long-settled immigrants and ethnic New Yorkers. While they did not service most middle- and upper-class New Yorkers, public markets still did a fine business in immigrant neighborhoods, particularly Essex Market, located on the Lower East Side. The produce at this market was a far better article than the foods offered by the corner grocers.

Indeed, by turns the corner groceries-cum-groggeries ceded some of their functions to other institutions. The most important of these institutions, of course, was the saloon. In the antebellum period, "saloon" (from the French "salon") served as a catchall term for a large public hall and applied to ice cream, billiard, drinking, and dining spaces. But after the Civil War, the term "saloon" came to be applied specifically to stand-alone drinking establishments, or bars. Even the liquor groceries morphed into saloons. City ordinances in the 1840s allowed groceries to sell liquor by the glass, and gradually the greengrocers separated from the liquor grocers, which became saloons.[40]

In postbellum Five Points, along the Bowery, in the Tenderloin around the West Thirties, and in other working-class entertainment districts, bawdy saloons, concert saloons, and dance halls took the place of liquor groceries in providing not just alcoholic beverages but also sociability, and economic and political connections to their (mostly male) patrons. In New York's tenement districts and other working-class neighborhoods around the country, saloons served as the workingmen's club, a respite from overcrowded tenement apartments and an important locus of male, working-class conviviality. In the 1880s, brewing companies addressed cutthroat competition by seeking novel ways to corner the market. One such way was to take over saloons, making agreements with their owners for exclusive distributorship deals. Other methods included helping to finance the opening of new saloons and owning the saloons outright. Like restaurants, saloons ran the gamut from barebones to high opulence (the latter reflecting the competition among the wealthy liquor interests).[41]

Illegal saloons (which essentially describes the antebellum groggeries that flaunted licensing laws by selling drinks by the glass and letting patrons imbibe them on premises) also continued to proliferate in postbellum New York, going by a number of names, including tippling shops, blind tigers, and blind pigs. But by the third decade of the nineteenth century, few of these drinking establishments bothered with the designation or function of groceries.[42]

In immigrant neighborhoods, the groceries competed with peddlers and carts for their neighbors' trade. Savvy immigrant shoppers sought bargains on produce by shopping late in the day or taking bruised produce from the pushcart peddlers. Polish immigrant Sadie Frowne describes the transactions that she and her roommate made at the markets. Although reflecting upon a slightly later period on the Lower East Side, Frowne's calculations would have applied to the 1870s and 1880s as well. "Some people who buy at the last of the market, when the men with the carts want to go home, can get things very cheap," Frowne explained. But these items "are likely to be stale" so she and her roommate did not risk it with such foods as fish, meat, milk, or fresh produce. But for less perishable items, including potatoes, tomatoes, onions, and cabbages, "we did buy that way and got good bargains."[43]

But pushcart markets were viewed differently depending on the eye of the beholder. While many immigrant shoppers saw them as symbols of abundance and possibility, many sanitary reformers and government officials considered the carts an unsanitary nuisance and continued to blame them for the epidemic disease rates in the crowded tenement wards.[44] Eventually, Mayor Fiorello La Guardia, himself the son of immigrants, would crack down on the pushcart vendors in the 1930s, creating indoor markets and demanding that the vendors be licensed and sell their goods in more sanitary (read: interior) conditions. Thus, the idea that food purchases *should* be made inside was codified into law in 1930s New York City.

Of course, as is often the case, custom did not follow law, and pushcart vendors continued to do a brisk trade on the streets of New York City for decades to come. The persistence of pushcart vendors and their customers in spite of the legal marginalization of the trade attests to the social and economic role these vendors played in the immigrant wards. More than supplying provisions, pushcarts and other immigrant businesses served as key mitigating institutions in the immigrant's settlement in New York City.

The same was true of ethnic restaurants. In addition to easing the immigrant's adjustment by providing the foods of home and social opportunities and outlets, they offered new New Yorkers entry into the public culture of the city. This culture increasingly included participation in public dining rituals for *all* New Yorkers, native-born and immigrant alike. For immigrant proprietors and patrons, immigrant restaurants and food shops thus served as a kind of middle ground between the old country and the new. But in their earliest iterations, ethnic restaurants—while connecting New York to the world in terms of the cuisine they served—did not actively connect most immigrant and native-born New Yorkers to each other. At first, ethnic restaurants catered mainly to the immediate population in immigrant neighborhoods. "Every nationality that helps to make up the cosmopolitan character of New York has its *own* eating and drinking places," a New York City guidebook remarked. They included several Chinese restaurants, numerous "Hebrew restaurants . . . on the East Side," along with "several Russian restaurants," some Polish, Spanish, and Italian offerings and even "one cheap Japanese restaurant."[45] The small basement restaurants that Italian, Hungarian, Chinese, and German New Yorkers frequented for a taste of home drew few native-born New Yorkers through their doors.

So while New York had the most diverse culinary offerings in the world, it took a while before the city's mainstream cuisine incorporated this variety. New York's culture became evermore worldly with some reticence. In 1872, the *New-York Times* complained that New York's food offerings did not live up to the city's diverse population. "It might be supposed that eclectic modes of cookery would spring up, wherein all the best customs of the various nations might be combined into one harmonious whole," the writer suggested. But this was not the case. While "New York is getting to be very cosmopolitan," the paper explained, "our cookery . . . is little better than that of the Middle Ages." Even the guidebooks that commented upon the variety of ethnic restaurants in New York mentioned them as curiosities rather than as serious contenders for the patronage of native-born New Yorkers and tourists. For example, *King's Handbook to New York City* described the city's several Chinese restaurants as "dingy, foul-smelling, and cheaply furnished," where "national viands of a mysterious character and national drinks are served at reasonable prices."[46]

Exceptions existed, of course. Some "foreign" cuisines fell on the right side of exotic and drew a mixed patronage. Even in the 1870s, French, German, and Hungarian restaurants attracted some American-born customers, especially when these restaurants were found outside of the immigrant neighborhoods. Gallic cuisine was considered the paragon of gastronomic culture, and the best American restaurants did not aim for an "American" style of cooking but rather for a French style. The exclusivity of French restaurants increased rather than waned as the nineteenth century progressed, and elite restaurants like Delmonico's insisted on a strictly French menu. This insistence verged on the ridiculous at times. For example, one of the items on Delmonico's menu was "Truite de Long Island," trout from the decidedly American Long Island Sound. Not all of New York's French restaurants served the elite however. Some of the midrange restaurants were owned and operated by Frenchmen and served a French menu to a cosmopolitan group of patrons. Eating French food thus did not involve a foray into the strangely ethnic realms occupied by Chinese and other cuisines.

The same was true of German food, which, although certainly not as established or familiar to New Yorkers as French food, was recognizable enough to the Anglo-Saxon palate to fall within the realm of acceptable cuisines. The German dominance of food trades may also have made their cuisine more tolerable to native-born diners. Some American-born New Yorkers experienced their first taste of German cooking not in a German restaurant strictly speaking but in the lager beer gardens and saloons that began to appear in New York in the 1840s. As early as 1856, *Frank Leslie's Illustrated Newspaper* reported on the German restaurants and beer gardens in New York, remarking, as most contemporary accounts did, on the German love of lager beer. "To gain an idea of the partiality of the German palate for this beverage, let the reader enter one of the German restaurants, and he will find that every order . . . is usually accompanied with the supplement '*und ein Glass Lager bier,*'" *Leslie's* explained. The writer doubted, however, "that it will ever become a favorite beverage with Young America," since "the liking for it [is] not . . . natural, but acquired."[47]

*Leslie's, Harper's Weekly,* the *New-York Times,* and other periodicals and newspapers that reported on the German beer gardens generally offered a positive assessment, celebrating the conviviality and sociability of these spaces, in contrast to the typical saloon or barroom. *Leslie's* attributed the pleasant atmosphere of the beer gardens to the fact that lager beer was accompanied by meals and not the strict centerpiece of the place. Germans ate their meals slowly and punctuated them with unhurried quaffs of lager beer. *Leslie's* suggested that American diners could take a page from their German neighbors. "There is something social and healthy about the custom of sitting down, and leisurely taking food, that of itself will do much, if generally adopted, to destroy one of our greatest national faults, 'fast eating!'" the writer explained.[48]

Another factor that contributed to the respectability of German beer gardens was their attention to decor. Despite the name, many beer gardens were, in fact, indoor spaces. The finest, which included Atlantic Garden on the Bowery, were enormous buildings which accommodated thousands of people. Atlantic Garden was "fitted up in imitation of a garden," and like its counterparts among the "better class" of beer gardens was "handsomely frescoed and otherwise adorned," explained an 1868 account. The atmosphere in the lager beer gardens, coupled with the seeming impossibility—to American observers—of growing drunk off lager beer, placed them among the few commercial spaces in New York City where women could maintain respectability even in the presence of liquor. Those women were largely German; middle-class American-born women did not venture into the lager beer gardens. But German women joined their husbands and even their children at the beer gardens on Sunday, making these venues family gathering spaces for New York's German population. Sunday at the Atlantic Garden found thousands of German families gathered under its roof, eating sausages, ham, pretzels, and sauerkraut, drinking lager beer, and listening to the music of German bands. Some beer gardens also contained bowling lanes, billiard halls, and several barrooms. Thus, like many other ethnic food establishments, the beer gardens served as community and social gathering spaces for German immigrants.[49]

Non-Germans, especially men, ventured to the lager beer saloons and gardens as well, and by the 1870s, the Atlantic Garden was a major attraction on the Bowery. While its clientele remained mostly German, it became popular with tourists and gained a reputation beyond the city for its atmosphere and even for its food. *Redfield's Traveler's Guide to New York* for 1871 even included the Atlantic Garden in its list of restaurants "where the strangers will find good fare." This inclusion was remarkable given that only sixteen restaurants made the list, among them New York's most famous—Delmonico's, Martinelli's, Dorlon's, and Maillard's.[50]

Traditional German restaurants also gained a foothold in New York and again, the fare was familiar enough, and the Germans had assimilated enough into New York culture, that Teutonic cuisine could resist the taint applied to some other more exotic offerings. German restaurants like Ermisch's, located near Wall Street (John and Nassau), offered German delicacies like lentil soup with bologna, Vienna sausage, hamburger, Wiener schnitzel, fish balls with red cabbage, dark German bread and, of course, "lager in foaming glasses." The restaurant drew not only German diners but also some French, Irish, Jewish, and Polish patrons as well as native-born customers, attracted by the hearty and abundant fare.[51]

At the other end of the spectrum, Germans also operated most of the city's delicatessens. German delicatessens initially opened in the 1860s selling smoked, pickled, and cured meats and vegetables, cheeses, and prepared dishes like meat pies and potato salad to the residents of Kleindeutschland. A subset of this restaurant type was the Jewish delicatessen, which offered kosher Jews a similar menu devoid of pork or pig products. By the end of the century, delicatessens had spread beyond the German neighborhood but were especially concentrated on the Lower East Side. Most delicatessen patrons were foreign-born, but some native-born New Yorkers might venture into these cookshops for a taste of Germany or eastern Europe.[52]

The native-born New Yorkers' embrace—or at least tolerance—of German beer gardens and restaurants did not necessarily reflect an acceptance of ethnic foodways by most New Yorkers. As noted, some cuisines, like some immigrants themselves, were sufficiently assimilated to American tastes to be palatable to native-born New Yorkers. And even German cuisine, though not as foreign or derided as some others, was seen as "exotic" by native-born commentators who ventured into German restaurants. They used such adjectives as "mysterious" and "peculiar" and "odd" to describe lentil soup, beef with macaroni, and hamburger steak. And one journalist characterized most German dishes as "distasteful to the native palate," although he allowed that the abundant cheap bread and red wine "will go far to remove the unpleasant taste that any of the foreign-flavored viands might have left in the mouth."[53]

Indeed, the development of "ethnic" restaurants highlights the complexities of cosmopolitanism in late nineteenth-century New York, which was replete with foreign foods and restaurants. Yet, of these foods and restaurants, few crossed the "boundaries of taste," as historian Donna Gabaccia terms the lines between ethnic foodways.[54] Even the most adventuresome native-born diners tried certain foreign restaurants with pinched nostrils. An item in the *New-York Times* serves to illustrate. In 1872, the newspaper published a small piece on "The Jewish Restaurant," entitled "A New Cuisine" and subtitled "Peculiar Food—Experiences of a Seeker after Novel Dishes." The author ventured into the Jewish quarter to sample the strange cuisine. He quickly found that he was the only non-Jew in the restaurant, with the possible exception of the waiter, who spoke with a "Cockney accent" and hailed from London. After several false starts with such exotic (and, to the diner, inedible) dishes as beet soup and brisket with raisins, the writer settled upon fried fish, which he found to be not just delicious but "a culinary anchor, after having been tossed about in a sea of hungry uncertainties." At the same time, the writer put forth his very willingness to try the Jewish restaurant as evidence that he was a sophisticated, urbane type, worthy of celebrating for his culinary adventurism. While he held the Jewish food at arm's length, the diner refused the waiter's entreaties to order roast beef since "roast beef was procurable at all times." And he eschewed the familiar mutton chop because "a man who would go to Turkey and not eat a kibob, ought to be ashamed of himself."[55]

The simultaneous attraction and revulsion to foreign cuisines was perhaps most pronounced in discussions of Chinese food and restaurants, perhaps because the Chinese seemed *so* exotic to native-born diners. Until the 1880s, a mere handful of New Yorkers came from China. The census of 1890 estimated a Chinese population of 1,970 people. And before the twentieth century, few non-Chinese New Yorkers ventured to Mott Street to sample the pigs' feet, oolong tea, and chop suey on offer at one of Chinatown's eight (by one account) restaurants. For native-born diners, a foray to Chinatown remained an exotic adventure in the 1880s. The chop suey craze, which brought scores of bohemian New Yorkers and tourists to Chinese restaurants, was yet forty years away. These restaurants thus served almost exclusively Chinese men (there were almost no Chinese women in New York in the 1880s) in second- and third-floor tenement settings.[56]

Even when written by culinary adventurers, native-born depictions of Chinese restaurants were generally dripping with sarcasm and condescension and a sense of cultural superiority. For example, in 1884 journalist Edwin H. Trafton determined to try Chung Fah Low, a Mott Street restaurant, with a group of friends. Trafton described Chung Fah Low as the "Chinese Delmonico's," a moniker applied to several nineteenth-century Chinese restaurants. But its "dingy, low-walled and ill-lighted" atmosphere with "small common wooden tables, two or three chairs and as many stools," distinguished its appointments considerably from that culinary mecca. And while its owner evinced a clear interest in catering to non-Chinese diners explaining "I can cook in every language," Chung Fah Low still was patronized by few non-Chinese New Yorkers.[57]

Trafton viewed the trip to Chung Fah Low more as science experiment than culinary opportunity, comparing the experience to "going up in a balloon; going down in a diving-bell," or simulating "the sensation of being hanged, drowned or guillotined." His first-person description of the restaurant is filled with such adjectives as "dread," "terrifying," mysterious," and "ghastly," and among his imagined translations of the Chinese characters adorning the walls are "It is a wise eater who can identify his own dog," "Do not spit on the floor," and "The American must not come."[58]

As for the food, Trafton declared it unrecognizable, "the flavors . . . unlike anything known to our more familiar gastronomy," and the main ingredients unidentifiable. Trafton's assessment was not all negative. He did allow that the restaurant was neat and tidy and the service prompt. In the end, Trafton appeared pleased with his experiment but not inclined to repeat it. Upon leaving Chung Fah Low, he and his fellow diners felt "a sense of devout thankfulness that we found ourselves in the open air," and headed straight to the Astor House for a nightcap. And after a restless night's sleep, Trafton confessed to his doctor that he had visited a Chinese restaurant and received a tongue-in-cheek prescription for a tumblerful of opium "every four hours until undertaker calls."[59]

Trafton's description of his Chinese dinner demonstrates clearly the fascination and yet discomfort with foreign food on the part of some native-born diners. His account also shows that culinary adventurism served as a badge of honor—however misguided—for the diner. Trafton was no provincial observer. He was a travel correspondent for *Leslie's* and other newspapers, reporting on his visits within and outside the United States. And he celebrated his willingness to visit Chung Fah Low as a sign of his open-mindednesss. And yet, his approach was not merely myopic but patronizing in the extreme.

Even positive accounts of Chinese restaurants held them apart as peculiar and lesser than their "American" counterparts. An 1888 article on the Chinese chef in *Harper's Weekly* offered a kinder assessment than Trafton of Chinese cooks. The article depicted the Chinese chef as a hardworking artist, his kitchen well ventilated and clean, and comparable to the great luxury hotels. But still, even here, the eating houses themselves were described as being marked with "strange dishes and stranger customs," characteristics by now well known to regular readers.[60]

This image of the interior of Chung Fah Low's Mott Street restaurant accompanied Edwin Trafton's 1884 article "A Chinese Dinner in New York." (Picture Collection, The New York Public Library, Astor, Lenox, and Tilden Foundations)

Rather than celebrate the cuisine, these depictions celebrated the diner, for his daring and adventurousness—his willingness to enter the second-floor restaurants and try the exotic, unrecognizable dishes on offer. Furthermore, in showing a disposition to be experimental and to incorporate "foreign" cuisines in their dining repertoires, native-born New Yorkers could display sophistication and status without taking much risk or expending much money. A similar process occurred in home design, as historian Kristin Hoganson suggests. Wealthy and upper-middle-class American homemakers, Hoganson argues, incorporated foreign decorative items and styles into their homes with the recognition of the power dynamics that opened those foreign markets to American purchasers but without the messy or dangerous interactions those power relations entailed.[61]

For late nineteenth-century New Yorkers, travel to foreign countries—the European tour—was not necessary to experience the exotic and foreign. Rather, it was a walk or elevated train ride away. "Without leaving the city," noted journalist L. J. Vance, the Manhattanite could "breakfast in London, lunch in Berlin, dine in Paris and sup in Vienna." In Gotham, one "could dine differently four times a day for a week, and have each repast composed of foreign dishes, served by foreign waiters, and eat with foreign-born men and women as his convives." In both cases, the food was secondary to the experience of trying out or dining in a given restaurant. These factors all contributed to the important role restaurants played in the contours of New York's nineteenth-century cosmopolitan public culture.[62]

One could assume that the embrace of spaghetti and chop suey on the part of native-born New Yorkers reflected an acceptance of these cultures. But clearly, the situation on the ground was far more complicated. A pluralistic culture certainly did emerge in New York City in the late nineteenth century, challenging Anglo-American hegemony in various areas from politics to residential patterns to culture. But we must not mistake a native-born interest in the foreign with the notion of cultural equality. Indeed, trying "exotic" cuisines, much like including oriental design elements in one's home decor or visiting the pygmy exhibit at the 1876 World's Fair, served for many as confirmation of their belief in the superiority of Anglo-American culture and civilization. As historian Andrew Haley cogently notes, an individual could eat "foreign" cuisine and remain a nativist.[63]

American-born diners in "foreign" restaurants thus confirmed their own cultural superiority first by their own adventurousness and second by their assessments of the cuisine, which was invariably found lacking. These accounts also offer the suggestion that the ability to partake of foreign cultures and foods was a mark of American prowess on the world stage. This assessment was applied to imported food as well. For example, in 1890 *Harper's Weekly* described the millions of workers around the world involved in food processing and production as "slaves" to the New Yorker's needs. They included "pig-tailed laborers working in the tea fields of China," "swarthy toilers gathering coffee in Java, and stripping the spice-trees of Sumatra," and countless workers "sweating under the tropical sun in two hemispheres." Thus, the language and imagery of imperialism and social Darwinism were marshaled to show the global reach of New York and its food culture. The foods and peoples of the world served as servants to New Yorkers' needs and desires, proof of American political and economic strength, and of the empire of gastronomy's imperial reach.[64]

Ethnic foods and cuisines made their way into mainstream New York foodways, but for most New Yorkers that eventuality occurred when immigrant proprietors and restaurateurs began to open restaurants in the city's nonimmigrant districts. These "ethnic" restaurants were significantly altered from the basement versions from which many of them sprouted. The menus at the uptown ethnic restaurants reflected attention to "American" tastes. They included both Americanized versions of foreign dishes and more familiar choices such as roasted meats and fried potatoes. As Haley describes it, middle-class diners "colonized" the foreign restaurant and foreign cuisine, demanding and receiving hybrid dishes that were modified for native-born tastes.[65]

This process was not unconscious. Contemporaneous commentators recognized the rounding out of the cuisine and analyzed the process insightfully. Describing uptown Italian restaurants in 1885, the *New-York Times* remarked: "It is a curious fact that, as the quality of the guests and food improves, the national dishes disappear, and the Italian cook shows a stronger inclination to a hybrid cuisine than to the unadulterated and savory dishes of his mother land." Thus, an adventurous or nostalgic diner in search of macaroni, spaghetti, or risotto had to visit the "humbler or newer restaurants" rather than "the gathering places of greater pretensions," the writer concluded.[66] In many cases, the native-born New Yorker's early embrace of "ethnic" cuisine reflected so watered-down a version of these dishes as to bear little resemblance to the original or its context. Like the small world exhibit or the food court at Disney's Epcot Center, New York's "ethnic" restaurants that catered to native-born New Yorkers reflected American tastes more than foreign cuisines.

Nonetheless, New York's restaurant culture *was* undeniably ethnicized in the second half of the nineteenth century, albeit in a hybridized fashion. Some of the most popularly frequented restaurants in Gilded Age Gotham had foreign names and proprietors. As more New Yorkers—native-born and immigrant alike—*chose* to eat out as a social event, they did so at foreign tables d'hôte which served Americanized versions of German, French, Hungarian, and Italian cuisine. The number of these restaurants grew from about five foreign tables d'hôte in the 1860s to more than two dozen in the 1880s, the most common being French, Hungarian, Italian, and German. Among the best-known were Morello's, Martinelli's, Donovan's, Jacques's, Marinetti's, and Moretti's, whose one-dollar table d'hôte included "wine and capital macaroni." One of the most popular tables d'hôte was available at the Hotel Hungaria on Union Square, which catered not just to middle-class patrons but also to artists and other bohemian New Yorkers.[67]

The tables d'hôte offered a middle ground between elite restaurants and the cheap businessmen's lunchroom. And they served as an alternative to the cheap and nasty restaurants that dominated the lower range of New York's mid-nineteenth-century public-dining hierarchy. At the table d'hôte restaurant, for a fixed price a diner could enjoy a digestible five-course meal. In 1885, the price of a table d'hôte dinner ranged from thirty cents for soup, fish, an entrée (appetizer), a roast, and a cup of coffee up to $1.25 which would afford the diner the same plus an additional entrée, salad, dessert, and a half bottle of wine ($7 to $30 in today's money). At Delmonico's, one would need to spend twice that price for the most modest meal. The food at the table d'hôte was not excellent but decent. A diner could find a "highly flavored" meal in which "tough or unsavory viands are unknown." And unlike the short-order houses, "dyspepsia is . . . unfamiliar to the regular frequenter" of the table d'hôte restaurant, the *New-York Times* explained approvingly.[68]

The late nineteenth-century tables d'hôte diverged from inexpensive antebellum restaurants in two ways. First, they catered to a new group of customers from the downtown lunchrooms. They were explicitly geared toward and patronized by people *choosing* to dine away from home rather than being forced to do so by schedule and proximity. According to the *New-York Times*, the tables d'hôte did not just draw "business men who cannot spare the time necessary to go home in the middle of the day." Rather, these establishments catered to "another class, who choose restaurants from preference."[69]

As a result, the table d'hôte restaurants also emphasized quality of food and the dining experience over speed, another big difference from the downtown restaurants. Even in the downtown districts, foreign tables d'hôte opened to serve a business clientele seeking a more leisurely and pleasant atmosphere than the short-order houses offered. Interestingly, as foreign tables d'hôte and other "ethnic" offerings emerged to cater to native-born New Yorkers, the old model of downtown eating house, replete with tepid vegetables, stringy meats, frenetic pace, and sullen waiters, came to be known as an American-style restaurant to distinguish it from the less rushed and more appetizing table d'hôte.[70]

In addition to eating in ethnic restaurants, native-born New Yorkers integrated some "ethnic" foods and preparations into their kitchens. One indicator is the "Household" section of the *New-York Times* and other newspapers and periodicals. Readers would write in and ask for recipes or advice for cooking certain foods, and their queries often turned to foreign foods that they had tasted in restaurants. For example, in 1876 a reader asked—and received an answer to—how to make Italian macaroni. A "mother" wrote in to ask "how to make the apple and peach cakes I see in most of the German bakeries." And "Brooklyn" inquired after "a receipt for German pancakes, such as can be found at some of the best German restaurants down town."[71] Again, the most common ethnicities mentioned were German, French, and Italian. No requests for chop suey or Chinese roast meats appeared in the "Household" column.

But by 1890, even before the opening of Ellis Island—the symbol of New York immigration—New York's food shops and restaurants had incorporated in complex and sometimes contradictory ways the foods and cuisines of the world. Ethnic foods and restaurants played a fundamental role in the life of the immigrant neighborhood and, in a hybridized form, contributed to the overall diversification, ethnicization, and sophistication of New York City's food culture. Ethnic foods and food vendors played a disproportionately large role in this process in the late 1800s. But in general, the roots that were laid earlier in the century in terms of the sophistication and complexity of New York's dining culture continued to sprout branches after the Civil War.

In the second half of the nineteenth century, the restaurants of Gotham—whether foreign or American—expanded their reach even further into the daily lives of New Yorkers so that almost all New Yorkers were dining out at least on occasion. Restaurants did not serve to dull class and other social distinctions. To the contrary, some New York restaurants became even more exclusive in the Gilded Age as conspicuous consumption for New York's elite included the ability to dine with frequency at Delmonico's and host (or at least attend) elaborate banquets and dinners for the Upper Ten.[72] But New York's restaurants *did* become increasingly inclusive in one sense—dining options continued to proliferate at every level of the social spectrum so that all New Yorkers participated in the city's restaurant life, albeit not under the same roof. The cheapest of these establishments, according to the *New-York Times*, served a diverse clientele including chorus singers, ballet dancers, foreign artisans, and young professionals while more expensive restaurants drew a "less distinctly foreign and considerably more stylish" patronage. Meanwhile, a middle swathe catered to young couples, New Yorkers entertaining visitors, and families who treated themselves to the occasional dinner out.[73]

Married women, in particular, had several more options in the late nineteenth century than those that had been available to their mothers or grandmothers. Many more "respectable" restaurants emerged to cater to middle-class New Yorkers in the late nineteenth century, including families. This development was rooted as much in the growth of the city as the emergence of short-order eating houses had been. The persistent housing crunch ensured that large numbers of workers continued to resort to hotel and boardinghouse living in the late nineteenth century. Families in these situations sought dining options away from home. Strictures still existed. Not until the twentieth century could respectable middle-class women dine alone in the evening without an escort. But increasingly they found options where they could enjoy an evening meal with their husbands and even their children without jeopardizing their reputations. The foreign tables d'hôte especially were among the first restaurants to cater to middle-class couples and families interested in dining out socially.

Middle-class women who desired a restaurant lunch without an escort continued to patronize restaurants that sought the ladies' trade, especially around Ladies' Mile. By the 1880s, the shopping district had moved uptown, stretching along Fifth Avenue from Astor Place to Madison Square. The large department stores of Ladies' Mile, including Macy's, O'Neill's, and Hearn's, also opened restaurants to cater to their female patrons. Macy's restaurant opened in 1878 and, according to the guidebooks, did a good business. These restaurants may not have been "first class in cooking or in service," as one guidebook put it. But they did serve an important function in offering a space for middle-class women alone to dine comfortably, and without fear of exposing themselves as inexperienced in public dining or, worse, tarnishing their reputations.[74]

Liquor continued to be a delineator for the respectability of a restaurant and while temperance restaurants were a relic of the past in the late nineteenth century, some liquor-free options did emerge where respectable men and especially ladies could feel comfortable dining. "Dairy" restaurants served cured meats, codfish cakes, and other light fare along with coffee, tea, and, of course, milk but eschewed liquor. A New York guidebook described "The Dairy Kitchen" near Union Square as "an enormous establishment where several thousand people are fed every day," for "moderate" prices.[75] These restaurants not only served women but often had female servers, a novelty in late nineteenth-century New York and one that was employed in part to create a comfortable space for women to dine in public.

In general, lunchroom options expanded in Gilded Age New York, and ladies could find far more choices for midday meals than could previous generations. One of the most popular lunch options both for ladies and businessmen and women was the Rotunda at the Astor House. An early

The Astor House Rotunda, an early version of a food court, was a major lunch draw in late nineteenth-century New York City. (Picture Collection, The New York Public Library, Astor, Lenox, and Tilden Foundations)

food court, the glass dome of the Rotunda covered "various stands around the room," where one could find "oysters and fish, made dishes, salads, sandwiches, etc., and in the adjoining room a good dinner *a la carte*." The food at the Rotunda was considered "first rate" and the prices "although not low are fairly reasonable." The St. Nicholas Hotel offered a similar, though not as popular, setup.[76]

Even the business-oriented eating houses eventually began to cater to women, especially the female white-collar workers who began to proliferate in the city in the second half of the nineteenth century. In 1885, a downtown restaurateur explained that five years before, the downtown restaurants had practically no female patrons. "But to-day we all provide special accommodation and special dishes for them, and their trade is well worth catering for." The women this proprietor referred to were, like the men, downtown workers engaged as secretaries, stenographers, and copyists. These women adrift favored such restaurants as Delmonico's on Broadway, Nash & Crook's, the restaurant in the Mills Building ("120 women [were] employed in clerical capacities" in the offices upstairs), and "the dairies on Broad-street."[77] Previously these women may have brought their lunches to work, but by turns they began to patronize public dining spaces like their male counterparts. Some downtown spaces—the club-like chophouses and the unsanitary short-order houses—were still male preserves. But the range of options available to different classes of New York women had expanded considerably over the nineteenth century.

Once female faces became more common sights in certain downtown eating houses, nonprofessional women came to join their working counterparts. The *Times* credited the Brooklyn Bridge, which brought ladies over from the leafy suburbs to the east, and the jewelry stores of John Street and Maiden Lane, which drew them downtown, for the influx of this new class of women in the downtown dining houses. They usually were accompanied by their male relations who took a break from the office to join their wives, daughters, and sisters for lunch.[78]

Toward the end of the nineteenth century, some working-class women also visited neighborhood saloons for lunch. The barrooms and back rooms of saloons were still largely a bastion for working-class men, and many respectable working-class women chose to bring their lunches to work or eat at cheap restaurants rather than brave the male space of the saloon. But some intrepid working-class women did begin to take advantage of the growing custom of the free lunch, offered in the saloons' back rooms beginning in the 1880s. Far more working-class men took advantage of the saloons' free lunches—meals on offer to anyone who purchased a five-cent glass of beer. The food for the free lunch—which could incorporate a range of meats, salted fish, salads, breads, and relishes but in New York more often consisted of soup and bread—was supplied by the liquor industry partly as a way to increase their customer base and partly to appease reformers who complained that the saloons encouraged excessive drunkenness. While the free lunch was intended to encourage more drinking in the saloons, it did come to serve—particularly toward the turn of the twentieth century—as an institution in working-class neighborhoods in New York and other industrial cities. Some poor men and women came to depend almost completely on the free lunch for their sustenance.[79]

All of these options and offerings contributed to New York's position as the restaurant capital of the nation. While it was, of course, not the only American city to boast several restaurants, New York did distinguish itself by the number, breadth, and range of restaurants as well as the practice of regularly dining out for many city residents. But New York was at the forefront of American food culture not just because it had more restaurants of more different kinds than any other place in the country, though that was certainly the case. Rather, New York was the nation's food capital because it served as a model for the food cultures of other US cities and towns. New York's role as the paragon of American gastronomy and restaurant culture became a national understanding, and New York served as both standard and beacon for the American restaurant. Restaurants opened in other cities on the "New York model," like Washington, DC's Gosling Restaurant, which advertised on a broadside that it would be "open for the accommodation of the public in New York style." Similarly, a booster from Auburn, New York, boasted in the pages of the *Literary World* that his city's main street featured "a restaurant—Leonard's—that would pass in New York."[80]

Delmonico's in particular became a shorthand for the standard in fine dining. City boosters from Louisville to Maysville boasted that their city had a restaurant on par with New York's most famous restaurant. And in a true expression of the link between imitation and flattery—and influence as well—a stock company formed in London "for the establishment in that city of a large restaurant similar in plan to Delmonico's in New York." Like the New York Delmonico's, the proposed restaurant aimed to "appeal chiefly to the wealthiest classes," and to distinguish itself in terms of design as well as cuisine.[81]

New York's position at the center of the nation's culinary culture also was reflected in the national press. By the turn of the twentieth century, magazines of regional cuisine such as *What to Eat*, published in the Midwest, and the *Southern Hotel Journal* employed New York–based correspondents who reported on food trends in Gotham. An 1888 article in the *St. Louis Globe-Democrat* entitled "Progress in Gastronomy" focused not on St. Louis's food culture but on that of New York, proclaiming: "Paris has long been accounted the culinary capital of the world; but within twenty-five years New York has rivaled it in this particular."[82] And among epicures, New York gained a reputation as a gourmand's oasis in the desert of American foodways.[83]

By the end of the nineteenth century then, New York's food culture reflected and refracted the many changes that the city had gone through in the act of becoming the nation's metropolis. The foodways of New York highlighted the growth of the city from a small seaport to an international nexus, arguably the most cosmopolitan city in the world. And in the late nineteenth and early twentieth centuries, many of the developments that New York had seen in terms of food supply and eating patterns spread beyond Manhattan to the rest of the country. The appetite of the metropolis thus became the appetite of the nation. And the roots of the food culture that New York developed in the nineteenth century are still sprouting buds in the city and the nation today.

# From the Broadway Shambles to New Amsterdam Market

On May 1, 2011, New York city council speaker Christine Quinn stood on a dais by the old Fulton Fish Market on South Street in Lower Manhattan and rang a brass bell to signal the season opening of the New Amsterdam Market. Spearheaded by urban planner Robert LaValva, the market, according to its mission statement, "is a reinvention of the *Public Market*, once a prevalent institution in the City of New York [r]evived for our present times and needs." Among its vendors are: "small businesses such as butchers, grocers, mongers, and other[s] who source, produce, distribute, and sell foods made with regional ingredients as well as carefully selected imports." Since 2007, the New Amsterdam Market has offered contemporary New Yorkers—who have thousands of choices in food purveyors—one more option. But this particular choice is a political and social one. New Amsterdam Market is as much a reclamation of a lost past and vision of a new food future in New York and the nation at large as it is a gastronomic pursuit. As Councilwoman Quinn herself put it: "Who knew that when you came today to buy arugula you would be making a profound political statement about the future of downtown Manhattan? But you are and we thank you very much."[1]

New Yorkers of the past like John Pintard and Thomas De Voe would likely approve of LaValva's New Amsterdam Market. The market's mission and self-image—as a community gathering point and locus of producer-consumer interaction that offers all the bounty of New York and its hinterlands—would certainly have rung true with these market boosters of old. And yet, for them and many of their contemporaries, the New Amsterdam Market would be downright confusing. First, the language of the market and many of its products, beginning with arugula and continuing with artisanal jam, ice cream, and cheese; tempeh; organic teas; heirloom citrus; fair trade molasses; small-batch coffee; responsibly raised, pasture-raised, and organic meats; and vintage-inspired handcrafted bicycles, would be utterly foreign to mid-nineteenth-century New Yorkers. And while De Voe missed the old patterns when the city grew and spread, many of his contemporaries—particularly those of the middle and upper classes—happily washed their hands of the filth and chaos of the public markets in favor of visiting local grocers and food vendors. When they considered the middlemen who separated them from their vendors, they usually did so in relation to the rising cost of foodstuffs, not a concern about "food miles" or the distance food traveled from producer to consumer and certainly not in terms of the harmful practices of industrial food processors that make "buying local" an attractive option to many contemporary New Yorkers.

Rather than regret the changes to their food supply, many mid-to-late-nineteenth-century New Yorkers of means celebrated the expansion of New York's hinterlands, the ever-growing list of food and dining options, and the extraordinary cosmopolitanism of their food culture. The fact that a large segment of today's New Yorkers seek out the most local of food options and visit farmers' markets as much for entertainment as for sustenance would strike their nineteenth-century counterparts as peculiar at best, ludicrous at worst. And yet, contemporary developments vis-à-vis New York City's (and the world's) food system from the organic and locavore movements to the rise of a new generation of food reformers concerned with industrial food-stuffs find their roots in Pintard's time.

Furthermore, the politicization of food that Christine Quinn alluded to in her comments at the opening of New Amsterdam Market reflects another important relationship between contemporary Gotham and the nineteenth-century city. In choosing to patronize the market, Quinn suggested, the shoppers she addressed made a political calculation that related to the sources of their foodstuffs and the practices involved in harvesting, slaughtering, processing, and transporting them. The vendors at the market embrace sustainable, organic, and fair trade practices in keeping with a contemporary ethos that suggests the closer consumers are to the producers of their food, the better for their health, for the environment, for the plants and animals that feed them, and for the workers who harvest, slaughter, and process their food.

Mast Brothers' chocolate serves as an example. These handcrafted candy bars are carefully made in Williamsburg, Brooklyn, from fair trade cocoa beans and other responsibly produced ingredients. In addition to sourcing their cocoa beans from sustainable farmers with whom they have direct relationships, the Mast brothers transported their cocoa beans from the Dominican Republic via a three-mast sailboat in an effort to lessen their environmental footprint and go "oil-free." Eventually, the company intends to transport all of their beans via sailing ship.[2] These practices come at a price and, in fact, the fresh, sustainable, and responsibly grown offerings at New Amsterdam Market are within reach of a very small segment of twenty-first-century New Yorkers. In a reversal of nineteenth-century patterns, contemporary wealthy residents are willing to pay considerably more money for locally grown and processed foodstuffs than they are for far-off, tropical fruits. Mast Brothers' chocolate bars cost nine dollars for a seven-and-a-half ounce bar. Sailing ships and fair trade practices are expensive. And Fleisher's Grass-Fed and Organic Meats, another of the market vendors, admits that its pasture-fed meats cost 15 percent more than "factory farm meats available at a supermarket chain," for a variety of reasons including the expense of the land, the need for more staffing to ensure proper treatment of the animals, and the longer life span of the cattle.[3]

The political vision of the New Amsterdam Market goes beyond sustainable practices, however, to ideas about the city itself. New Amsterdam Market, which seeks a permanent home in the old Fulton Fish Market (vacant since 2005 when the market moved to Hunts Point in the Bronx), is fighting a battle against the real estate developer Howard Hughes Corporation, whose vision for the old Fulton Market site involves not an open-air market but rather retail shops, luxury condominiums, and a 495-foot-tall hotel. In 2013, the city granted the Hughes Corporation rights to the site, and to determine whether the New Amsterdam Market will continue to use the building. For the 2013 season, the market was on hiatus, holding several festival days instead of the regular weekly market that it has conducted since 2007.

Proponents of the market, with LaValva at the forefront, argue that the site of the old Fulton Fish Market *should* be used not for real estate development but for a reclamation of an older public culture that (they think) characterized preindustrial New York. "By bringing residents back to the Seaport," the market's mission statement explains, "we are reviving . . . a rare fragment of our city's first port and oldest commercial neighborhood—as a thriving, public destination for all New Yorkers."[4] Market proponents see this destination as a direct contrast to development and renewal projects that obliterate rather than celebrate the historical character of the city's neighborhoods. And they also seek a return not only to the food provisioning patterns of past New Yorkers but to the residential and social patterns as well. Thus, the New Amsterdam Market—and initiatives like it—shows the strong political, economic, and social implications of food and eating in today's New York City just as *Urban Appetites* shows those implications in nineteenth-century Gotham.

The developments that this book addresses—the shift from public markets to private retail food shops as the main provisioners for individuals' food needs; the intertwining of class and geography to determine access and the quality of an individual's food supply; the growing distance between producer and consumer of foodstuffs and other consumer products; the instances of and concerns over tainted and adulterated foods; the industrialization of the food supply; the rise and proliferation of restaurants and other commercial, public dining options as well as the role of these spaces in New York's public culture; and the cosmopolitanization of foodways—occurred in other US cities and towns in the late nineteenth and early twentieth centuries. New York was unique in the timing and scope of the changes but not in their occurrence.

Large cities like Philadelphia, Boston, and Baltimore experienced similar transformations in their public markets and the rise of private food shops to service the retail needs of individual food shoppers. Meanwhile, newer cities like Chicago, Minneapolis, and San Francisco developed geographies of provisioning that were similar to older, East Coast urban areas—central wholesale and terminal markets that stocked retailers and restaurateurs who then serviced the retail needs of individual consumers. Like New York, these cities developed neighborhoods that were stratified according to class and function, and the best, most sanitary, and most expensive food shops were found in the more expensive neighborhoods. And tainted food scandals were not exclusive to New York City in the early nineteenth century. A series of swill-milk scandals also occurred in Chicago and Cincinnati, and Chicago's meatpacking industry offered the muck for the rake in Upton Sinclair's novel *The Jungle*. The result was federal legislation regulating the meatpacking industry and pure-food-and-drug laws during the Progressive Era.[5] Food manufacturing was nationalized as certain cities cornered particular food industries, meatpacking in Chicago and grain processing in Minneapolis, for example.

The restaurant culture modeled in New York City went national in the early twentieth century, when restaurants became commonplace in cities and towns around the country. New York restaurants served as a model for dairies, delicatessens, businessmen's restaurants, tables d'hôte, and first-class establishments from Portland, Maine, to San Diego, California. New York's cosmopolitan dining culture also spread throughout the country. By the 1920s, every city and even many towns had at least one Italian and one

Chinese restaurant and perhaps a few other ethnic options as well. By the early twentieth century, the celebration of cosmopolitan dining became a national concern forwarded by a rising middle class that gained hegemony over the shape of mainstream American culture.[6] Middle-class women from Maine to California also listened to (or at least were exposed to) the advice of ladies' magazines and other prescriptive writers about turning the food spaces of their homes into consumer spaces in the service of domesticity. Thus, in the twentieth century, the appetite of the metropolis became the appetite of the nation.

In addition to showing New York's role in forecasting and shaping national foodways, these developments illustrate the strong connections between changing foodways and larger social, cultural, political, economic, and technological shifts. This book's approach—to explore the interplay between food and larger structural developments—thus has interpretive application to a variety of historical contexts, including the protests of New York Jewish women against rising kosher-meat prices in 1902, the eventual regulation and slow deregulation of the American food industry in the twentieth century, the lunch counter sit-ins during the African American civil rights movement, the rise of the organic food movement, and the current globalization of our food supply.

The links between foodways and social, economic, and technological change have significant salience today in communities from New York City to Lagos, Nigeria. Concerns about "food deserts" and the strong links between geography and class in determining the quality of one's food supply are quite current in today's American urban discourse. But all too often policy makers and commentators look at these developments as new ones, related only to the economic, social, and political developments of the last decade or two. A typical approach is presented in a 2010 *Newsweek* article on social class and food habits in the United States which asserts: "Modern America is a place of extremes, and what you eat for dinner has become the definitive marker of social status; as the distance between rich and poor continues to grow, the freshest, most nutritious foods have become luxury goods that only some can afford."[7] These discussions must be informed by an understanding of the past—both the past that contributed to the development of disparities tied to food, class, and geography, and the past that demonstrates the ways in which food interacts with social class and geography in various times and places to shape social experience.

In the last thirty to forty years, the American food system has undergone major changes. The rise of agribusiness and genetically modified organisms (GMOs), the consolidation of food production into the hands of a very few multinational corporations, and the extraordinary lobbying power of these corporations to determine the quality, derivation, and content of our food supply have appeared evermore pervasive. So too the distance between producer and consumer grows ever wider and many consumers attempt to narrow it by shopping at farmers' markets or CSAs (community sponsored agriculture). Along with the consolidation of the food industry and the rise of factory farms have come frequent tainted food scares including salmonella and E. coli outbreaks in meat, peanut butter, tomatoes, and spinach to name a few. Recent years have even seen a series of tainted-milk scandals originating in China that recall Frank Leslie's 1858 swill-milk exposé.

A host of contemporary food reformers have demanded stricter government regulation, fewer industrial processes applied to food, and the narrowing of the distance between producer and consumer. These issues are very much rooted in contemporary geopolitics and economics. But they reverberate with examples from the past, recalling similar (though not identical) issues, concerns, and developments witnessed in New York 150 to 200 years ago. And as did those developments, contemporary food issues touch not only on nutrition and diet but on economics, politics, global culture, social class and socioeconomic status, popular culture, and many other areas.

Parallel developments are transpiring in industrializing and rapidly urbanizing communities worldwide. In burgeoning economies like the cities of India, residents are experiencing a transformation of eating habits. Dining out in restaurants, once a completely foreign concept, reserved only for special occasions, is now a regular occurrence for middle-class Indians.[8] And megacities of more than ten million people like Lagos, Nigeria, and São Paulo, Brazil, are experiencing similar (if magnified) problems of rapid growth and strong inequities that New York experienced 150 years ago with similar effects on the food supply, food distribution channels, and the linking of class and geography to determine access to quality foodstuffs.

In some ways, we have come full circle as reformers, consumers, and some policy makers seek to undo the processes put into motion two centuries ago in the markets, streets, restaurants, homes, and government bodies of New York. Contemporary farmers' markets, organic and locavore movements, slow-food organizations, advocacy groups for better quality foods in poor neighborhoods, and others hearken back to a golden age of sorts in the recent past, when producers and consumers were very connected, when farmers were responsible husbands of the land, using sustainable farming techniques and few industrial processes. These reformers harbor a strong sense of nostalgia and an assumption of a lost golden age of food production and agrarian responsibility.

When Michael Pollan, author of *The Omnivore's Dilemma* and *In Defense of Food* and perhaps the most well known of today's reformers, offers a manifesto in defense of "real food—the sort of food our great grandmothers would recognize as food," removed from industrial processes and professional nutrition advice—he ignores, or fails to realize, the fact that many of our grandmothers and great-grandmothers also worried about the quality and derivation of their food supply, which had already been touched by industrial processes and political chicanery.[9] Likewise, the documentary *Food, Inc.*, an exposé of the American food industry that serves as a modern-day version of *The Jungle*, offers a rose-colored view of mid-twentieth-century American food processing and agriculture that suggests industrialization and agribusiness is new to this generation.[10]

These approaches are problematic because by failing to see the long roots of our current food system, they offer unrealistic solutions to addressing its problems.[11] In seeking to undo these changes by simply advocating local or organic food systems (unrealistic for all but the wealthiest Americans as dietary staples) or the deindustrialization of the food supply, these reformers ignore the important fact that our food system is intertwined not simply with recent political and economic decisions, but with urban, industrial, social, and economic structures that have long been in place. This is not to argue that the American food system does not desperately need reform but rather to suggest that the reformers would do well to take a long view of the trajectory of these developments in trying to figure out how effectively to remedy them.

And these developments do indeed have a long trajectory. *Urban Appetites* traces the evolution of retail food shops in Manhattan, restaurants in Gotham, cookstoves and sideboards in the kitchens and dining rooms of middle-class New Yorkers, the swill-milk distilleries and slaughterhouses of the west side, the cafés of Little Italy, the groceries of Chinatown, and the pushcart markets of the Lower East Side. Their roots lay in the urbanization of New York in the nineteenth century, in its rise as the nation's metropolis and food capital. Its urban appetites fostered a major transformation of food, eating, and daily life in New York City. The many effects are visible today.

INTRODUCTION

1. "NYCFood," New York City's food policy page, accessed January 3, 2013, http://www.nyc.gov/html/nycfood/html/home/home.shtml.

2. Junius Henri Browne, *The Great Metropolis: A Mirror of New York* (Hartford, CT: American Publishing Company, 1869), 260.

3. "How the City Is Fed," *Christian Union* 42, no. 14 (October 2, 1890): 428–29.

4. On various approaches to the history of New York City in the nineteenth century, see Edwin G. Burrows and Mike Wallace, *Gotham: A History of New York City to 1898* (New York: Oxford University Press, 1999); Timothy Gilfoyle, *A Pickpocket's Tale: The Underworld of Nineteenth-Century New York* (New York: W. W. Norton, 2006); Tyler Anbinder, *Five Points: The Nineteenth-Century New York Neighborhood That Invented Tap Dance, Stole Elections, and Became the World's Most Notorious Slum* (New York: Free Press, 2001); David M. Henkin, *City Reading: Written Words and Public Spaces in Antebellum New York* (New York: Columbia University Press, 1998); Kenneth D. Ackerman, *Boss Tweed: The Corrupt Pol Who Perceived the Soul of Modern New York* (New York: Carroll and Graf, 2005); David Quigley, *Second Founding: New York City, Reconstruction, and the Making of American Democracy* (New York: Hill and Wang, 2005); Sven Beckert, *The Monied Metropolis: New York City and the Consolidation of the American Bourgeoisie, 1850–1896* (New York: Cambridge University Press, 2006); Thomas Kessner, *Capital City: New York and the Men behind America's Rise to Dominance, 1860–1900* (New York: Simon and Schuster, 2001); Timothy Gilfoyle, *City of Eros: New York City, Prostitution and the Commercialization of Sex, 1790–1920* (New York: W. W. Norton, 1992); Edward Spann, *The New Metropolis: New York City, 1840–1857* (New York: Columbia University Press, 1981); Christine Stansell, *City of Women: Sex and Class in New York, 1790–1860* (Urbana: University of Illinois Press, 1987); Sean Wilentz, *Chants Democratic: New York City and the Rise of the American Working Class, 1788–1850* (New York: Oxford University Press, 1984); Elizabeth Blackmar, *Manhattan for Rent, 1785–1850* (Ithaca, NY: Cornell University Press, 1989); George Chauncey, *Gay New York: Gender, Urban Culture, and the Making of the Gay World* (New York: Basic Books, 1995); Patricia Cline Cohen, *The Murder of Helen Jewett* (New York: Vintage, 1999); Amy Gilman Srebnick, *The Mysterious Death of Mary Rogers: Sex and Culture in Nineteenth-Century New York* (New York: Oxford University Press, 1997); Leslie M.

Harris, *In the Shadow of Slavery: African Americans in New York City, 1626–1863* (Chicago: University of Chicago Press, 2004).

5. On American food history, see Andrew Haley, *Turning the Tables: Restaurants and the Rise of the American Middle Class, 1880–1920* (Chapel Hill: University of North Carolina Press, 2011); Harvey Levenstein, *Revolution at the Table: The Transformation of the American Diet* (New York: Oxford University Press, 1988) and *Paradox of Plenty: A Social History of Eating in Modern America* (New York: Oxford University Press, 1993); James McWilliams, *A Revolution in Eating: How the Quest for Food Shaped America* (New York: Columbia University Press, 2007); Roger Horowitz, *Putting Meat on the American Table: Taste, Technology, Transformation* (Baltimore: Johns Hopkins University Press, 2005); Warren Belasco, *Appetite for Change: How the Counterculture Took on the Food Industry* (New York: Pantheon, 1990); Donna Gabaccia, *We Are What We Eat: Ethnic Food and the Making of Americans* (Cambridge, MA: Harvard University Press, 2000); Hasia Diner, *Hungering for America: Italian, Irish, and Jewish Foodways in the Age of Migration* (Cambridge, MA: Harvard University Press, 2003).

6. On the eighteenth-century consumer revolution, see Cary Carson, Ronald Hoffman, and Peter J. Albert, eds., *Of Consuming Interests: The Style of Life in the Eighteenth Century* (Charlottesville: University Press of Virginia, 1994); T. H. Breen, *The Marketplace of Revolution: How Consumer Politics Shaped American Independence* (New York: Oxford University Press, 2005); Richard Bushman, *The Refinement of America: Persons, Houses, Cities* (New York: Alfred A. Knopf, 1992). On mass consumption, see Lizabeth Cohen, *A Consumer's Republic: The Politics of Mass Consumption in Postwar America* (New York: Vintage, 2003); William Leach, *Land of Desire: Merchants, Power, and the Rise of a New American Culture* (New York: Vintage, 1994); Elaine Abelson, *When Ladies Go A-Thieving: Middle-Class Shoplifters in the Victorian Department Store* (New York: Oxford University Press, 1989); Andrew Heinze, *Adapting to Abundance: Jewish Immigrants, Mass Consumption, and the Search for American Identity* (New York: Columbia University Press, 1990); John F. Kasson, *Amusing the Million: Coney Island at the Turn of the Century* (New York: Hill and Wang, 1978); David Nasaw, *Going Out: The Rise and Fall of Public Amusements* (New York: Basic Books, 1993); Stephen Nissenbaum, *The Battle for Christmas: A Cultural History of America's Most Cherished Holiday* (New York: Vintage, 1996); Kathy Peiss, *Cheap Amusements: Working Women and Leisure in Turn-of-the-Century New York* (Philadelphia: Temple University Press, 1986); Nan Enstad, *Ladies of Labor, Girls of Adventure* (New York: Columbia University Press, 1999).

7. To be sure, there are many popular histories of New York's restaurant and dining culture and immigrant foodways including William Grimes, *Appetite City: A Culinary History of New York* (New York: North Point Press, 2010); Jane Ziegelman, *97 Orchard: An Edible History of Five Immigrant Families in One Tenement* (New York: Harper, 2011); Michael and Ariane Batterberry, *On the Town in New York: The Landmark History of Eating, Drinking, and Entertainments from the American Revolution to the Food Revolution*, revised ed. (New York: Routledge, 1999); John Mariani, *America Eats Out: An Illustrated History of Restaurants, Taverns, Coffee Shops, Speakeasies, and Other Establishments That Have Fed Us for 350 Years* (New York: William Morrow, 1991) and *How Italian Food Conquered the World* (New York: Palgrave Macmillan, 2011); Mark Kurlansky, *The Big Oyster: History on the Half-Shell* (New York: Random House, 2006). And a few scholars have begun to look at certain elements of New York's food culture in the nineteenth century, especially Haley, *Turning the Tables*; Gergely

Baics, "Feeding Gotham: A Social History of Urban Provisioning, 1780–1860" (PhD dissertation, Northwestern University, 2009); Thomas David Beal, "Selling Gotham: The Retail Trade in New York City from the Public Market to Alexander T. Stewart's Marble Palace, 1625–1860" (PhD dissertation, SUNY Stony Brook, 1998). An excellent collection of studies on the food culture of New York City, though it is interdisciplinary and scarce on history, is Annie Hauck-Lawson and Jonathan Deutsch, eds., *Gastropolis: Food and New York City* (New York: Columbia University Press, 2010).

8.  See, for example, Rebecca Spang, *The Invention of the Restaurant: Paris and Modern Gastronomic Culture* (Cambridge, MA: Harvard University Press, 2000); Levenstein, *Revolution at the Table*; Belasco, *Appetite for Change*, McWilliams, *A Revolution in Eating*; Gabaccia, *We Are What We Eat*; Haley, *Turning the Tables*. Many of these works draw on anthropological studies by scholars like Sidney Mintz and Mary Douglas.

9.  On public culture see Marguerite S. Shaffer, ed., *Public Culture: Diversity, Democracy, and Community in the United States* (Philadelphia: University of Pennsylvania Press, 2008); Henkin, *City Reading*; Mary Ryan, *Women in Public: Between Banners and Ballots, 1825–1880* (Baltimore: Johns Hopkins University Press, 1990).

10. For an explanation of conspicuous consumption and leisure see Thorstein Veblen, *The Theory of the Leisure Class* (1899; reprint, New York: Penguin, 1994).

11. Ryan, *Women in Public*; Amy G. Richter, *Home on the Rails: The Railroad and the Rise of Public Domesticity* (Chapel Hill: The University of North Carolina Press, 2005); Katherine C. Grier, *Culture and Comfort: Parlor-Making and Middle Class Identity* (Washington, DC: Smithsonian Institution Press, 1997); Andrew Sandoval-Strausz, *Hotel: An American History* (New Haven, CT: Yale University Press, 2008); Barbara Penner, "'Colleges for the Teaching of Extravagance': New York Palace Hotels," *Winterthur Portfolio* 44 (Summer–Autumn 2010): 159–92; Mona Domosh, "Those 'Gorgeous Incongruities': Polite Politics and Public Space on the Streets of 19th-Century New York," *Annals of the Association of American Geographers* 88, no. 2 (1998): 209–26.

12. For many years historians of nineteenth-century women argued that middle-class white women and men occupied "separate spheres"—the woman's sphere domestic and private, and the man's sphere commercial, political and public. In recent years, scholars have complicated this dichotomy significantly, many arguing for its rejection. But the notion of separate spheres has persisted, in part because it was unquestionably forwarded as an ideological position by many nineteenth-century writers and advisers even if it did not reflect the lived reality of American women. Influential works on separate spheres include Barbara Welter, "The Cult of True Womanhood: 1820–1860," *American Quarterly* 18 (Summer 1966): 151–74; Nancy Cott, *The Bonds of Womanhood: "Woman's Sphere" in New England, 1780–1835* (New Haven, CT: Yale University Press, 1977); Carl Degler, *At Odds: Women and the Family in America from the Revolution to the Present* (New York: Oxford University Press, 1980); Kathryn Kish Sklar, *Catharine Beecher: A Study in American Domesticity* (New Haven, CT: Yale University Press, 1973). For a more positive interpretation of separate spheres in creating supportive networks for women, see Carroll Smith-Rosenberg, "The Female World of Love and Ritual: Relations between Women in Nineteenth-Century America," *Signs* 1 (Autumn 1975): 1–29; Blanche Wiesen Cook, "Female Support Networks and Political Activism: Lillian Wald, Crystal Eastman, Emma Goldman," *Chrysalis* (1977): 43–61. In a pivotal article published in 1988, Linda Kerber surveyed the paradigms of women's history and complicated the idea of separate spheres. See Kerber, "Separate Spheres, Female Worlds, Woman's Place: The Rhetoric of Woman's History,"

*Journal of American History* 75, no. 1 (June 1988): 9–39. For a more recent rejection of separate spheres as an organizing principle see the 2001 special issue of the *Journal of the Early Republic* 21 (Spring 2001), edited by Mary Kelley, with contributions by Julie Roy Jeffrey, Laura McCall, and Carol Lasser.

13. On the history of department stores, see Leach, *Land of Desire*; Abelson, *When Ladies go a'Thievin*; and Susan Porter Benson, *Counter Cultures: Saleswomen, Managers, and Customers in American Department Stores, 1890–1940* (Urbana: University of Illinois Press, 1987).

14. On the creation of shopping districts, see Beal, "Selling Gotham"; Mona Domosh, "Shaping the Commercial City: The Retail Districts of Nineteenth Century New York and Boston." *Annals of the Association of American Geographers* 80, no. 2 (1990): 268–84.

15. On the culture of empire in the late nineteenth century, see Robert Rydell, *All the World's a Fair: Visions of Empire at American International Expositions, 1876–1918* (Chicago: University of Chicago Press, 1987); Kristin Hoganson, *A Consumer's Imperium: The Global Production of American Domesticity, 1865–1920* (Chapel Hill: University of North Carolina Press, 2007); Catherine Cocks, *Doing the Town: The Rise of Urban Tourism in the United States, 1850–1915* (Berkeley: University of California Press, 2003), especially 174–203; Gail Bederman, *Manliness and Civilization: A Cultural History of Gender and Race in the United States* (Chicago: University of Chicago Press, 1996), 1–44; Kasson, *Amusing the Million*.

CHAPTER ONE

1. John Pintard, *Letters from John Pintard to His Daughter Eliza Noel Pintard Davidson, 1816–1833, in Four Volumes* (New York: New-York Historical Society, 1941), 1:215, 329; 2:217.

2. Historian Gergely Baics includes these calculations of Pintard's market habits in "Feeding Gotham: A Social History of Urban Provisioning, 1780–1860" (PhD dissertation, Northwestern University, 2009), 114.

3. Pintard, *Letters*, 1:297; 2:41. See also 3:162.

4. Pintard refers to Stickler the grocer several times in his *Letters*, including: 2:193, 301; 311; 4:42. The reference to Mrs. King appears in 3:261. An example of Pintard's interaction with other market vendors can be found in 1:335: "A good woman in the market this morn$^g$ from whom I was purchasing some thyme for winters use, when I told her the price was high, remarked that *Time* was scarce. I told her, that was too true with me."

5. Pintard, *Letters*, 2:301.

6. Ibid., 1:317.

7. Percy Wells Bidwell and John I. Falconer, *History of Agriculture in the Northern United States, 1620–1860* (1925; reprint, New York: Peter Smith, 1941), 89–90; James McWilliams, *A Revolution in Eating: How the Quest for Food Shaped America* (New York: Columbia University Press, 2005), 193–96; Charles L. Sachs, *Made on Staten Island: Agriculture, Industry, and Suburban Living in the City* (Staten Island, NY: Staten Island Historical Society, 1988), 20; Kenneth Roberts and Anna M. Roberts, trans. and eds., *Moreau de St. Méry's American Journey, 1793–1798* (Garden City, NY: Doubleday, 1947), 172.

8. William Smith, *The History of the Late Province of New-York, from Its Discovery, to the Appointment of Governor Colden, in 1762* (New York: Collections of the New-York Historical Society, vol. 4, 1829), 263; Roberts and Roberts, *Moreau de St. Méry's*

*American Journey*, 166–67; William Strickland, *Journal of a Tour in the United States of America 1794–5*, ed. J. E. Strickland (New York: New-York Historical Society, 1971), 41; Bidwell and Falconer, *History of Agriculture*, 84; Roger Horowitz, *Putting Meat on the American Table: Taste, Technology, Transformation* (Baltimore: Johns Hopkins University Press, 2005), 20; Ulysses Prentiss Hedrick, *A History of Agriculture in the State of New York* (New York: New York Agricultural Society, 1933); J. Ritchie Garrison, "Farm Dynamics and Regional Exchange: The Connecticut Valley Beef Trade, 1670–1890," *Agricultural History* 56, no. 1 (1982): 3–21.

9. Timothy Dwight, *Travels in New England and New York, in Four Volumes* (London: William Baynes and Son, 1823), 3:289–90, 457 (on street-manure income). On eighteenth-century market production, see McWilliams, *A Revolution in Eating*, 195–96; Bidwell and Falconer, *History of Agriculture*, 89.

10. "A List of Farms on New York Island, 1780," *New-York Historical Society Quarterly Bulletin* (1917): 8–11.

11. *New-York Packet*, February 2, 1790, 3.

12. *New York Gazette and General Advertiser*, December 16, 1801, 4. See also *New-York Packet*, February 2, 1790, 3; *Daily Advertiser*, August 13, 1790, 4; *Daily Advertiser*, May 7, 1796, 3.

13. Roberts and Roberts, *Moreau de St. Méry's American Journey*, 166–67.

14. *Daily Advertiser*, February 17, 1790, 2.

15. *Spectator*, July 6, 1803, 4. See also *Daily Advertiser*, August 13, 1790, 4. Hundreds of advertisements published in the early national period for farms near New York boasted of their fecundity and proximity to the New York markets.

16. Roberts and Roberts, *Moreau de St. Méry's American Journey*, 155–57, 172–73; Pintard, *Letters*, 2:301; 3:123–24, 174–75. On the Buttermilk Market, see Thomas F. De Voe, *The Market Book: A History of the Public Markets of the City of New York* (1862; reprint, New York: Augustus M. Kelly, 1970), 408.

17. De Voe, *Market Book*, 82, 186–89, 322, 366–67; Bidwell and Falconer, *History of Agriculture*, 108–9; Horowitz, *Putting Meat on the American Table*, 20; Roger Horowitz, "The Politics of Meat Shopping in Antebellum New York City," in *Meat, Modernity and the Rise of the Slaughterhouse*, ed. Paula Young Lee (Durham: University of New Hampshire Press, 2008), 169–70; Jared N. Day, "Butchers, Tanners, and Tallow Chandlers: The Geography of Slaughtering in Early-Nineteenth-Century New York City," in Lee, *Meat, Modernity*, 181–87; J. Ritchie Garrison, "Farm Dynamics and Regional Exchange: The Connecticut Valley Beef Trade, 1670–1850," *Agricultural History* 61, no. 3 (Summer 1987): 13–15.

18. Thomas F. De Voe, *The Market Assistant: Containing a Brief Description of Every Article of Human Food Sold in the Public Markets of the Cities of New York, Boston, Philadelphia, and Brooklyn; including the Various Domestic and Wild Animals, Poultry, Game, Fish, Vegetables, Fruits, &c., &c. with Many Curious Incidents and Anecdotes* (New York: Riverside Press, 1867), 203. On the oyster trade in the eighteenth century, see William Smith, *The History of the Province of N.Y. from the First Discovery to the Year MDCCXXXII* (London, 1757), 676; Adolph B. Benson, ed., *Peter Kalm's Travels in North America / the English version of 1770, revised from the original Swedish* (New York: Wilson-Erickson, 1937), 237; *The Independent Reflector* (New York: James Parker, 1752–53); Mark Kurlansky, *The Big Oyster: History on the Half-Shell* (New York: Ballantine Books, 2006), 62, 88–98.

19. The 1686 Dongan Charter included provisions for establishing a ferry service between New York City and Long Island, requiring the ferry master to operate two

small boats for passengers and two large ones for farm produce and livestock. The city farmed out ferry leases on a five- or seven-year basis. A. Everett Peterson, *New York as an Eighteenth-Century Municipality, Prior to 1731* (New York: Longmans, Green, 1917), 124–50; Mary L. Booth, *History of the City of New York* (New York: W. R. C. Clark, 1867), 262–65.

20. *Niles' Weekly Register,* May 30, 1826; Brian Cudahy, *Over and Back: The History of Ferryboats in New York Harbor* (New York: Fordham University Press, 1990), 24; De Voe, *Market Book,* 186–67, 195–98, 322, 341; Robert Greenhalgh Albion, *The Rise of New York Port* (1939; reprint Hamden, CT: Archon Books, 1961), 125; Edwin G. Burrows and Mike Wallace, *Gotham: A History of New York City to 1898* (New York: Oxford University Press, 1999), 36, 449.

21. Roberts and Roberts, *Moreau de St. Méry's American Journey,* 169.

22. De Voe, *Market Book,* 187–95; *New York Journal* quotation on 187.

23. George Rogers Taylor, *The Transportation Revolution, 1815–1860* (New York: Harper and Row, 1951), 5, 16, 132–33.

24. Bidwell and Falconer, *Agricultural History,* 139; De Voe, *Market Book,* 322, 335, 341, 348, 408.

25. *Minutes of the Common Council of the City of New York, 1675–1776,* 8 vols. (New York: Dodd, Mead, 1905), 7:264–65; De Voe, *Market Book,* 183, 407, 410, 422. On market vendors and structures, see Helen Tangires, *Public Markets and Civic Culture in Nineteenth-Century America* (Baltimore: Johns Hopkins University Press, 2003), 26–47, 55–64.

26. Pintard, *Letters,* 2:124.

27. Ibid; *New York Gazette,* January 21 and 23, 1821; De Voe, *Market Book,* 495.

28. De Voe, *Market Book,* 325, 347.

29. *Minutes of the Common Council* (1766–1883), 7: 338; Murray Hoffman, *A Digest of the Charters, Statutes and Ordinances of, and Relating to, the Corporation of the City of New York,* Vol. 2 (New York: Edmund Jones, 1866), 641; "The Public Markets: True Value of the Markets to the City," *New-York Daily Times,* January 23, 1855, 2.

30. Pintard frequently comments on his early market schedule, on rising "before the dawn" to begin his marketing. At one point in his letters, he tells Eliza: "My summer hour is ½ p. 5 w$^h$ gives me every advantage to look after my private business, market & c" (Pintard, *Letters,* 1:67). See also 1:35, 57, 206, 219, 313; 2:35, 68, 81.

31. De Voe, *Market Book,* 346.

32. Theophilus Eaton, *Review of New-York, or Rambles through the City* (New York: J. Low, 1813), 29–30. For historians' analysis of the public markets as democratic spaces, see Tangires, *Public Markets and Civic Culture.* Roger Horowitz also analyzes the butchers in the context of republicanism and the moral economy in "Politics of Meat Shopping," 167–77 and *Putting Meat on the American Table,* 18–26. Horowitz and two other historians, Jeffrey Pilcher and Sydney Watts, explore these developments in an international context in "Meat for the Multitudes: Market Culture in Paris, New York City, and Mexico City over the Long Nineteenth Century," *American Historical Review* 109, no. 4 (2004): 1055–83. In his excellent unpublished dissertation on urban provisioning in antebellum New York City, "Feeding Gotham," Gergely Baics complicates this trajectory from "moral economy" to laissez-faire ethos governing the markets. Baics's quantitative study shows how spatial and temporal changes to daily life (geographic growth of the city and changing market and provisioning schedules) contributed to the decline of municipal regulation of the markets. Baics does not disagree with the shift from moral economy to laissez-faire politics, but he

does place greater emphasis on social and economic factors than on ideological ones in bringing about the shift.

33. Baics, "Feeding Gotham," 56–58; De Voe, *Market Assistant*, 199–200. For examples of private residents requesting public markets and raising funds for their erection or repair see *Minutes of the Common Council, 1675–1776,* 4:179, 354–55, 413–14, 423–24, 426–27; 5:56, 162, 167–68, 352; 6:325; 7:312, 326, 350–51; *Minutes of the Common Council of the City of New York, 1784–1831,* 19 vols. (New York: Published by the City of New York, 1917), 1:29, 135, 220.

34. On market regulations, see Tangires, *Public Markets and Civic Culture,* 3–25.

35. *Minutes of the Common Council, 1784–1831,* 1:237, 239.

36. De Voe, *Market Book,* 73–74; *Minutes of the Common Council, 1675–1776,* 4:84, 106, 109–10; 5:85–86; 6:116, 338–42; 7:113, 260.

37. See, for example, *Minutes of the Common Council, 1730–1776,* 7:260, 262, 265. *Minutes of the Common Council, 1784–1831,* 1:233, 235.

38. Baics, "Feeding Gotham," 21.

39. *Minutes of the Common Council of the City of New York, 1784–1831,* 1:387. For an example of a butcher stripped of and returned to his license, see 2:270, 272. See also 2:312, 380–81, 383, 386, 409, 462, 476, 477, 628, 631; 3:21, 231, 486. For butchers' applications—granted and rejected—for stands in the public markets, see *Minutes of the Common Council, 1784–1831,* vol. 1 (1784–1793): 339, 557, 758; vol. 2 (1793–1801): 27, 34, 270, 466, 479, 483, 524, 566, 582, 609, 611, 614, 631, 632, 649, 656, 712; vol. 3 (1801–1805): 30, 38, 45, 170, 192, 195, 207, 211, 218, 224, 233, 236, 248, 251, 259, 262, 269, 272, 284, 302, 329, 346, 368, 384, 386, 417, 423, 432, 444, 458, 462, 474, 475, 476, 477, 478, 482, 490, 515, 519, 565, 580, 586, 592, 607, 611, 661, 684, 689, 707, 728, 733, 742; vol. 4 (1805–1808): 57, 86, 90, 102, 108, 116, 123, 134, 137, 139, 191, 199, 233, 249, 250, 260, 275, 292, 338, 373, 377, 499, 506, 575, 579, 615, 691, 713, 727. The significant increase over time in the number of petitions for licenses and stands (many rejected) suggests that the number of apprenticed butchers was rapidly exceeding the number of stalls, a factor that would eventually contribute to the de-licensing of the butchers in 1843. The Common Council also remarked on the insufficient number of stalls for licensed butchers in March 1803, *Minutes of the Common Council,* 3:221. Applications for licenses continue but in most cases, they are requesting a license for a vacated stall or the transfer of stalls between two licensed butchers rather than new stalls to new butchers. Vol. 5 (1808–1809): 41, 101, 235, 251, 287, 436, 448, 526, 533, 550, 556, 568, 591, 598, 618, 623, 656, 694, 790; vol. 6 (1810–1811): 7, 95, 113, 186, 218, 332, 388, 439; vol. 7 (1812–1814): 77, 104, 214, 230, 768; vol. 8 (1814–1817): 109, 164, 174, 187, 237, 245, 265, 371, 432, 455, 560, 576, 583, 601, 720; vol. 9 (1817–1818): 404, 765; vol. 10 (1818–1820): 2, 71, 355, 360, 399, 570; vol. 11 (1820–1821): 290, 626, 636, 671, 710, 714, 738, 753, 776; vol. 12 (1821–1823): 33, 47, 56, 109, 113, 128, 133, 135, 139, 146, 173, 188, 195, 203, 236, 318, 337, 345, 358, 386, 465, 471, 489, 508, 524, 548, 568, 581, 591, 614, 624, 644, 687, 703.

40. Baics, "Feeding Gotham," 64–65.

41. *Laws and Ordinances Ordained and Established by the Mayor, Aldermen and Commonalty of the City of New-York* (New York: Hugh Gaine, 1793), 7.

42. Ibid., 154–64.

43. One such example is George Meserve Jr., a young butcher who had served an apprenticeship under his father. Meserve's case illustrates the hierarchy of butchers as well as the public-private nature of the city's eighteenth-century markets. In 1795, along

with several other young butchers, Meserve petitioned the city to expand a part of Fly Market where they were offered shirk stands. These butchers asked the Common Council to expand the lower market and build official butchers' stalls. In 1796, a new building was added to the Fly Market, a handsome brick structure with fourteen new butchers' stands, sold at a public auction on the fourteenth of March. George Meserve purchased stall number 68, for the price of 320 pounds. Meserve's connections to the butchers of New York through his father, a noted butcher, surely helped him in securing an official stall. *Minutes of the Common Council, 1784–1831*, 2:301–2; De Voe, *Market Book*, 82, 199–201. See also Bidwell and Falconer, *Agricultural History*, 140; Thomas David Beal, "Selling Gotham: The Retail Trade in New York City from the Public Market to Alexander T. Stewart's Marble Palace, 1625–1860" (PhD dissertation, SUNY Stony Brook, 1998), 113, 320–42; Horowitz, "Politics of Meat Shopping," 170–72.

44. Baics, "Feeding Gotham," 46; *Minutes of the Common Council, 1784–1815*, 3:42, 363. On butchers and residents of underserved areas seeking to take advantage of this loophole, see *Minutes of the Common Council, 1784–1831*, 4:11, 559; 5:116, 136, 265, 412, 493, 679, 714; 7:746; 8:34, 83, 482, 601; 9:393, 414, 461, 645, 655; 10:71, 360; 12:16, 36, 56, 84, 113, 228.

45. Howard Rock, *Artisans of the New Republic: The Tradesmen of New York City in the Age of Jefferson* (New York: New York University Press, 1979), 186–97.

46. On the city's laws protecting the butchers' monopoly and butchers' complaints when the city failed to prosecute offenders, see *Minutes of the Common Council*, 3:313–14, 344, 464; 4:61, 404, 445, 487, 493; 5:199, 648, 661; 6:399; 7:83, 775; 8:187, 601, 626; 9:691; 10:8–9, 61; 11:505; 12:202, 668, 671, 687. It is significant that butchers' petitions defending their monopoly occurred only as the number of licensed butchers outpaced the number of available market stalls, which prompted licensed butchers to seek a livelihood outside of the market system—and outside of the law. See *Minutes of the Common Council*, 3:221–23, on the crisis of too many butchers.

47. The licensed butchers especially protested against the city's policies on leasing market stalls. Even though the stalls were technically the city's property to lease to butchers, butchers developed a proprietary position toward their stalls. They thus protested when the city closed down markets, denying them their stalls or when—as they did with the new Fulton Market—the Common Council leased new market stalls on the open market rather than giving priority to already settled butchers. The widows and children of butchers also frequently petitioned (and often successfully) for the right to "inherit" their deceased husbands' and fathers' butchers' stalls and to operate them on their own. For petitions and complaints on these matters, see *Minutes of the Common Council*; on butchers' stands going to widows or heirs, or butchers trafficking in stalls, see *Minutes of the Common Council*, 2:476, 477, 479, 524; 3:170, 202; 4:93, 377, 382; 6:338; 7:115, 270; 8:550; 12:438, 764. On Fulton Market, see 12:38, 47, 56, 148, 165, 166, 197, 319, 338, 405, 568. See also Rock, *Artisans of the New Republic*, 207–29; Horowitz, "Politics of Meat Shopping," 167–77; Baics, "Feeding Gotham," especially 38–112.

48. *Minutes of the Common Council, 1784–1831*, 6:337–39; Peterson, *Eighteenth-Century Municipality*, 80–82.

49. Christine Stansell, *City of Women: Sex and Class in New York, 1789–1860* (New York: Alfred A. Knopf, 1986), 14–15; Tyler Anbinder, *Five Points: The 19th-Century New*

*York City Neighborhood That Invented Tap Dance, Stole Elections, and Became the World's Most Notorious Slum* (New York: Free Press, 2001), 129–31.

50. Samuel Wood, *Street Cries of New York* (1808; reprint, with five extra cries from the 1814 edition, New York: Harbor Press, 1931), quotation on 29. See also Mahlon Day, *The New-York Cries in Rhyme* (New York: Mahlon Day, 1825).

51. Allan Nevins, ed., *The Diary of George Templeton Strong*, 4 vols. (New York: Macmillan, 1952), 2:149. For another romanticized recollection of New York street vendors, see Charles Haswell, *Reminiscences of an Octogenarian, 1816–1860* (New York: Harper and Brothers, 1896), 35.

52. Mahlon Day, *New York Street Cries in Rhyme* (1825; reprint, with a new introduction by Leonard S. Marcus, New York: Dover Publications, 1977), 18; Stansell, *City of Women*, 13; Anbinder, *Five Points*, 129–31; Harlow, *Old Bowery Days: The Chronicles of a Famous Street* (New York: D. Appleton, 1931), 175. Reformer Solon Robinson titled an 1854 exposé of New York street life *Hot Corn: Life Scenes in New York Illustrated* and filled it with sad tales of desperate street youths, the most iconic of them the hot-corn girl. Solon Robinson, *Hot Corn: Life Scenes in New York Illustrated* (New York: DeWitt and Davenport, 1854).

53. *Minutes of the Common Council, 1730–1776*, 4:106.

54. Ibid., 109–10.

55. *Minutes of the Common Council, 1730–1776*, 6:260, 339; *Minutes of the Common Council, 1784–1831*, 1:233, 235.

56. For petitions to and discussions of forestallers' abuses in the papers of the Common Council, see *Minutes of the Common Council of the City of New York, 1784–1831*, 1:233, 235; De Voe, *Market Book*, 425; Robert Ernst, *Immigrant Life in NYC, 1825–1863* (1949; reprint, Port Washington, NY: Ira J. Friedman, 1965), 84.

57. *Minutes of the Common Council, 1730–1776*, 4:109–10.

58. *Minutes of the Common Council, 1675–1776*, 5:16, 435; 6:336–42, 360–75, 415; 7:181. See also Peterson, *Eighteenth-Century Municipality*, 68.

59. De Voe, *Market Book*, 234, 373–74, 379; Peterson, *Eighteenth-Century Municipality*, 79–80.

60. Pintard, *Letters*, 1:10, 124, 187, 317; 2:348; De Voe, *Market Book*, 379–80.

61. De Voe, *Market Book*, 380.

62. Pintard, *Letters*, 1:317; 2:277, 284.

63. J. P. Brissot de Warville, *New Travels in the United States of America, 1788* (Cambridge, MA: Belknap Press, 1964), 142–43.

64. Roberts and Roberts, *Moreau de St. Méry's American Journey*, 155; An 1807 guidebook to New York City likewise described fifty-two kinds of fish found in the markets of the city, as well as eight types of "quadrupeds," five kinds of "amphibious creatures," fourteen types of shellfish, and fifty-one different birds. Samuel Mitchill, *The Picture of New York, or the Travellers' Guide through the Commercial Metropolis of the United States* (New York: I. Riley, 1807), 129. And "A List of the Fish That Is Brought to the New York Market," published in the January 4, 1804, edition of the *New York Daily Advertiser* includes fifty-six varieties of fish.

65. See, for example, Amelia Simmons, *American Cookery, or the Art of Dressing Viands, Fish, Poultry, and Vegetables, and the Best Modes of Making Pastes, Puffs, Pies, Tarts, Puddings, Custards and Preserves, and All Kinds of Cakes, from the Imperial Plumb to Plain Cake. Adapted to this Country, and All Grades of Life. By Amelia Simmons, an American Orphan* (Albany, NY: Charles R. and George Webster, 1796); *New American Cookery*

*or Female Companion, Containing Full and Ample Directions. . . . by an American Lady* (New York: D. D. Smith, 1805); *A New System of Domestic Cookery Formed upon Principles of Economy, and Adapted to the Use of Private Families. By a Lady* (Boston: William Andrews, 1807).

66. Pintard's letters suggest this seasonality. See, for example, 1:36, 119, 124, 297, 345; 2:28, 41, 68, 277, 348; 3:161, 172. See also Baics, "Feeding Gotham," 121, 124; De Voe, *Market Book*, 217, 373.

67. Beal, "Selling Gotham," 249, 273–79.

68. *New York Morning Post*, January 16, 1790, 1.

69. *Commercial Advertiser*, June 8, 1802, 3; *New-York Evening Post*, July 19, 1802, 3.

70. *Daily Advertiser*, December 24, 1794, 1.

71. See, for example, Pintard, *Letters*, 2:106, 120, 193, 311. See also Beal, "Selling Gotham," 392–94.

72. Beal, "Selling Gotham," 399.

73. Ibid., 216–33.

74. Reporter for the *American*, quoted in De Voe, *Market Book*, 354. See also Baics, "Feeding Gotham," 133, 138.

75. On the public markets as gathering places for African Americans, see Leslie Harris, *In the Shadow of Slavery: African Americans in New York City, 1626–1863* (Chicago: University of Chicago Press, 2003), 41–42; Thelma Foote, "Black Life in Colonial Manhattan, 1664–1786," (PhD dissertation, Harvard University, 1991), 236–39; Beal, "Selling Gotham," 207–8.

76. Shane White, "The Death of James Johnson," *American Quarterly* 51, no. 4 (December 1999): 762–63; Baics, "Feeding Gotham," 270–73; De Voe, *Market Book*, 344; W. T. Lhamon Jr., *Raising Cain: Blackface Performance from Jim Crow to Hip Hop* (Cambridge, MA: Harvard University Press, 1998), 22–28.

77. Pintard, *Letters*, 1:80, 139, 248, 250, 299, 317, 337, 343, 355; 2:41, 46, 49, 217, 225, 280, 301, 311, 313, 316, 321, 334, 335, 352, 367; 3:124, 127, 160, 161–62, 175, 190, 207, 256, 284, 298; 4:1, 8, 12, 16–17, 116, 121; Baics, "Feeding Gotham," 122.

78. Lorena Walsh, "Consumer Behavior, Diet, and the Standard of Living in Late Colonial and Early Antebellum America, 1770–1840," in *American Economic Growth and Standards of Living Before the Civil War*, ed. Robert E. Gallman and John Joseph Wallis (Chicago: University of Chicago Press, 1992), 218. On heavy meat eating among Americans and New Yorkers in particular, see Baics, "Feeding Gotham," 124–25, 192–93; Rock, *Artisans of the New Republic*, 177–80; Horowitz, "The Politics of Meat Shopping," 172; Horowitz, *Putting Meat on the American Table*, 18–19; and Horowitz, Pilcher, and Watts, "Meat for the Multitudes," 1055–83, for a comparative perspective.

79. Walsh, "Consumer Behavior," 218, 242.

80. Baics, "Feeding Gotham," 124–25.

81. In "Feeding Gotham," 192–93, Gergeley Baics calculates: "In the late 1810s, New Yorkers on average ate between 85.9 to 92.1 pounds of beef, 16.9 to 19.6 pounds of veal, 28.6 to 34.1 pounds of lamb and mutton, and 10.7 to 13.5 pounds of pork—for all categories of meat, the year of 1816 representing the upper, while the year of 1818 the lower bound. On the whole, annual per capita consumption of fresh red meat was 159.3 pounds in 1816 and 142 pounds in 1818." These figures are based on sales of meats in the markets, so they do not include preserved meats or fresh meats purchased at illegal meat shops or from peddlers.

82. Richard Stott, ed., *History of My Own Times, by William Otter* (Ithaca, NY: Cornell University Press, 1995), 25–26.

83. On preservation abilities and storage space, see Walsh, "Consumer Behavior," 9; Elizabeth Blackmar, *Manhattan for Rent, 1785–1850* (Ithaca, NY: Cornell University Press, 1989), 123.

84. Pintard, *Letters*, 1:36, 345. Pintard made these provisions each November, as his letters reflect. See, for example, 1:250, 341; 2:316.

85. Susannah Carter, *The Frugal Housewife, or Complete Woman Cook* (New York: G. R. Waite, 1803), 188–201.

86. Walsh, "Consumer Behavior," 9–10, 12; Blackmar, *Manhattan for Rent*, 123.

CHAPTER TWO

1. James Fenimore Cooper, *Notions of the Americans as Picked Up by a Travelling Bachelor* (1825; reprint, New York: Frederick Ungar Publishing Company, 1963), 136–41.

2. *New York Mercury*, March 9, 1856.

3. Transporting wheat by land from Buffalo to New York City, for example, cost three times the value of the product; moving corn cost six times its worth; and oats cost an astonishing twelve times more in transportation costs than on the open market.

4. Percy Wells Bidwell and John I. Falconer, *History of Agriculture in the Northern United States, 1620–1860* (Washington, DC: Carnegie Institution, 1925), 181; George Rogers Taylor, *The Transportation Revolution, 1815–1860* (New York: Harper and Row, 1951), 133–37.

5. John Pintard, *Letters from John Pintard to His Daughter Eliza Noel Pintard Davidson, 1816–1833, in Four Volumes* (New York: New-York Historical Society, 1941), 1:61; 2:78.

6. Thomas F. De Voe, *The Market Assistant, Containing a Brief Description of Every Article of Human Food Sold in the Public Markets of the Cities of New York, Boston, Philadelphia, and Brooklyn; including the Various Domestic and Wild Animals, Poultry, Game, Fish, Vegetables, Fruits, &c., &c. with Many Curious Incidents and Anecdotes* (New York: Riverside Press, 1867), 186.

7. Ibid.

8. Pintard, *Letters*, 3:123–24.

9. Brian Cudahy, *Over and Back: The History of Ferryboats in New York Harbor* (New York: Fordham University Press, 1990), 24, 38–42, 340; Robert Greenhalgh Albion, *The Rise of New York Port* (1939; reprint Hamden, CT: Archon Books, 1961), 145–47.

10. Cudahy, *Over and Back.*, 62; Carl W. Condit, *The Port of New York: A History of the Rail and Terminal System from the Beginnings to Pennsylvania Station* (Chicago: University of Chicago Press, 1980), 60–62; Thomas F. De Voe, *The Market Book: A History of the Public Markets of the City of New York* (1862; reprinted, New York: Augustus M. Kelley, 1970), 195–98; Edwin G. Burrows and Mike Wallace, *Gotham: A History of New York City to 1898* (New York: Oxford University Press, 1999), 36, 449.

11. De Voe, *Market Book*, 187–95; Burrows and Wallace, *Gotham*, 449.

12. Marc Linder and Lawrence S. Zacharias, *Of Cabbages and Kings County: Agriculture and the Formation of Modern Brooklyn* (Iowa City: University of Iowa Press, 1999), 32; Joseph Camp Griffith Kennedy, *Preliminary Report on the Eighth Census* (Washington, DC: Government Printing Office, 1862,), clxvi, 218, quotation on 105.

13. Taylor, *Transportation Revolution*, 137.

14. *Long Island Railroad Broadside*, April 1, 1841.

15. De Voe, *Market Assistant*, 186–87; De Voe, *Market Book*, 515.

16. For comments on food from distant ports, see *Leslie's Illustrated Newspaper* 1, no. 26 (June 7, 1856): 407; 2, no. 41 (September 20, 1856): 235; "Our Family Market Report," *New York Herald*, February 25, 1859; March 19, 1859; De Voe, *Market Assistant*, 145.

17. *Frank Leslie's Illustrated Newspaper* 4, no. 1 (January 5, 1856): 50.

18. Bidwell and Falconer, *History of Agriculture*, 228–29, 422; "Extract from the Address [of John King]," *Transactions of the New York State Agricultural Society* 12 (1852): 536.

19. Bidwell and Falconer, *History of Agriculture*, 224–27; Roger Horowitz, *Putting Meat on the American Table: Taste, Technology, Transformation* (Baltimore: Johns Hopkins University Press, 2005), 20; Roger Horowitz, "The Politics of Meat Shopping in Antebellum New York City," and Jared N. Day, "Butchers, Tanners, and Tallow Chandlers: The Geography of Slaughtering in Early Nineteenth-Century New York City," both in *Meat, Modernity, and the Rise of the Slaughterhouse*, ed. Paula Young Lee (Durham: University of New Hampshire Press, 2008), 169–70, 181–82; J. Ritchie Garrison, "Farm Dynamics and Regional Exchange: The Connecticut Valley Beef Trade, 1670–1850," *Agricultural History* 61, no. 3 (Summer 1987): 13–15; De Voe, *Market Book*, 186–89.

20. The system of overland droving continued until the 1850s when railroads took over. Bidwell and Falconer, *History of Agriculture*, 177–78. See also De Voe, *Market Book*, 411.

21. "The Fruit Culture," *Charleston Mercury*, July 19, 1858, 1.

22. John Pintard noted the advantages these nearby hinterlands enjoyed when he remarked to his daughter: "Long Island, Westchester, Dutchess & Orange Counties by their proximity & water intercourse possess great advantages, & always will be the garden of N York." Pintard, *Letters*, 3:123–24.

23. Joseph C. G. Kennedy, *Agriculture of the United States in 1860; Compiled from the Original Returns of the Eighth Census* (Washington, DC: Government Printing Office, 1864), vii; Linder and Zacharias, *Cabbages and Kings County*, 32–33; *Transactions of the New York State Agricultural Society* 12 (1852): 536, 545.

24. Bidwell and Falconer, *History of Agriculture*, 242; Ulysses Prentiss Hedrick, "History of Agriculture," in *History of the State of New York in Ten Volumes*, ed. Alexander Flick (New York: Columbia University Press, 1935), 8:97–105.

25. Kennedy, *Agriculture of the United States in 1860*, vii, x. The interest in domestic commercial agriculture also spurred the formation of agricultural societies in American cities, including New York. These societies included some farmers but also many merchants and others interested in the commercial potential for improved agricultural techniques. John Pintard was among these nonfarming agricultural society folks. He remarked several times to Eliza about the progress made by the agricultural societies. For example, in July 1821, he exalted "the great abundance of fine vegetables with which our market is supplied. What used to be rare is now redundant, owing to the great exertion of our A[gri]cultural & horticultural societies." After the 1830s, agricultural societies declined in rural areas (with the loss of state funding in laissez-faire Jacksonian America) but remained strong in the vicinity of New York where the commercial imperative encouraged their persistence. These societies encouraged agricultural education and the use of innovative farming techniques to enhance production. Pintard, *Letters*, 2:68; 3:14. See also Bidwell and Falconer, *History of Agriculture*, 184–85, 198–201, 208–16; Kennedy, *Agriculture of the United States in 1860*, xii–xv.

26. Kennedy, *Agriculture of the United States in 1860*, vii, x.

27. "Poudrette for Sale," *New-York Tribune*, May 18, 1842, 3; Edward Spann, *The New Metropolis: New York City, 1840–1857* (New York: Columbia University Press, 1981), 131.

28. *Documents of the Board of Aldermen of the City of New York* (New York: Chas. King, 1843), 9:163–69.

29. *New-York Tribune*, March 10, 21, 1855, and March 9, 1853. Spann, *New Metropolis*, 168–69.

30. These numbers jumped significantly by 1860 especially for the latter counties, when the statistics were as follows: Queens County (886,934), New York County (392,828), Kings County (319,134), Richmond County (20,227), Westchester County (200,540), Orange County (48,815), Dutchess County (20,880), Putnam County (1,070). These numbers are especially striking when compared to other New York counties. Even those that are relatively close to New York City, like Dutchess and Orange Counties, produced a combined value of market produce of only about $10,000. Nearby Putnam County sent out a mere $274 worth of market produce in 1850. 1860 census data (compiled and analyzed in 2004) from Historical Census Browser, accessed November 4, 2010, from the University of Virginia, Geospatial and Statistical Data Center, http://fisher.lib.virginia.edu/collections/stats/histcensus/index.html. *Leslie's Illustrated* describes one local farmer and his yield: "A farmer in Germantown, NJ, claims that he makes $7,000 a year clear profit from twelve acres of land. He raises principally early vegetables for the markets, and uses about $2,000 worth of fertilizers on his land. From a patch sixteen feet by one hundred and eighty feet, he has sold $50 worth of plant this season, and can sell more from the same patch." *Leslie's Illustrated Newspaper* 4, no. 85 (July 11, 1857): 83.

31. Kennedy, *Agriculture of the United States in 1860*, vii.

32. De Voe, *Market Assistant*, 186–87; Pintard, *Letters*, 3:123; advertisement for hothouse grapes, *Home Journal* 26, no. 437 (June 24, 1854): 3; Richard Osborn Cummings, *The American and His Food* (New York: Arno Press, 1970), 57–59.

33. For contemporary descriptions of the ice harvest, see "Our Ice-Harvest," *Circular* 4, no. 52 (January 17, 1856): 206; "A Day among the Ice," *Knickerbocker; or New York Monthly Magazine* 47, no. 3 (March 1856): 315; "Ice: And the Ice Trade," *Merchants' Magazine and Commercial Review* 33, no. 2 (August 1, 1856): 174–75; J. T. Trowbridge, "Among the Ice-Cutters," *Our Young Folks: An Illustrated Magazine for Boys and Girls* 3, no. 1 (January 1867): 1–7; "The Ice Business," *Maine Farmer* 35, no. 8 (January 31, 1867): 2; L. S. Brockett, "Ice," *Appleton's Journal* 5, no. 100 (February 25, 1871): 231–32. See also Cummings, *American and His Food*, 36–39.

34. *Massachusetts Ploughman and New England Journal of Agriculture*, 7, no. 21 (February 19, 1848): 2.

35. "A Day among the Ice," *Knickerbocker*, 315.

36. Dorothy Smith, "Ice Harvesting on Staten Island," *Staten Island Historian* 1, no. 3 (July 1938): 17–23; "A Day among the Ice," *Knickerbocker*, 315.

37. "Ice: And the Ice Trade," *Merchants' Magazine*, 171.

38. "Facts and Opinions," *Literary World*, August 10, 1850, 115.

39. *Minutes of the Common Council of the City of New York, 1784–1831* (New York: Published by the City of New York, 1917), 10:225; "The Mild Weather and the Ice Trade of New York," *New York Herald*, January 22, 1858, 1; "A Day among the Ice," *Knickerbocker*, 315; "Ice: And the Ice Trade," *Merchants' Magazine*, 174–75.

40. *Saturday Evening Post* 19 (June 13, 1840): 4; "Improved Refrigerator," *Scientific American*, 2, no. 25 (June 16, 1860): 400.

41. Thomas B. Smith, "Improved Refrigerators," *American Agriculturist* 7, no. 11 (November 1848): 332. For an example of the range of commercial refrigerators on offer see "Alligretti Iceberg: The Antiseptic Refrigerator," Trade Catalogues, Manuscripts Collection, American Antiquarian Society.

42. De Voe, *Market Book*, 347, 349.

43. De Voe, *Market Assistant*, 191, 203–4.

44. *Leslie's Illustrated Newspaper*, 1, no. 22 (May 10, 1856): 343. For references to southern and Caribbean fruit in New York's markets, see for example, "Market Report," *New York Herald*, June 30, 1842; July 19, 1845; May 9, 1846; June 20, 1846; June 2, 1855; March 27, 1858; July 17, 1858; April 16, 1859; April 30, 1859; May 21, 1859. In *Leslie's Illustrated Newspaper*, see market reports for May 10, 1856; June 7, 1856; September 20, 1856; October 11, 1856; April 4, 1857. See also "New York Provision Markets," *New York Herald*, January 18, 1853, 3; and "What It Costs to Feed New York," *New York Herald*, January 18, 1853, 4.

45. "Provision Market" reports from *New York Herald*, June 30, 1842; March 30, 1844; July 19, 1845; June 20, 1846; January 23, 1855. On Virginia oysters in New York, see *New York Herald*, January 23, 1853; March 12, 1853.

46. "Supply of Fruit and Vegetables in New York," *New York Herald*, July 24, 1853, 4.

47. De Voe, *Market Assistant*, 145.

48. Ibid., 27. Gergely Baics addresses the impact of transportation development on seasonal variations in New York's meat trade in "Feeding Gotham: A Social History of Urban Provisioning, 1780–1860" (PhD dissertation, Northwestern University, 2009), 128.

49. *Leslie's Illustrated Newspaper* 3, no. 71 (April 18, 1857): 310.

50. "Family Marketing," *New York Herald*, June 2, 1855, 8.

51. *Leslie's Illustrated Newspaper* 3, no. 55 (December 27, 1856): 51.

52. "Supply of Fruit and Vegetables in New York," *Herald*, 4. Virtually all fruits and vegetables were available for longer periods of time than before the transportation revolution. Thus New Yorkers could enjoy asparagus, string beans, cucumbers, tomatoes, grapes, peaches, and strawberries as early as April; cabbage, onions, and cherries in May; and tomatoes as late as November. Of course, they would pay a premium for these more exotic items. Just as New Yorkers today can eat fresh berries, for example, year-round—from local growers in June, from California in the fall, and from Chile and Mexico the rest of the year—so too the nineteenth-century New Yorker could enjoy fresh fruits from distant ports throughout the year: for a price. At the same time, in season these treats were more abundant and cheap. Strawberries, for example, could be purchased for a mere three cents per basket at the height of the season in 1853, a significant savings over the seventy-five-cent baskets of early-season Baltimore berries. "New York Provision Market," *Herald*, 3; "The Strawberry Trade," *New York Herald*, June 17, 1853, 4; De Voe, *Market Assistant*, 325–91.

53. *Leslie's Illustrated Newspaper* 1, no. 22 (May 10, 1856): 343.

54. "Family Marketing," *Herald*, 8.

55. Robert A. Margo and Georgia C. Villeflor, "The Growth of Wages in Antebellum America: New Evidence," *Journal of Economic History* 47, no. 4 (December 1987): 893–94. For wages, see also "House Rents in Town," *New-York Daily Times*, September 16, 1852, 2; "Living on $600 a Year," *New-York Daily Tribune*, November 8, 1853,

4; "Life of the City Poor: Labor and Its Wants in Cities," *New-York Daily Tribune*, August 22, 1853, 6; "A Laborers' Strike," *New-York Tribune*, May 1, 1852, 4.

56. "The Market Men and the Long Island and Other Farmers," *New York Herald*, July 15, 1855, 1; De Voe, *Market Book*, 448.

57. "Victualling the Metropolis," *New York Herald*, February 5, 1853, 4; "The Washington Market," *New York Herald*, March 23, 1854, 2.

58. "City Intelligence," *New York Herald*, December 2, 1848, 2.

59. Undated 1842 petition about speculators and overcrowding in Washington Market, signed by William B. Jenkins and ten others, City Clerk (filed papers), 1842; "Petition to the Common Council," May 29, 1843, City Clerk Approved Papers, 1843, "Markets" folder, New York City Municipal Archives. See also "Washington Market," *New-York Daily Tribune*, June 19, 1844, 1; "Washington Market—Meeting of the Gardeners of New York," *New York Herald*, June 14, 1858, 8.

60. Spann, *New Metropolis*, 126.

61. "Provision Market," *New York Herald*, November 6, 1841, 3; See also *Herald*, June 10, 1843, 2; March 3, 1844, 4; July 19, 1845, 8; *Herald*, September 24, 1842, 7, 2.

62. This trend toward separate work and residential space had begun in the first decade of the nineteenth century; according to city directories, only one-tenth of New York's merchants or professionals had offices separate from their homes in 1800 as compared to more than half a decade later.

63. Diana DiZerega Wall, *The Archaeology of Gender: Separating the Spheres in Urban America* (New York: Plenum Press, 1994), 52–53; Burrows and Wallace, *Gotham*, 655–56, 727–28; Eric Homberger, *The Historical Atlas of New York City: A Visual Celebration of 400 Years of New York City's History*, rev. ed. (New York: Henry Holt, 2005), 76; Stuart Blumin, *The Emergence of the Middle Class: Social Experience in the American City, 1790–1860* (New York: Cambridge University Press, 1989), 149–53.

64. De Voe, *Market Book*, 559–90.

65. *Minutes of the Common Council, 1784–1831*, 12:84, 113, 228.

66. Baics, "Feeding Gotham," 91; On butchers' petitions to sell on streets outside of markets or residents' petitions for meat markets in underserved areas, see *Minutes of the Common Council, 1784–1831*, 4:11, 559; 5:116, 136, 265, 412, 493, 679, 714; 7:746; 8:34, 83, 482, 601; 9:393, 414, 461, 645, 655; 10:71, 360; 12:16, 36, 56, 84, 113, 228; 19:686. For Daniel Hyde's address, see *Minutes of the Common Council, 1784–1831*, 11:506.

67. Board of Aldermen Docs., Document 60, February 22, 1841, 7:710–11.

68. De Voe, *Market Book*, 382; Petition in City Clerk, "Filed Papers," Municipal Archives, Market File, 1841. For examples of unlicensed butchers appealing fines, see *Minutes of the Common Council 1784–1831*, 12:16, 36.

69. Beal, "Selling Gotham: The Retail Trade in New York City from the Public Market to Alexander T. Stewart's Marble Palace, 1625–1860" (PhD dissertation, SUNY Stony Brook, 1998), 398–99.

70. "Gossip with Readers and Correspondents," *Knickerbocker; or New York Monthly Magazine* 54, no. 2 (August 1859): 207.

71. Beal, "Selling Gotham," 393–99, 424.

72. William Bobo, *Glimpses of New-York City. By A South Carolinian (Who Had Nothing Else to Do)* (Charleston: J. J. McCarter, 1852), 136.

73. Burrows and Wallace, *Gotham*, 823.

74. "City Items," *New-York Tribune*, July 13, 1854.

75. On the deregulation of the markets in the context of the shift from patrician to laissez-faire politics, see Baics, "Feeding Gotham"; Horowitz, *Putting Meat on the American Table*, 21–22; Horowitz, "Politics of Meat Shopping," and Day, "Butchers, Tanners, and Tallow Chandlers," both in Lee, *Meat, Modernity*; Helen Tangires, *Public Markets and Civic Culture in Nineteenth-Century America* (Baltimore: Johns Hopkins University Press, 2003); Beal, "Selling Gotham," 304–70.

76. Petition in City Clerk, "Filed Papers," Municipal Archives, Market File, 1841. For examples of unlicensed butchers appealing fines, see *Minutes of the Common Council 1784–1831*, 12:16, 36.

77. Burrows and Wallace, *Gotham*, 632; Horowitz, "Politics of Meat Shopping," 175–77.

78. William Knapp, *"I Die a True American!" Life of William Poole with a Full Account of the Terrible Affray in Which He Received His Death Wound* (New York: Clinton T. DeWitt, 1855); Herbert Asbury, *The Gangs of New York: An Informal History of the Underworld* (1927; reprint, New York: Paragon House, 1990), 87–101.

79. For a discussion of the murder of Bill the Butcher as an example of the rise of nativism in the face of craft degradation in 1850s New York City, see Elliott J. Gorn, "'Good-Bye Boys, I Die a True American': Homicide, Nativism, and Working-Class Culture in Antebellum New York City," *Journal of American History* 74, no. 2 (September 1987): 388–410. For contemporaneous accounts of the murder and discussion of the rowdiness and violence of native-born butchers' culture, see "Fatal Termination of the Shooting Affray at Stanwix Hall," *New York Herald*, March 8, 1855, 9; "The News," *New York Herald*, March 10, 1855, 4.

80. "Common Council," *New York Herald*, January 31, 1843, 1; February 14, 1843, 1; De Voe, *Market Book*, 382, 532–34.

81. *Evening Post*, December 9, 1840.

82. *New-York Tribune*, July 8, 1843.

83. "Provision Market," *New York Herald*, June 30, 1842, 3.

84. Baics, "Feeding Gotham," 95–96, 99.

85. "Provision Market," *New York Herald*, November 6, 1841, 3. See also "Provision Market," *New York Herald*, June 30, 1842, 3.

86. "Common Council," *New York Herald*, September 6, 1842, 5.

87. Chas. H. Haswell, *Reminiscences of New York by an Octogenarian (1816 to 1860)* (New York: Harper and Brothers, 1896), 378.

88. Horowitz, "Politics of Meat Shopping," 177; Beal, "Selling Gotham," 354–57.

89. Advertisement, *New York Herald*, August 26, 1867.

90. See, for example, "Provision Market," *New York Herald*, June 10, 1843, 2; March 30, 1844, 4; August 17, 1844, 3; June 20, 1846, 4; January 23, 1847, 4.

91. "Municipal Reform," *New-York Times*, February 22, 1860, 6.

92. De Voe, *Market Assistant*, 21.

93. Among the grocers Dustan mentions regularly are Newton, Stranahan, Van Warts, Mr. Driggs, Shadrack Smith, the German grocer Brunje, Mrs. King, and Underhill & W. Caroline Dustan diary, Manuscripts Collection, New York Public Library, March 24, 1856; May 3, 1856; July 29, 1856; August 1, 1856; August 6, 1856; October 14, 1856; October 31, 1856; November 1, 1856; November 11, 1856; November 14, 1856; November 18, 1856, December 23, 1856; December 24, 1856; December 31, 1856; January 9, 1857; January 24, 1857; January 27, 1857; February 17, 1857; April 18, 1857; May 16, 1857; May 23, 1857; May 27, 1857; June 6, 1857; June 12, 1857; June 13, 1857; June 16, 1857; June 17, 1857; June 24, 1857; August 5, 1857; August 12, 1857; August 19, 1857; August 29, 1857; March 4, 1864;

March 19, 1864; April 1, 1864; June 7, 1864; June 25, 1864; July 30, 1864; August 6, 1864; October 19, 1864; October 24, 1864. NB: NYPL has catalogued Dustan's diary with the incorrect spelling of "Dunstan."

94. Dustan diary, May 7, 1864; May 31, 1864; June 4, 1864; June 18, 1864; November 23, 1864; February 3, 1865. Dustan does mention going to Jefferson Market a few times, usually when she is passing by on her errands through the city: January 3, 1857; May 16, 1857; June 16, 1857; June 23, 1857.

95. For visits to Ridley's and Stuart's, see ibid., March 6, 1856; July 8, 1857; February 20, 1864; July 6, 1864; October 19, 1864; December 20, 1864; December 31, 1864; January 13, 1865; January 30, 1865. Dustan records visits to Pinsent's, Lyon's, and Taylor's on June 25, 1857; July 10, 1857; July 24, 1857; July 25, 1857; August 1, 1857; August 7, 1857; August 14, 1857; February 2, 1864; February 22, 1864; July 2, 4, and 5, 1864. And her trips to Walduck's, Wall's, and Stuart's take place on October 13, 1856; October 27, 1856; December 29, 1856; December 31, 1856; January 7, 1857; June 25, 1857; March 31, 1864; February 25, 1865.

96. Pintard, *Letters*, 1:215, 247–48, 253, 272, 282, 285, 301; 2:156, 208; 3:256; 4:1. Louise's confection-making (or at least Pintard's recording of it) drops off considerably over time. One explanation is that she begins to have children and so has less spare time for the arduous process of confection making. Another explanation is that by the 1830s, like Dustan, she begins to purchase sweetmeats and confections rather than making them. Pintard alludes to this possibility in a notation on September 21, 1831, when Louise hosts a party at her home. Of the refreshments, Pintard writes: "How different dear mother observed from our times when every thing was prepared in the family. Now all is provided abroad [at a shop]. Easy, but expensive" (3:280).

97. Dustan diary, June 12, 1857; July 24, 1857; August 15, 1857; February 6, 1864; August 6, 1864.

98. Ibid., June 9, 1856; June 10, 1856; June 12, 1856; July 5, 1856; July 9, 1856; July 23, 1856; June 9, 1857; June 22, 1857. Milkman: January 19, 1857.

99. Ibid., June 13, 1857; June 16, 1857; June 17, 1857; August 19, 1857.

100. Ibid., November 4, 1856; June 24, 1857.

101. Ibid., June 10, 1857.

102. Ibid., May 16, 27, and June 2, 1857; July 8, 1857; March 11, 1864.

103. Henry Ward Beecher, *Eyes and Ears* (Boston: Ticknor and Fields, 1863), 358–59.

104. Joel H. Ross, MD, *What I Saw in New-York* (Auburn, NY: Derby and Miller, 1851), 198–99.

105. "Marketing," *New-York Times*, February 16, 1858, 4.

106. "The Market Gardeners before the Mayor," *New-York Daily Times*, May 29, 1855; "Mayor Wood on the Price of Vegetables," *New-York Daily Times*, June 8, 1855, 4; "Marketmen and Middlemen," *New-York Daily Times*, June 14, 1855, 4. See also "Municipal Reform," *Times*, 6.

107. As is the case today, the hotels and restaurants of antebellum New York were major customers at the city's wholesale markets. But some hotels were so large that they were early models of vertical integration, supplying their own food needs. The Astor House, for example, had its own ice stores and even its own farm and dairy, established in the mid-1850s. "Created and built up solely to supply the hotel with eggs, butter, milk (the real genuine article), fowls, hams, meats, vegetables, and fruits—in short, all the necessaries and luxuries of a hotel bill of fare." "Astor House Farm and Dairy," *Frank Leslie's Illustrated Newspaper* 6, no. 136 (July 10, 1858): 91.

108. "What It Costs to Feed New York—Washington Market and Its Business," *Herald*, 4.

109. De Voe, *Market Book*, 452; "New York Provision Markets," *Herald*, 3.

110. "Victualling the Metropolis," *Herald*, 2.

111. Ibid.

112. De Voe, *Market Book*, 452; "New York Provision Markets," *Herald*, 3; *Frank Leslie's Illustrated Newspaper* 9, no. 215 (January 14, 1860): 101.

113. John Sturtevant, "Recollections of a Resident of New York City from 1835 to 1905," Diaries, Manuscripts Collection, New York Public Library. See also Paul Prowler, "Glimpses of Gotham," *National Police Gazette* 35, no. 128 (March 6, 1880): 15.

114. "How New York Is Fed," *Scribner's Monthly* 14, no. 6 (October 1877): 732; "Characters in Washington Market," *Appleton's Journal of Literature, Science and Art* 7, no. 166 (June 1, 1873): 604.

115. "Hotel Life—How the Guests Are Fed," *Frank Leslie's Illustrated Newspaper* 15 (December 1860): 58.

116. "How We Get Our Ducks," *Frank Leslie's Illustrated Newspaper* 3, no. 59 (January 24, 1857): 125.

117. "Marketmen and Middlemen," *Times*, 4.

118. "Our Markets," *Frank Leslie's Illustrated Newspaper* 3, no. 77 (May 30, 1857): 403.

119. "Astor House Farm and Dairy," *Leslie's*, 91.

120. De Voe, *Market Assistant*, 7.

121. Ibid., 21–22.

122. Ibid., 25.

123. Roger Horowitz makes a connection between licensed market butchers' resistance to changes to the butchering trade and the increased immigrant makeup of the city's nonmarket butchers in "Politics of Meat Shopping," 174–76.

124. See, for example, Gorn, "'Good-Bye Boys: I Die a True American'"; Richard Stott, *Workers in the Metropolis: Class, Ethnicity, and Youth in Antebellum New York City* (Ithaca, NY: Cornell University Press, 1990), 244–53.

125. "The Pugilists' Encounter. Death of William Poole. Post-Mortem Examination-Corner's Investigation," *New-York Daily Times*, March 9, 1855, 1; "'I Die a True American!' Life of William Poole, With a Full Account of the Terrible Affray in Which He Received His Death Wound* (New York: Clinton T. De Witt, 1855), 7–8; "The Stanwix Hall Tragedy," *New-York Daily Times*, March 12, 1855, 1; *New York City Directory for 1847 and 1848* (New York: John R. Doggett Jr. Publisher, 1847), 328; *Doggett's New York City Directory for 1848–1849* (New York: John Doggett Jr., 1848), 328; *The New York City Directory for 1850–1851* (New York: Doggett and Rode, 1850), 403.

126. Gorn, "'Good-Bye Boys: I Die a True American,'" 392–400; Stott, *Workers in the Metropolis*, 34–68.

127. "The Pugilists' Encounter," 1.

CHAPTER THREE

1. "Washington Market in Christmas-Time," *Harper's Weekly*, December 30, 1865, 823–24; See also Junius Henri Browne, *The Great Metropolis: A Mirror of New York* (Hartford, CT: American Publishing Company, 1869), 408.

2. "Washington Market in Christmas-Time," *Harper's*; Browne, *Great Metropolis*, 405.

3. On the growing contrasts between poor New Yorkers and their middle-class and wealthier counterparts, see Edwin G. Burrows and Mike Wallace, *Gotham: A History of New York City to 1898* (New York: Oxford University Press, 1999), 460–61, 475–76, 587–88, 712–34, 744–48, 786–90; Edward Spann, *The New Metropolis: New York City, 1840–1857* (New York: Columbia University Press, 1981), 67–75, 94–116;

Elizabeth Blackmar, *Manhattan for Rent, 1785–1850* (Ithaca, NY: Cornell University Press, 1989), 72–108, 115, 138–48; Stuart Blumin, *The Emergence of the Middle Class: Social Experience in the American City, 1790–1860* (Cambridge: Cambridge University Press, 1989), 138–91.

4. Gergely Baics, "Feeding Gotham: A Social History of Urban Provisioning, 1780–1860" (PhD dissertation, Northwestern University, 2009), 230–33, 235.

5. Citizens' Association of New York, *Report of the Council of Hygiene and Public Health of the Citizens' Association of New York upon the Sanitary Condition of the City* (New York: D. Appleton, 1866), 59, 137–38; Tyler Anbinder, *Five Points: The Nineteenth-Century New York Neighborhood That Invented Tap Dance, Stole Elections, and Became the World's Most Notorious Slum* (New York: Free Press, 2001), 191.

6. On associations between grocers and liquor in the temperance literature, see, for example: "A Conversation between a Grocer and a Keeper of a Gambling House," *New York Evangelist* 1, no. 3 (April 17, 1830): 11; Letter from "Philanthropist," in *New York Evangelist* 1, no. 3 (April 17, 1830): 11; "New York City Temperance Society," *New York Evangelist* 1, no. 7 (May 15, 1830): 27; "The Temperance Cause in New York City," *Religious Intelligencer* 14, no. 53 (May 29 1830): 843; "Letter to a Friend on Temperance," *Religious Intelligencer* 17, no. 5 (June 30, 1832): 73; "Diary of a Drunkard," *Universalist Watchman, Repository, and Chronicle* 4, no. 10 (June 30, 1832): 80. On temperance grocers, see "Testimony of a Temperance Grocer," *Boston Recorder* 17, no. 13 (March 28, 1832): 49; "Temperance Grocers," *Christian Watchman* 15, no. 1 (January 3, 1834): 3; "National Temperance Convention," *Religious Intelligencer* 18, no. 2 (June 8, 1833): 24; "Grievances of a Temperance Grocer," *Christian Advocate and Journal* 21, no. 17 (December 2, 1846): 68.

7. On antebellum middle-class culture, see Blumin, *Emergence of the Middle Class*, especially 1–16; Mary Ryan, *The Cradle of the Middle Class* (New York: Cambridge University Press, 1983), especially 11–15, 155–85. On working-class culture, see Christine Stansell, *City of Women: Sex and Class in New York 1789–1860* (Urbana: University of Illinois Press, 1987), especially 1–18, 89–101; Sean Wilentz, *Chants Democratic: New York City & The Rise of the American Working Class, 1788–1850* (New York: Oxford University Press, 1984), 255–62; Richard Stott , *Workers in the Metropolis: Class, Ethnicity and Youth in Antebellum New York City* (Ithaca, NY: Cornell University Press, 1990), 191–276; Elliott J. Gorn, "'Good-Bye Boys, I Die a True American': Homicide, Nativism, and Working-Class Culture in Antebellum New York City," *Journal of American History* 74, no. 2 (September 1987): 388–410. On the temperance movement and middle-class ideology, see Scott C. Martin, *Devil of the Domestic Sphere: Temperance, Gender, and Middle-Class Ideology, 1800–1860* (DeKalb: Northern Illinois University Press, 2008).

8. George Foster, "New York in Slices—Liquor Groceries," *New-York Tribune*, October 5, 1848, 2; *New-York Tribune*, February 9, 1847, 3.

9. Citizens' Association, *Report of the Council of Hygiene and Public Health*, 138.

10. "The Holidays," *New-York Tribune*, December 25, 1851, 4; and "Holiday Gifts," *New-York Daily Times*, December 30, 1851, 2; *Leslie's Illustrated Newspaper* 9, no. 229 (April 21, 1860): 329; Solyman Brown, ed., *The Citizen and Strangers Pictorial and Business Directory for the City of New York and Its Vicinity* (New York: Charles Spalding, 1853), 111. See also "Marketmen and Middlemen," *New-York Daily Times*, June 14, 1855, 4; ad for "Essence of Coffee," *New-York Daily Times*, February 18, 1852, 3; ad for Thomas R. Agnew, "Fine Groceries," *New York Observer and Chronicle* 43, no. 17 (April, 27, 1865).

11. Article from *Clipper*, October 3, 1868, quoted in Anbinder, *Five Points*, 191.

12. [George G. Foster], *New York in Slices; By an Experienced Carver* (New York: W. F. Burgess, 1849), 81. On grocers selling adulterated liquors, see "Adulterations in Wine," *New York Observer and Chronicle* 24, no. 5 (January 31, 1846): 20.

13. George Foster, "New York in Slices—The Immigrants," *New-York Tribune*, July 8, 1848, 2; Unpublished Bultman memoir, quoted in Stanley Nadel, *Little Germany: Ethnicity, Religion, and Class in New York City, 1845–1860* (Urbana: University of Illinois Press, 1990), 40.

14. "Walks among the New York Poor: The Street-Boys," *New-York Daily Times*, September 28, 1853, 2; Foster, *New York in Slices*, 81.

15. Frank Beard, *The Night Side of New York: A Picture of the Great Metropolis after Nightfall* (New York: J. C. Haney, 1866), 20–24; Foster, *New York in Slices*, 82; As early as the 1830s, Frances Trollope had commented on the presence of these "ladies" in the Corlaer's Hook grocery she visited in the 1830s. See "Leaves from Mrs. Trollope's Journal," *New-York Mirror: A Weekly Gazette of Literature and the Fine Arts* 10, no. 6 (August 11, 1832): 46.

16. G[eorge] G. Foster, *New-York by Gas-Light: With Here and There a Streak of Sunshine* (New York: Dewitt and Davenport, 1850), 60.

17. Matthew Hale Smith, *Sunshine and Shadows in New York* (Hartford, CT: J. B. Burr, 1868), 276.

18. "Liquor Groceries," *Harbinger, Devoted to Social and Political Progress*, 7, no. 25 (October 21, 1848): 195; Citizens' Association, *Report of the Council of Hygiene*, 54.

19. Citizens' Association, *Report of the Council of Hygiene*, 40, 59, 71, 313. Quotations on 59.

20. Foster, *New York in Slices*, 81, 79.

21. "Liquor Groceries," *Harbinger*, 195; Foster, *New-York by Gas-Light*, 61. See also Foster, *New York in Slices*, 82.

22. John Doherty Ely, *Report on the Sanitary Condition of the City of New York* (New York: n.p., 1859), 75; Citizen's Association, *Report of the Council of Hygiene*, 201–2.

23. Browne, *Great Metropolis*, 99.

24. "Broadway and the Bowery," *New-York Daily Times*, August 9, 1852, 2.

25. "The Joy of Growing Up Italian," anonymous memoir in Oblate Sisters of the Sacred Heart of Jesus, Villa Maria Teresa, Hubbard, Ohio, *La Cucina dell'Amore: The Kitchen of Love* (Youngstown, Ralph R. Zerbonia, 1990, xxi), quoted in Donna Gabaccia, *We Are What We Eat: Ethnic Food and the Making of Americans* (Cambridge, MA: Harvard University Press, 2000), 73.

26. *Documents of the Board of Aldermen of the City of New York* (New York: Chas. King, 1843), 6:363–77.

27. Baics, "Feeding Gotham," 239, 238. See also A. K. Gardner, MD, "Reports on the Varieties and Conditions of the Meats Used in the City of New-York," *New York Journal of Medicine and Collateral Sciences* 10, no. 1 (January 1853): 48–57. For a detailed discussion of the slaughterhouses and the call to centralize them along the lines of Paris or Mexico City, see Roger Horowitz, Jeffrey M. Pilcher, and Sydney Watts, "Meat for the Multitudes: Market Culture in Paris, New York City, and Mexico City over the Long Nineteenth Century," *American Historical Review* 109, no. 4 (2004): 1055–83. On slaughterhouses in New York, see also Jared N. Day, "Butchers, Tanners, and Tallow Chandlers: The Geography of Slaughtering in Early Nineteenth-Century New York City," in *Meat, Modernity, and the Rise of the Slaughterhouse*, ed. Paula Young Lee (Durham: University of New Hampshire Press, 2008), 178–97.

28. Baics, "Feeding Gotham," 230–33, 235.

29. Robert Hartley, *An Historical, Scientific and Practical Essay on Milk, as an Article of Human Sustenance* (New York: Jonathan Leavitt, 1842), 108–9; "Spurious Milk: Highly Important to the Public," *New York Herald*, August 20, 1854, 3.

30. "The Milk Trade of New York," *Merchants' Magazine and Commercial Review* 28, no. 6 (June 1, 1853): 686; *Majority and Minority Reports of the Select Committee of the Board of Health, Appointed to Investigate the Character and Condition of the Sources from Which Cows' Milk Is Derived, for Sale in the City of New York, Together with the Testimony and the Chemical and Microscopical Analyses of Milks. Also, Letters from Distinguished Physicians, &c., &c., &c.* (New York: Charles W. Baker, Printer to the Common Council, 1858), 8.

31. "Milk Trade of New York," *Merchants' Magazine*, 684, 686.

32. Ibid., 686, 687; "Adulteration of Milk in the City of New York," *Farmer's Register: A Monthly Publication* 4, no. 5 (September 1836): 279; Samuel R. Percy, *On the Food of Cities. Read before the Medical Society of the State of New York at Its Annual Meeting, February 1864* (New York, 1864), 91; Ely, *Report on Sanitary Condition*, 177.

33. See, for example, "Adulteration of Milk in the City of New York," *Farmer's Register*, 279.

34. Hartley, *Essay on Milk*, 107, 108, 110.

35. Ibid., 107–15; "Milk Trade of New York," *Merchants' Magazine*, 686–70; "Our Exposure of the Swill Milk Trade," *Leslie's Illustrated Newspaper*, May 29, 1858, 407; Ely, *Report on Sanitary Condition*, 99.

36. "Exposure of Swill Milk," *Leslie's*, 407; Citizens' Association, *Report of the Council of Hygiene*, 311–12; "Milk Trade of New York," *Merchants' Magazine*, 686; Ely, *Report on Sanitary Condition*, 177.

37. On Tammany Hall and municipal corruption in general and of the markets in particular, see Burrows and Wallace, *Gotham*, 822–29; Spann, *New Metropolis*, 313–400.

38. "New York Provision Markets," *New York Herald*, January 18, 1853, 3; Ely, *Report on Sanitary Condition*, 9, 88–90.

39. The city council did periodically investigate and take action on such charges. In September 1855, for example, Councilman Healy was charged with demanding $1,000 in bribes from Washington Market farmers, "on their application to the Common Council for a stand or position for their wagons in West-st." *New-York Daily Tribune*, September 24, 1855, 7.

40. "The Management of the Public Markets," *New York Herald*, February 17, 1858, 1.

41. For details of the investigation, see the following articles in the *New York Herald*: "The News," December 15, 1857, 4; "The News," December 22, 1857, 4; "The Washington Market Investigation," December 23, 1857, 2; "The Washington Market Investigation," December 25, 1857, 1. In the *New-York Daily Tribune*, see "Washington Market Affairs," December 22, 1857, 7; "The Alleged Abuses at Washington Market," December 23, 1857, 7; "The West Washington Market Investigation," December 25, 1857, 7.

42. "Washington Market Investigation," *Herald*, December 23, 1857, 2; "Management of the Public Markets," *Herald*, 1; Ely, *Report on Sanitary Condition*, 177. For another instance of fraud the following year, see "The West Washington Market Case Again," *New York Herald*, October 27, 1859, 10; and "The Washington Market Blackmailing Affair," *New-York Daily Tribune*, October 27, 1859, 8. See "Our Albany Correspondence," *New York Herald*, May 7, 1858, 2; "The Washington Market Difficulty," *New-York Daily Tribune*, May 8, 1858, 7; "The Latest News," *New York Herald*, February 11,

1859, 4; "Washington Market Matters," *New-York Times*, February 9, 1860, 8; "West Washington Market," *New-York Times*, May 4, 1860, 2, 4; "Motion to Set Aside the West Washington Market Judgment," *New-York Times*, May 16, 1860, 2; "The West Washington Market Case," *New-York Times*, July 7, 1860, 3; "State Lands around the City—West Washington Market," *New-York Times*, July 27, 1860, 4; "The West Washington Market Case: The Troubles Not Yet Ended," *New-York Times*, August 17, 1860, 8; "West Washington Market," *New-York Times*, August 21, 1860, 8; "The West Washington Market Property," *New-York Times*, January 8, 1861, 4.

43. "The Old City Government and the New," *New York Herald*, January 10, 1852, 4; "Municipal Reform," *New-York Times*, February 22, 1860, 6.

44. "Washington Market Affairs," *Tribune*, 7; "Washington Market," *New-York Daily Tribune*, June 19, 1844, 1.

45. "Provisions and Extravagance," *New-York Daily Times*, November 9, 1852, 4.

46. "Meats, Milk, and Fruits," *New-York Daily Times*, May 25, 1852, 2.

47. "Provisions and Extravagance," *Times*, 4. See also "The Scramble for Food," *New-York Daily Tribune*, June 9, 1855, 4.

48. "The Scramble for Food," *Tribune*, 4; Foster, *New York in Slices*, 42.

49. See series of Petitions to the Common Council, City Clerk, Filed Papers, 1842, 1843. "Markets" folder, Municipal Archives, New York City.

50. Petition to the Common Council, May 29, 1843, City Clerk Approved Papers, 1843, "Markets" folder, Municipal Archives, New York City. See also "Washington Market," *Tribune*, 1. Farmers also complained about the laws that were geared toward preventing crowding on the sidewalks outside of the market buildings—statutes that required country vendors to unload all of their merchandise by 9:00 a.m. In June 1858, a group of Long Island and New Jersey farmers, primarily Germans, met to devise strategies to resist these laws and the fines the city levied when they were broken. See "Washington Market—Meeting of the Gardeners of New York," *New York Herald*, June 14, 1858, 8.

51. "The Market Gardeners before the Mayor," *New-York Daily Times*, May 29, 1855, 4; "Mayor Wood on the Price of Vegetables," *New-York Daily Times*, June 8, 1855, 4; "Venders of Vegetables," *New-York Daily Times*, August 15, 1855, 4. See also "The Market and the Market Gardeners," *New-York Daily Times*, May 31, 1855, 4; "Marketmen and Middlemen," *Times*, 4.

52. Ibid.

53. "Market Report," *New York Herald*, September 24, 1842, 7. In yet another market report, the *Herald*'s reporter declared Washington Market "not fit for a lady to go into," due to its "very filthy condition." The *Herald* included complaints about the terrible state of Washington Market in its market reports through the 1840s and 1850s. See, for example, *New York Herald*, July 15, 1843, 3; March 30, 1844, 4; July 19, 1845, 8; August 1, 1846, 4; January 13, 1850, 1; January 18, 1853, 3; July 17, 1857, 3; February 19, 1859, 8. See also "The New Central Park—The New Croton Reservoir—The New Washington Market—The New Emigrant Depot at Castle Garden—The New City Hall," *New York Herald*, July 18, 1855, 4.

54. "A Good Move," *New-York Daily Times*, April 6, 1853, 4; "Marketmen and Middlemen," *Times*, 4; "Municipal Reform," *Times*, 6.

55. Citizens' Association, *Report of the Council of Hygiene*, 16; "Characters in Washington Market," *Appleton's Journal of Literature, Science and Art* 7, no. 166 (June 1, 1872): 604.

56. Citizens' Association, *Report of the Council of Hygiene*, xliv, xcii. On today's mortality rates, see New York City Department of Health and Mental Hygiene statistics, accessed August 8, 2013, https://a816-healthpsi.nyc.gov/SASStoredProcess/guest?_PROGRAM =%2FEpiQuery%2FVS%2Fqnycvs1&topic=OverallMortality&years=2007.

57. "Our Family Market Report," *New York Herald*, February 26, 1859, 8; Citizens' Association, *Report of the Council of Hygiene*, 11. See also "Municipal Reform," *Times*, 6. *Appleton's Journal* also expressed concern about water damage thanks to holes in the roof and shingle damage. "In rainy weather the stalls and stands are drenched with rain . . . causing, annually, destruction and consequent loss of enough valuable articles, damaged by water, to build a splendid and convenient edifice," the writer declaimed. "Characters in Washington Market," *Appleton's Journal*, 604.

58. "Extraordinary Developments of the Administration of Justice in New York," *New York Herald*, March 7, 1844, 8. For coverage of these proposals, see also: *New York Herald*: December 2, 1848, 2; December 28, 1849, 2; January 12, 1850, 1; January 13, 1850, 2; October 16, 1851, 7; December 30, 1851, 34; December 31, 1851, 1; March 31, 1853, 2; April 22, 1854, 54; June 20, 1856, 8; July 17, 1857, 3; June 18, 1859, 1.

59. "Marketing," *New-York Times*, February16, 1858, 4; "The Market Gardeners before the Mayor," *Times*, 4; "Mayor Wood on the Price of Vegetables," *Times*, 4; "Marketmen and Middlemen," *Times*, 4. See also "Municipal Reform," *Times*, 6.

60. "The Manhattan Market," *New-York Times*, June 8, 1880, 3; "Manhattan Market Gone: Destroyed at Midnight by Fire," *New-York Times*, September 9, 1880, 1.

61. "Exposure of Swill Milk," *Leslie's*, 407.

62. Ibid.

63. Tuomey's market associations continued well beyond this point; according to his obituary in the *New-York Times*, at the end of his life, Tuomey died on his way to the butchers' stall he had operated in Washington Market for the past eight months. "Suddenly Dropping Dead: Alderman Tuomey's Varied Career Brought to a Close," *New-York Times*, May 3, 1877, 8.

64. "The Swill Milk Committee Render Their Report at Last," *Leslie's Illustrated Newspaper*, July 10, 1858, 90.

65. "The Swill Milk Investigating Committee," *Leslie's Illustrated Newspaper*, June 12, 1858, 24; *Majority and Minority Reports of the Select Committee of the Board of Health*, 61.

66. *Majority and Minority Reports of the Select Committee of the Board of Health*, 31–68, 67.

67. Ibid., 81, 189.

68. Ibid., 158, 162.

69. "Our Exposure of the Swill Milk Trade," *Leslie's Illustrated Newspaper*, September 12, 1858, 22; June 12, 1858, 22. See also "Swill Milk Committee Render Their Report," *Leslie's*, 90.

70. "Marketmen and Middlemen," *Times*, 4; Burrows and Wallace, *Gotham*, 627–28; Baics, "Feeding Gotham," 100–104.

71. Roy Rosenzweig and Elizabeth Blackmar, *The Park and the People: A History of Central Park* (Ithaca, NY: Cornell University Press, 1992), 211–37; Spann, *New Metropolis*, 169–72; Burrows and Wallace, *Gotham*, 790–95.

72. "Swill Milk Committee Render Their Report," *Leslie's*, 90; *Majority and Minority Reports of the Select Committee of the Board of Health*, 9.

73. *Majority and Minority Reports of the Select Committee of the Board of Health*, 21–28; "Our Exposure of the Swill Milk Trade," *Leslie's Illustrated Newspaper*, July 24, 1858, 120; "The Swill Milk Question—Important Movement of Alderman Tucker," *Leslie's Illustrated Newspaper*, September 18, 1858, 248.

74. "New York Items," *Maine Farmer* 26, no. 24 (June 3, 1858): 2; "Pure Country Milk," *New-York Times*, May 15, 1858, 5; "Pure Milk," *New-York Times*, June 10, 1858, 8; "What Is American Solidified Milk?," *New-York Times*, March 28, 1859, 5; "Milk for Babes," *Leslie's Illustrated Newspaper*, May 15, 1858 ; advertisements and announcements in *Leslie's Illustrated Newspaper*, May 22, 1858, 400; May 29, 1858, 416; June 5, 1858, 16; June 12, 1858, 32; June 19, 1858, 48; "Dalson's American Solidified Milk," *New-York Daily Times*, January 27, 1856, 5; "New-York Condensed Milk Company," *New-York Times*, May 12, 1858, 5; "Borden's Condensed Milk," *New-York Times*, April 2, 1859, 5; Fulton Coffee and Dining Rooms," *Leslie's Illustrated Newspaper*, May 15, 1858, 384; "The Astor House Farm and Dairy," *Leslie's Illustrated Newspaper*, July 10, 1858, 91; "Astor House, New York," *Leslie's Illustrated Newspaper*, July 10, 1858, 94.

75. "They Ought to Be Beaten," *New-York Times*, October 29, 1878, 8; also "Suddenly Dropping Dead," *Times*, 8.

76. "Swill Milk Nuisance," *New York Observer and Chronicle* 36, no. 22 (June 3, 1858): 174.

77. Samuel M. Percy, MD, "On the Food of Cities," *Transactions of the Medical Society of the State of New York, for the Year 1864* (Albany, NY: Comstock and Cassidy, Printers, 1864), 77, 86.

78. Percy, "Food of Cities," 86, 87–88; Citizens' Association, *Report of the Council of Hygiene*, 264.

79. Citizens' Association, *Report of the Council of Hygiene*, 263–64.

80. On pure-food-and-drug laws as a response to late nineteenth-century industrialization, see Michael E. McGerr, *A Fierce Discontent: The Rise and Fall of the Progressive Era in America, 1870–1920* (New York: Oxford University Press, 2005), 160–63; Joshua David Hawley, *Theodore Roosevelt: Preacher of Righteousness* (New Haven, CT: Yale University Press, 2008), 160–61.

CHAPTER FOUR

1. "Outline Sketches of New-York," *Home Journal*, September 9, 1854, 2; Junius Henri Browne, *The Great Metropolis: A Mirror of New York* (Hartford, CT: American Publishing Company, 1869), 260.

2. Jürgen Habermas, *The Structural Transformation of the Public Sphere*, trans. Thomas Burger and Frederick Lawrence (Cambridge, MA: MIT Press, 1989); David Conroy, *In Public Houses: Drink and the Revolution of Authority in Colonial Massachusetts* (Chapel Hill, NC: Omohundro Institute of American Culture, 1995).

3. Mary Ryan, *Women in Public: Between Banners and Ballots* (Baltimore: Johns Hopkins University Press, 1990), 58–80, quotation on 62.

4. Rebecca Spang, *The Invention of the Restaurant: Paris and Modern Gastronomic Culture* (Cambridge, MA: Harvard University Press, 2000), 85–86.

5. Andrew Sandoval-Strausz, *Hotel: An American History* (New Haven, CT: Yale University Press, 2008), 65.

6. Browne, *Great Metropolis*, 263.

7. Of course, taverns had long existed, but they served more as places of lodging and drinking than of eating. Those who stayed in the taverns received meals with lodging, but they could not separate the two and had no options for commercial meals out-

side of the tavern. Male residents of various stripes might visit taverns for drinking, socializing, and transacting business, and the taverns' public rooms hosted balls and assemblies. But with few exceptions, only travelers ate their meals in these establishments. City residents tended to take all of their meals at home, then located near or in the same structures as their places of work. On taverns see Sharon V. Salinger, *Taverns and Drinking in Early America* (Baltimore: Johns Hopkins University Press, 2002); Kym S. Rice, *Early American Taverns: For the Entertainment of Friends and Strangers* (Chicago: University of Chicago Press, 1983); Richard Pillsbury, *From Boarding House to Bistro* (Boston: Unwin Hyman, 1990), 18; Edwin G. Burrows and Mike Wallace, *Gotham: A History of New York City to 1898* (New York: Oxford University Press, 1999), 338–39.

8. The predominant history of the French restaurant is Rebccca Spang's *Invention of the Restaurant*. While Spang offers a more particularized definition of the restaurant than I do, I share her designation of a restaurant as a free-standing establishment with a fixed menu. And her claim that the restaurant played a central role in the civic, social, economic, and political life of Paris applies to the restaurants of nineteenth-century New York City as well. Indeed, New York served as an American Paris in terms of its restaurant culture.

9. Abram Dayton, *Last Days of Knickerbocker Life in New York* (New York: G. P. Putnam's Sons, 1897), 145–48; *Longworth's New York City Directory for 1810* (New York: Longworth, 1810).

10. John Pintard described a typical pattern when telling his daughter Eliza about her sister's stepson's daily schedule in New York in 1829: "He is to begin his career by going down to the store in Nassau S$^t$ near Pine, before breakfast, sweep[ing] the counting room, & return[ing] to breakfast," Pintard explained. After returning to the office, the young man would "attend to duty till 2, come home to dine, return & lock up at evening." John Pintard, *Letters from John Pintard to His Daughter Eliza Noel Pintard Davidson, 1816–1833, in Four Volumes* (New York: New-York Historical Society, 1941), 3:90.

11. "House Rents in Town," *New-York Daily Times*, September 16, 1852, 2; "Living on $600 a Year," *New-York Daily Tribune*, November 8, 1853, 4; "Life of the City Poor: Labor and Its Wants in Cities," *New-York Daily Tribune*, August 22, 1853, 6; "A Laborers' Strike," *New-York Tribune*, May 1, 1852, 4; Elizabeth Blackmar, *Manhattan for Rent, 1785–1850* (Ithaca, NY: Cornell University Press, 1989), 192–95.

12. "The Summer Hotels," *Nation*, September 11, 1884, 217; Frederick Marryat, *A Diary in America with Remarks on its Institutions*, ed. Sydney Jackman (New York: Alfred A. Knopf, 1962), 390.

13. Wendy Gamber, *The Boardinghouse in Nineteenth-Century America* (Baltimore: Johns Hopkins University Press, 2007), 3; On clerks, see Thomas Augst, *The Clerk's Tale: Young Men and Moral Life in Nineteenth-Century America* (Chicago: University of Chicago Press, 2003).

14. "New-York Daguerreotyped," *Putnam's Monthly Magazine of American Literature, Science, and Art* 1, no. 4 (April 1853): 366; "The Eating Houses—How New Yorkers Sleep Up Town and Eat Down Town," *New-York Daily Times*, November 6, 1852, 8. See also "Dining Down Town," *Home Journal*, 2, no. 413 (January 7, 1854): 2; "The Serious Comedy of the Restaurant," *Frank Leslie's Illustrated Newspaper*, November 10, 1866, 115.

15. Calvin Pollard Diaries, 1841–1842, New-York Historical Society, Manuscript Collections; Allan Nevins, ed., *The Diary of George Templeton Strong*, 4 vols. (New York:

Macmillan Company, 1952), 1:364; T. Barry Davies, comp. and ed., *Letters from America, 1853–1860* (Upton-upon-Severn, Worcs: Self Publishing Association, 1991), 19; "The Eating-Saloons of New-York," *New-York Tribune*, November 10, 1866, 2. See also "The Eating Houses," *Times*, 8; and the *Water Cure Journal*, May 1857, 111, for a letter from "A Bachelor" lamenting the reliance of boardinghouse residents on restaurants for their daily subsistence.

16. Dayton, *Knickerbocker Life*, 46–47.

17. Sandoval-Strausz, *Hotel*, 168–69; *Albion*, July 18, 1840, 236. See also "Change in New-York Habits," *New York Weekly Mirror*, October 12, 1844; "New York Hotels," *Daily Picayune*, April 11, 1865. For mention of specific European Plan hotels, see "New-York Daguerreotyped," *Putnam's*, 360. Advertisements for European Plan hotels can be found in *Spirit of the Times*, August 7, 1841, 274; August 13, 1853, 312; October 14, 1854, 419; *Independent*, August 2, 1855; *Charleston Mercury*, September 5, 1854 and May 11, 1849; *New York Herald*, September 6, 1865.

18. *New-York Daily Times*, June 1, 1852, 3; *Independent*, August 13, 1857, 5; "The Astor House Restaurant," *Daily Picayune*, May 8, 1857, 9; "Hotels on the European Plan," *New York Observer and Chronicle*, August 9, 1855, 254; *Home Journal*, March 29, 1856, 3. See also "The Astor House, New York," *Daily Picayune*, July 25, 1857, 1.

19. O. L. Holley, *A Description of the City of New York with a Brief Account of the Cities, Towns, Villages, and Places of Resort within Thirty Miles. Designed as a Guide for Citizens and Strangers to All Places of Attraction in the City and Its Vicinity* (New York: J. Disturnell, 1847), 55; Browne, *Great Metropolis*, 261; "New-York Daguerreotyped," *Putnam's*, 366; Davis, *Letters from America*, 30–31. An 1858 Sabbatarian count of New York's restaurants listed 487 restaurants, along with "3,409 liquor shops and drinking saloons," and "1,244 confectionery and cigar stores." "Sabbath Observance," *Columbus Gazette*, March 12, 1858, 4. See also "Eating Houses," *Times*, 8; "Financiering," *Literary World* 12 (January 1, 1853): 6.

20. Dayton, *Knickerbocker Life*, 124–25, 134–38; Foster, *New-York by Gas-Light: With Here and There a Streak of Sunshine* (New York: Dewitt and Davenport, 1850), 217; "Outline Sketches," *Home Journal*, 4; "Eating Houses," *Times*, 8, noted that at 12.5 cents for a full meal, the sixpenny eating houses catered to "thousands of mechanics and others." For ads and notices for restaurants that drew merchants, see *Independent*, August 13, 1857, 5; *Knickerbocker*, June 1849, 554; "Pieri's Splendid Restaurant," *New York Herald*, February16, 1845; "New-York Daguerreotyped," *Putnam's*, 366–67; *Albion*, January 22, 1859, 48. Sherwood's and Fisher's were two restaurants associated with sporting men. "From the Docket of a Late Sheriff," *Knickerbocker*, January 1853, 59–64; "Gossip of the Last Knickerbocker," *Spirit of the Times*, May 27, 1848, 165; *Spirit of the Times*, October 1, 1859, 406. For a story that links restaurants and bachelor life, see "Slippers. A Wife's Stratagem," *Godey's Lady's Book*, February 1856, 136–41.

21. "New-York Daguerreotyped," *Putnam's*, 367; William Ferguson, *America: By River and Rail, or Notes by the Way on the New World and Its People* (London: James Nisbet, 1856), 50.

22. "The Eating-Saloons of New York," *Tribune*, 2. See also Foster, *New-York by Gas-Light*, 216–17; "Outline Sketches," *Home Journal*, 2; "New-York Daguerreotyped," *Putnam's*, 366–67; "Our Restaurants," *New-York Tribune*, July 6, 1868, 3; Browne, *Great Metropolis*, 260–66.

23. [George G. Foster], *New York in Slices; By an Experienced Carver* (New York: W. F. Burgess, 1849), 67.

24. "Dining for Fifteen Cents," *New-York Tribune*, February 20, 1881, 2; "Eating-Saloons," *Tribune*, 2; "How to Be Neat, Elegant, and Economical," *Albion* 37, no. 4 (January 22, 1859): 47.

25. *New York Herald*, February 8, 1855. Ads seeking partners in restaurant ventures appeared frequently in the *Herald* and other newspapers. See, for example, *New York Herald*, May 2, 1855; March 18, 1856; March 20, 1856; May 25, 1856; May 12, 1861; *New-York Times*, June 25, 1858; October 14, 1859; April 28, 1864. Junius Browne also claimed that nearly all restaurants in New York "do a successful business, and many make their proprietors rich in a very few years." Browne, *Great Metropolis*, 261.

26. "Our Restaurants," *Tribune*, 3.

27. For descriptions of the short-order eating houses, see Dayton, *Knickerbocker Life*, 120–22; Foster, *New-York by Gas-Light*, 214–18; "New-York Daguerreotyped," *Putnam's*, 361; Captain Basil Hall, *Travels in North America in the Years 1827 and 1828* (Edinburgh: Cadell, 1829), 32–34; "Of Dinners and Dining Places," *Harper's Weekly*, March 7, 1857, 147–48; "Eating Houses," *Times*, 8; "Eating-Saloons," *Tribune*, 2.

28. "Of Dinners and Dining Places," *Harper's*, 147; "Culinary Reform," *Memphis Daily Appeal*, November 18, 1865; Hall, *Travels in North America*, 32–34. See also "Our Restaurants," *Tribune*, 3.

29. "Eating Houses," *Times*, 8. According to one proprietress, some failed to honor the agreement. Mrs. C. F. Fish announced in the *New-York Daily Times* (November 1, 1852, 4) that she would be returning her prices to six pence a plate "to suit the wishes of her patrons and to protect herself against dishonorable competitors who have not stood up to their agreement." On specie and liquor pricing see *New York Herald*, February 15, 1851; April 4, 1858; *Daily Dispatch*, September 28, 1853; *Louisville Daily Journal*, July 16, 1862.

30. "New York Eating Houses," *Louisville Daily Journal*, August 17, 1855. Likewise, the *Tribune* declared: "A good saloon in a good location has from five to six hundred customers at breakfast, perhaps eight hundred at dinner, and about six hundred at supper." The *Tribune* estimated a daily consumption of five hundred to six hundred pounds of beef, "100 to 150 pounds of veal, 100 pounds of mutton, about as much of pork, and about as much lamb in its season; 100 pounds of fish; from 100 to 200 pounds of poultry in Winter, $30 to $50 worth of various vegetables, 300 loaves of wheat bread, 100 loaves of French and 25 loaves of Graham bread; from 400 to 500 rolls; 100 gallons of coffee; 50 gallons of tea; 300 to 400 quarts of milk; from 100 to 150 pounds of butter, from $30 to $50 worth of dried, canned, and fresh fruits," and two thousand pounds of ice per week. "Our Restaurants," *Tribune*, 3.

31. Foster, *New-York by Gas-Light*, 215; "Of Dinners and Dining Places," *Harper's*, 147; "Culinary Reform," *Memphis Daily Appeal*; "Humanizing Influence of the Central Park," *New York Herald*, October 2, 1859, 4. Abram Dayton makes a similar assessment of the short-order houses in *Knickerbocker Life*, 121.

32. "Culinary Reform," *Memphis Daily Appeal*; Horatio P. Batcheler, *Jonathan at Home: or, a Stray Shot at the Yankees* (London: W. H. Collingridge, 1864), 56. More commentary on food bolting can be found in James Boardman, *America, and the Americans* (London: Longman, Rees, Orme, Brown, Green, and Longman), 1833, 25; Thomas Nichols, *Forty Years of American Life* (London: J. Maxwell, 1864), 287–88; "Blancard's Five O'Clock Table," *Spirit of the Times*, November 4, 1848, 433; Dayton, *Knickerbocker Life*, 48–49, 126. Likewise, New York journalist Junius Browne viewed patrons "standing elbow to elbow, or perched on stools, using knives, and forks, and spoons; talking with their mouths full; gesticulating with their heads, and arms, and bodies;

eating as if they were on the eve of a journey round the World, and never expected to obtain another meal." Browne, *Great Metropolis*, 252.

33. "Our Restaurants," *Tribune*, 3; "Eating-Saloons," *Tribune*, 2–3.

34. Foster, *New York in Slices*, 70–71; "New-York Daguerreotyped," *Putnam's*, 366; Dayton, *Knickerbocker Life*, 120–21.

35. "Eating-Saloons," *Tribune*, 2; Dayton, *Knickerbocker Life*, 123–25; Foster, *New-York in Slices*, 69; Samuel Ward, "Unpublished History of Delmonico's," 1, Rare Books and Manuscripts Collection, New York Public Library.

36. On hotels and their ordinaries, see Sandoval-Strausz, *Hotel*, especially 65–67, 168–72; Molly W. Berger, "A House Divided: The Culture of the American Luxury Hotel, 1825–1860," in *His and Hers: Gender, Consumption, and Technology*, ed. Roger Horowitz and Arwen Mohun (Charlottesville: University Press of Virginia, 1998), 46; and "The Modern Hotel in America, 1829–1939," (PhD dissertation, Case Western University, 1997); Carolyn Brucken, "In the Public Eye: Women and the American Luxury Hotel," *Winterthur Portfolio* 31, no. 4 (Winter 1996): 215–17; Meryle Evans, "Knickerbocker Hotels and Restaurants, 1800–1850," *New-York Historical Society Quarterly* 36 (1952): 377–410; Jeffrey Williamson, *The American Hotel* (New York: Arno Press, 1975); Doris Elizabeth King, introduction to *Never Let People Be Kept Waiting: A Textbook on Hotel Management*, by Tunis G. Campbell (Raleigh, NC: D. E. King, 1973).

37. Capt. Oldmixon, R. N., *Transatlantic Wanderings: or, A Last Look at the United States* (London: Geo. Routledge, 1855), 26. See also "A French Visitor's Idea of the Astor House," *New Mirror*, August 9, 1843.

38. "A French Visitor's Idea of the Astor House, " *New Mirror*; William Chambers, *Things As They Are in America* (1854; reprint, New York: Negro Universities Press, 1986), 182, 189; Williamson, *American Hotel*, 196–99; Michael and Ariane Batterberry, *On the Town in New York from 1776 to the Present* (New York: Charles Scribner's Sons, 1973), 63–64. Evans, "Knickerbocker Hotels," 379–81, 390.

39. "New-York Daguerreotyped," *Putnam's*, 362. For travelers' descriptions of New York hotels, see Chambers, *Things As They Are in America*, 177–90; William Ferguson, *America by River and Rail: Or Notes by the Way on the New World and Its Peoples* (London: James Nisbet, 1856), 51–53; Charles MacKay, *Life and Liberty in America: Sketches of a Tour in the United States and Canada, in 1857–8* (London: Smith, Elder, 1859), 37–46; Marryat, *A Diary in America*, 373–79.

40. Ferguson, *America by River and Rail*, 52; Nichols, *Forty Years of American Life*, 11.

41. "A French Visitor's Idea of the Astor House, " *New Mirror*; Chambers, *Things As They Are in America*, 182; "New Kind of Hotel Up Town," *New York Weekly Mirror*, December 7, 1844.

42. "New Kind of Hotel Up Town," *Weekly Mirror*; "Change in New-York Habits," *New York Weekly Mirror*, October 12, 1844; "A French Visitor's Idea of the Astor House," *Weekly Mirror*; Nichols, *Forty Years of American Life*, 14; Chambers, *Things As They Are in America*, 182.

43. *Tribune* quoted in Evans, "Knickerbocker Hotels," 394; "The Astor House, New York," *New York Weekly Mirror*, November 9, 1844.

44. On segmentation of the theater and other areas of nineteenth-century culture, see Lawrence Levine, *High Brow, Low Brow: The Emergence of Cultural Hierarchy in America* (Cambridge, MA: Harvard University Press, 1990); Richard Butsch, "Bowery B'hoys and Matinee Ladies: The Re-Gendering of Nineteenth-Century American Theater Audiences," *American Quarterly* 46, no. 3 (September 1994): 374–405.

45. On the development of the aristocratic restaurant and some of the codes mentioned, see Andrew Haley, *Turning the Tables: Restaurants and the Rise of the American Middle Class, 1880–1920* (Chapel Hill: University of North Carolina Press, 2011), 23–29, 34–37.

46. Dayton, *Knickerbocker Life,* 147.

47. The *Gazette* article was reprinted in the *Workingman's Advocate,* December 18, 1830, 1.

48. Dayton, *Knickerbocker Life,* 147. One such youth was banker Samuel Ward who remembered entering "its charmed precincts" for the first time "with something of awe" in 1829 when Delmonico's was still a café. He recalled spending his Saturdays there years later, "the day of pastime and pocket money the culminat of the college week." Ward, "Unpublished history," 1, 2. Ward's fellow Columbia alumnus George Templeton Strong also enjoyed meals at Delmonico's while a student and afterward. Strong was so frequent a guest at Delmonico's that he grew close to the proprietor. Strong made a special trip to the restaurant to announce his engagement to Ellen Ruggles and reported in his diary that he "took [Delmonico's] breath away with the news." Nevins, *Strong Diary,* 1:74; 2:315. Not everyone was impressed by Delmonico's. In 1832, famed Knickerbocker and former mayor Philip Hone wrote in his diary: "Went yesterday to dine at Delmonico's, a French restauranteur in William Street, which I had heard was upon the Parisian [or French] plan and very good. We satisfied our curiosity but not our appetites." Allan Nevins, ed., *The Diary of Philip Hone, 1828–1851* (1927; reprint, New York: Dodd, Mead, 1969), 33.

49. "Original Sketches of the Metropolis," *New-York Mirror, a Weekly Gazette of Literature and the Fine Arts,* August 22, 1840, 69–70; See also Foster, *New York in Slices,* 72–75; Dayton, *Knickerbocker Life,* 139–48; Henry Collins Brown, *Delmonico's: A Story of Old New York* (New York: Valentine's Manual, 1928), 15–18, 48–51; Lately Thomas, *Delmonico's: A Century of Splendor* (Boston: Houghton Mifflin, 1967), 3–62.

50. Dayton, *Knickerbocker Life,* 139; Brown, *Delmonico's,* 15–18, 48–51; Thomas, *Delmonico's,* 3–62.

51. Ward, "Unpublished History," 6.

52. Ibid., 8.

53. Foster, *New York in Slices,* 69; Dayton, *Knickerbocker Days,* 145.

54. *Tribune* reporter, quoted in Lately, *Delmonico's,* 84–85; Dayton, *Knickerbocker Days,* 145; Ward, "Unpublished History," 8.

55. Dayton, *Knickerbocker Life,* 141–42.

56. "The Great Thoroughfares As Seen on the Day before Election," *New York Herald,* November 4, 1856, 1; "The Mayor Elect Receiving the Returns at Delmonico's," *New York Herald,* December 7, 1859, 8; Dayton, *Knickerbocker Life,* 139, 141–42.

57. "Eating-Saloons," *Tribune,* 2; Dayton, *Knickerbocker Life,* 139–48; Thomas, *Delmonico's,* 82–86. See also "Lorenzo Delmonico Dead," *New-York Times,* September 4, 1881, 7. For Delmonico's as a restaurant model, see *Knickerbocker,* September 1855, 29.

58. Foster, *New-York by Gas-Light,* 113–14.

59. "Up among the Nineties," *Harper's Weekly,* August 15, 1868, 520–21.

60. William M. Bobo, *Glimpses of New-York City. By A South Carolinian (Who Had Nothing Else To Do)* (Charleston: J. J. McCarter, 1852), 158–59.

61. "Our Restaurants," *Tribune,* 3; "Outline Sketches," *Home Journal,* 2; Nevins, *Diary of Philip Hone,* 587; Dayton, *Knickerbocker Life,* 128–33; "Thomas Downing Obituary," *New-York Times,* April 12, 1866, 5; "Funeral of the Late Thomas Downing," *New-York Times,* April 14, 1866, 8. For references to African American and Irish waiters, see

Nichols, *Forty Years of American Life*, 12; Isabella L. Bird, *The Englishwoman in America* (London: John Murray, 1856), 353; "From the Docket of a Late Sheriff," *Knickerbocker*, 60–61; "Little-or-Things," *Home Journal*, April 12, 1856,: 4; *Knickerbocker*, January 1857, 94; *Spirit of the Times*, December 15, 1855, 520, 522. On waiter girls, see Ferguson, *America by River and Rail*, 49; "Editorial Melange," *Gleason's Pictorial Drawing-Room Companion* 6, no. 12 (March 25, 1854): 191.

62. "The Man about Town: Of Dinners and Dining Places," *Harper's Weekly*, March 7, 1857; "Eating-Saloons," *Tribune*, 2.

63. "Humanizing Influence of Central Park," *New York Herald*, October 2, 1859, 4. Advertisements for respectable inexpensive restaurants appear, for example, in the *New York Herald*, September 24, 1840; May 26, 1842; April 10, 1849; *Albion* 37, no. 4 (June 22, 1859): 4.

64. "Eating-Saloons," *Tribune*, 2. See also "Lager Bier," *Frank Leslie's Illustrated Newspaper* 2, no. 9 (June 28, 1856): 35; "Lager Bier," *Frank Leslie's Illustrated Newspaper*, October 4, 1856, 278.

65. See, for example, advertisements for Vauxhall Garden in the *New York Daily Advertiser*, December 7, 1799, 3; May 14, 1803, 2. Newlywed and New York transplant Eliza Southgate Bowne describes visits to several pleasure gardens in a letter to her sister, dated June 6, 1803: *Letters of Eliza Southgate, Mrs. Walter Bowne* (New York: DeVinne Press, 188?), n.p.

66. Dayton, *Knickerbocker Life*, 122, 147–48, 159–62.

67. Foster, *New-York by Gas-Light*, 133.

68. Ibid.

69. *Carroll's New York City Directory to the Hotels of Note, Places of Amusement, Public Buildings . . . Etc.* (New York: Carroll, 1859), 15.

70. Downing ad, *New York Herald*, May 26, 1842; "The Brother Perkins' Restaurant," *New York Herald*, April 10, 1849; See also, advertisements in *Morris' National Press: A Journal for Home*, February 21, 1846, 3; *Yankee Doodle*, October 10, 1846, 11; *Albion*, January 22, 1859, 48; an advertisement for Gosling's Restaurant in the *New York Herald*, June 5, 1857, announcing the opening of a new space, with "two large saloons, each 160 feet deep," housing "a restaurant for the accommodation of gentlemen alone, and for ladies accompanied by gentlemen; also a separate dining saloon for gentlemen, oyster and lunch room, smoking room, &c."; and an ad for a Railroad Restaurant, with a separate ladies' saloon in *Home Journal*, August 31, 1850, 3. An ad for Thompson's can be found in O. A. Bullard, *Views in New York City, Embracing Many of the Most Celebrated Public Buildings in the Empire City, with a Description of Each* (New York: s.n., 1857), 22. In another example, by the 1860s, Delmonico's reserved the second floor of its Chambers Street establishment (the grand salle à manger that Sam Ward had reserved for the luminaries of the 1840s) for ladies. "Eating-Saloons," *Tribune*, 2; "Our Restaurants," *Tribune*, 3.

71. Bullard, *Views in New York City*, 39.

72. Ryan, *Women in Public*, 62.

73. On the public parlor, see Katherine C. Grier, *Culture and Comfort: Parlor-Making and Middle Class Identity* (Washington, DC: Smithsonian Institution Press, 1997). On semipublic spaces, see Ryan, *Women in Public*, 60–94; On the railroad, see Amy G. Richter, *Home on the Rails: The Railroad and the Rise of Public Domesticity* (Chapel Hill: University of North Carolina Press, 2005), especially 58–111. On parlor culture, see Karen Halttunen, *Confidence Men and Painted Women: A Study of Middle-Class Culture*

*in America* (New Haven, CT: Yale University Press, 1982). On public parlors in hotels see Sandoval-Strausz, *Hotel*, 171–73; and Brucken, "In the Public Eye," 215–17. See also Mona Domosh, "Those 'Gorgeous Incongruities': Polite Politics and Public Space on the Streets of 19th-Century New York," *Annals of the Association of American Geographers*, 88 no. 2 (1998): 209–26.

74. Chambers, *Things As They Are*, 177; Bird, *Englishwoman in America*, 353–54; *Gleason's Pictorial*, July 1, 1854, 415. See also Bullard, *Views in New York*, 39–40; *Boston Herald*, June 24, 1853.

75. Bobo, *Glimpses of New-York City*, 154; Bullard, *Views in New York*, 40. Eventually, in 1859, Thompson closed his restaurant and retired, allegedly at the behest of Taylor who offered him $4,000 per annum for the next ten years for eliminating his competition. See "Editor's Easy Chair," *Ballou's Pictorial Drawing Room Companion* 17, no. 8 (August 20, 1859), 126.

76. *Taylor's International Hotel and Saloon* (New York: s.n., 1853); Bullard, *Views in New York*, 39–40; "New-York Daguerreotyped," *Putnam's*, 363; "A Large Business," *Gleason's Pictorial*, November 19, 1853, 333; Bird, *Englishwoman in America*, 353–54; "Broadway at Night," *Leslie's Illustrated Newspaper*, September 11, 1858, 226. Like some contemporary New York restaurants—the Rainbow Room comes to mind—Taylor's eventually came to be visited mainly by tourists as fashionable New Yorkers moved on to other options. An English traveler wrote in 1864: "Taylor's saloon is very grand, but in nowise fashionable. . . . It is for the most part frequented by country people and strangers, who are attracted by its external magnificence. As to ladies, you see none of any position there, though many with very pretty faces." Batcheler, *Jonathan at Home*, 52.

77. Foster, *New-York by Gas-Light*, 133–34; Bird, *Englishwoman in America*, 353–54.

78. Tunis Campbell, *Hotel Keepers, Head Waiters, and Housekeepers' Guide* (Boston: Coolidge and Wiley, 1848), 41–42.

79. Foster, *New-York by Gas-Light*, 65, 66.

80. Bobo, *Glimpses of New-York City*, 153–59, quotation on 159; "Another 'Institution' Gone: Taylor's Saloon Closed—the International Hotel Furniture at Auction," *New-York Times*, July 31, 1866, 8; Browne, *Great Metropolis*, 266.

81. "Another 'Institution' Gone," *Times*, 8.

82. Andrew Haley makes this point as well in *Turning the Tables*, 151.

83. On working-class women and commercial entertainments, see Christine Stansell, *City of Women: Sex and Class in New York 1789–1860* (Urbana: University of Illinois Press, 1987); Kathy Peiss, *Cheap Amusements: Working Women and Leisure in Turn-of-the-Century New York* (Philadelphia: Temple University Press, 1986); Nan Enstad, *Ladies of Labor, Girls of Adventure* (New York: Columbia University Press, 1999).

84. Charles Dickens, *American Notes* (London: Chapman and Hall, 1850), 57–60; *New York Herald*, October 30, 1854; Ernest A. Mackay, *The Civil War and New York City* (Syracuse, NY: Syracuse University Press, 1990), 13. For descriptions of visits to New York's oyster cellars, see Foster, *New-York by Gas-Light*, 73–74; Browne, *Great Metropolis*, 202–4; Nichols, *Forty Years of American Life*, 269; MacKay, *Life and Liberty*, 24–28; Oldmixon, *Transatlantic Wanderings*, 28; Boardman, *America, and the Americans*, 87–88; Bird, *Englishwoman in America*, 353; Dayton, *Knickerbocker Life*, 133–34. See also Mark Kurlansky, *The Big Oyster: History on the Half-Shell* (New York: Random House, 2006), 157–71.

85. "Death of a Private Citizen of New York," *Christian Recorder*, April 21, 1866; "Thomas Downing Obituary," *Times*, 5; "Politics of the Free Colored People of New York," *National Era*, October 6, 1859; "The Negro in the Metropolis," *New York Herald*, January 25, 1861, 3. On Downing, see also John H. Hewitt, "Mr. Downing and His Oyster House: The Life and Good Works of an African-American Entrepreneur," *New York History* 74, no. 3 (July 1993): 229–33; Kurlansky, *Big Oyster*, 162–70; Dayton, *Knickerbocker Life*, 128–33; "Funeral of the Late Thomas Downing," *Times*, 8. Another oyster house which served New York's elite and middle classes was Dorlon's, located in Fulton Market. For a description, see Browne, *Great Metropolis*, 202–4.

86. Nichols, *Forty Years of American Life*, 269.

87. Foster, *New-York by Gas-Light*, 123, 73; N. P. Willis, "Letter from the Astor," *Godey's Lady's Book* 26 (May 1843): 227–28.

88. On sporting men's culture, see Timothy Gilfoyle, *City of Eros: New York City, Prostitution, and the Commercialization of Sex, 1790–1920* (New York: W. W. Norton, 1992), 92–116. On bachelors' association with restaurants, see *New York Herald*, November 18, 1853; December 6, 1853; *Daily Dispatch*, October 12, 1864; Foster, *New-York by Gas-Light*, 73–74. *The Spirit of the Times*, a magazine aimed at wealthy sporting men, contained many ads and notices for oyster saloons including mention of private rooms. See, for example, the following issues and pages: May 27, 1848, 165; January 29, 1853, 599; October 1, 1859, 406. See also "Gossip of the Last Knickerbocker," *Spirit of the Times*, 165; *New York Herald*, April 15, 1851. Sherwood's and Fisher's association with sporting men is addressed in "From the Docket of a Late Sheriff," *Knickerbocker*, 59–64. On private rooms and vice, see George Ellington, *The Women of New York* (New York: New York Book Company, 1870), 272–77.

89. See for example: "Slippers," *Godey's Lady's Book*, 136–41; "Life in Cities," *Home Journal* 29, no. 179 (July 14, 1849): 4; H. Hastings Weld, "A Young Man's Temptations," *Gleason's Pictorial Drawing-Room Companion* 5, no. 7 (August 13, 1853): 106; Francis A. Durivage, "The Gold Fiend," *Flag of Our Union* 11, no. 32 (August 9, 1856): 1; Alice B. Neal, "Ruth Norton's Trial of Patience," *Godey's Lady's Book*, June 1852, 474–50; "Hartley Coleridge," *National Magazine* 1, no. 1 (July 1852): 71–72; "The Awful Calamity," *New York Evangelist* 21, no. 41 (October 10, 1850): 162; "The Story of the Lucky Doctor," *Prisoner's Friend: A Monthly Magazine Devoted to Criminal Reform, Philosophy* 25, no. 6 (December 9, 1848): 41.

90. Gilfoyle, *City of Eros*, 112.

91. Frank Beard, *Night Side of New York: A Picture of the Great Metropolis after Nightfall* (New York: J. C. Haney, 1868), 75.

92. Beard, *Night Side*, 78; Gilfoyle, *City of Eros*, 112. For ads and commentary on private rooms, see "Gossip of the Last Knickerbocker," *Spirit of the Times*, 165; *Spirit of the Times*, January 29, 1853, 599; October 1, 1859,: 406; Ellington, *Women of New York*, 272–77. The periodical literature, both the Evangelical and the mainstream press, often linked restaurants and vice. See, for example, "The Awful Calamity," *New York Evangelist*, 162; Neal, "Ruth Norton's Trial of Patience," *Godey's Lady's Book*, 474–79; "Hartley Coleridge," *National Magazine*, 71–72; Weld, "A Young Man's Temptations," *Gleason's Pictorial*, 106–7; Durivage, "The Gold Fiend, or Shadows on the Hearthstone," *Flag of Our Union*, 1; "Letter to Reverend Dr. Bellows," *Christian Inquirer*, March 13, 1858, 1; "A Glance at Our Moral and Social Condition," *United States Democratic Review*, October 1858, 317.

93. On Butter-Cake Dick's, see Foster, *New-York by Gas-Light*, 112–19, 218–19; Beard, *Night Side*, 74–75; "The Herald Establishment: Its Rise and Progress," *New York Her-*

*ald,* July 31, 1854, 1; "Origin of the Sinker," *Summary* 76 (December 26, 1908): 5. (William Grimes kindly shared his transcription of this source with me.) Other references to Butter-Cake Dick's are included in "Mathematical," *John-Donkey,* February 26, 1848, 135; "Celebration of the Seventy-Second Anniversary of the Glorious 4th," *John-Donkey,* July 15, 1848, 27.

94. Beard, *Night Side,* 49–50, 74–75; Foster, *New-York by Gas-Light,* 112–19. A close competitor to Butter-Cake Dick's was Meschutt's. Located first on the Bowery, it eventually grew into a small chain with outlets around downtown. Meschutt's eschewed the lard and served a lighter variety of butter cake than did Dick Marshall, "to be buttered by the customer himself to suit his taste." "Origin of the Sinker," *Summary,* 5.

95. The article "Dining for Fifteen Cents," *New-York Tribune,* February 20, 1881, 2, recalled the cake-and-coffee shops of the antebellum period; "Men Who Live Downtown," *New-York Times,* December 4, 1881, 3; Beard, *Night Side,* 50–52; Paul Prowler, "Glimpses of Gotham," *National Police Gazette* 35, no. 116 (December 13, 1879): 116.

CHAPTER FIVE

1. "The Two Mothers," *New York Observer and Chronicle* 33, no. 13 (March 29, 1855): 100.

2. On servants and the home as a place of work, see Faye Dudden, *Serving Women: Household Service in Nineteenth Century America* (Middletown, CT: Wesleyan University Press, 1983); Jeanne Boydston, *Home & Work: Housework, Wages, and the Ideology of Labor in the Early Republic* (New York: Oxford University Press, 1990); Elizabeth Blackmar, *Manhattan for Rent, 1785–1850* (Ithaca, NY: Cornell University Press, 1989), 109–48; Karen Halttunen, *Confidence Men and Painted Women: A Study of Middle-Class Culture in America* (New Haven, CT: Yale University Press, 1982). See also Katherine C. Grier, *Culture and Comfort: People, Parlors, and Upholstery, 1850–1930* (Rochester, NY: Strong Museum, 1988).

3. Thorstein Veblen, *The Theory of the Leisure Class* (1899; reprint 1994, New York: Penguin Classics), 69–85. More recent historians like Stuart Blumin have identified a distinctive middle class in the nineteenth century, defined by a series of characteristics including consumption patterns. Stuart Blumin, *The Emergence of the Middle Class: Social Experience in the American City, 1790–1860* (Cambridge: Cambridge University Press, 1989), 138–91.

4. Diana DiZerega Wall, *The Archaeology of Gender: Separating the Spheres in Urban America* (New York: Plenum Press, 1994), 34.

5. On construction and layout of eighteenth- and nineteenth-century homes, see Charles Lockwood, *Bricks and Brownstones: The New York Row House, 1783–1929* (New York: McGraw Hill, 1972), 14–26, 70–75; Richard Bushman, *The Refinement of America: Persons, Houses, Cities* (New York: Alfred A. Knopf, 1992), 103–27; Blackmar, *Manhattan for Rent,* 47–48; Russell Lynes, *The Domesticated Americans* (New York: Harper and Row, 1963).

6. Clifford Clark, "Domestic Architecture as an Index to Social History: The Romantic Revival and the Cult of Domesticity in America, 1840–1870," *Journal of Interdisciplinary History* 7, no. 1 (Summer 1976): 33–56; and "The Vision of the Dining Room: Plan Book Dreams and Middle Class Realities," in *Dining in America, 1850–1900,* ed. Kathryn Grover (Amherst: University of Massachusetts Press, 1987), 149–51.

7. Mary Ryan, *The Cradle of the Middle Class* (New York: Cambridge University Press, 1983). Clifford Clark argues for the dining room's importance within this paradigm in "Vision of the Dining Room," 147–55.

8.  Calvert Vaux, *Villas and Cottages: A Series of Designs Prepared for Execution in the United States* (1857; reprint, New York: Da Capo Press, 1968), 18. See also 145.

9.  "Table-Talk," *Appleton's Journal*, 5, no. 116 (June 17, 1871): 714; "Our Dining-Rooms," *New-York Times*, January 10, 1875, 4.

10.  Clarence Cook, "Decoration and Furniture," *Art Amateur* 11, no. 2 (July 1884): 41.

11.  John Pintard, *Letters from John Pintard to His Daughter Eliza Noel Pintard Davidson, 1816–1833, in Four Volumes* (New York: New-York Historical Society, 1941), 2:314.

12.  William Ross, Esq., Architect, "Street Houses of the City of New York," *Architectural Record*, July 9, 1899, 54–55. First published in the *Architectural Magazine and Journal of Improvement in Architecture, Building and Furnishing and the Various Arts and Trades Connected Therewith* (London: Longman, Rees, Orme, Brown, Green and Longman, 1835). Mrs. Frances Trollope, *Domestic Manners of the Americans*, vol. 2, 2nd ed. (London: Whittaker, Trencher, 1832), 193; Lockwood, *Bricks and Brownstones*, 14; "The Modern Home," *Art Amateur*, 11, no. 2 (July 1884): 40.

13.  Pintard, *Letters*, 2:275. See also 2:266.

14.  Caroline Dustan diary, April 25, 1856; May 3, 1856; May 5, 1856, Rare Books and Manuscripts Collection, New York Public Library.

15.  "Correspondence," *Friends' Intelligencer*, 41, no. 2 (February 23, 1884): 22.

16.  "Mr. and Mrs. Woodbridge: A Story of Domestic Life," *Godey's Lady's Book, and Ladies' American Magazine* 22 (January 1841): 3.

17.  Vaux, *Villas and Cottages*, 18.

18.  For domestic environmentalism and housing reform, see Grier, *Culture and Comfort*, 5; Clark, "Domestic Architecture as an Index to Social History," 33–56.

19.  "Our Dining-Rooms," *New-York Times*, January 10, 1875, 4.

20.  "Table-Talk," *Appleton's*, 714.

21.  James Fenimore Cooper, *Notions of the Americans as Picked Up by a Travelling Bachelor* (1825; reprint, New York: Frederick Ungar Publishing Company, 1963), 146–49; Catharine E. Beecher, *A Treatise on Domestic Economy, for the Use of Young Ladies at Home, and at School* (New York: Harper and Brothers, 1845), 261; Sereno Todd, *Todd's Country Homes and How to Save Money* (New York: Published by the Author, 1868), 29; see also "The Skeleton in the Closet," *New-York Tribune*, March 3, 1876.

22.  Grier, *Culture and Comfort*, 108–16. On the parlor, see also Halttunen, *Confidence Men and Painted Women*.

23.  Elizabeth E. Lea, *Domestic Cookery*, 5th ed. (Baltimore: Cushings and Bailey, 1853), 286.

24.  Grier, *Culture and Comfort*, 8.

25.  "Mr. and Mrs. Woodbridge," parts 1–4, *Godey's Lady's Book* 22 (serialized from January to April 1841): 2–6; 74–8, 109–14, 168–74.

26.  For similar tales, see "Best Rooms versus Happy Homes," *Ladies' Repository* 25, no. 9 (September 1865): 522–23; Alice B. Neal, "Furnishing; or Two Ways of Commencing Life," *Godey's Lady's Book and Magazine* 41 (November 1850): 299.

27.  Clark, "Vision of the Dining Room," 156–57; Grier, *Culture and Comfort*.

28.  "Advice to Housekeepers," *Godey's Lady's Book and Magazine* 68 (April 1864): 392. See also "How to Economize and Conduct a Home," *Godey's Lady's Book and Magazine* 58 (March 1859): 231; "The Kitchen," *Ladies' Repository* 18 no. 1 (January 1858): 33–34.

29.  Grier, *Culture and Comfort*, ix.

30.  Veblen, *Theory of the Leisure Class*, 84.

31.  Ibid., 83.

32. "Furniture and Equipage," *Register of PA*, 6, no. 10 (September 4, 1830): 155. On shifting styles of furniture from the eighteenth to the nineteenth century and the development of the dining room, see Helen Comstock, *American Furniture* (New York: Viking Press, 1962); Charles F. Montgomery, *American Furniture: The Federal Period* (New York: Viking Press, 1966); John T. Kirk, *American Furniture* (New York: Harry N. Abrams, 2000); Myrna Kaye, *There's a Bed in the Piano: The Inside Story of the American Home* (Boston: Little Brown, 1998); *Cabinet Maker's Album of Furniture: Comprising a Collection of Designs for the Newest and Most Elegant Styles of Furniture* (Philadelphia: Henry Carey Baird, 1868).

33. "Gross's Patent Extension Table," *Scientific American* 13, no. 19 (January 16, 1858): 148; Abram Dayton, *Last Days of Knickerbocker Life in New York* (New York: G. P. Putnam's Sons, 1897), 19. See also "The Dining Room," *Godey's Lady's Book*, February 1850, 152. For additional extension table patents, see "Improvement in Extension Tables," *Scientific American* 18, no. 11 (March 14, 1868): 168. See also *Scientific American* 1, no. 50 (September 1, 1849): 398; 17, no. 17 (October 26, 1867): 265; 18, no. 3 (January 18, 1868): 38.

34. "Sideboard Refrigerator," *Scientific American*, 32, no. 22 (May 29, 1875): 341.

35. Eliza Leslie, *The House Book, or, a Manual of Domestic Economy for Town and Country* (Philadelphia: Carey and Hart, 1844), 250; Samuel Sloan, *City and Suburban Architecture; Containing Numerous Designs and Details for Public Edifices, Private Residences, and Mercantile Buildings* (Philadelphia: J. B. Lippincott, 1859), plates 19, 50. *Godey's Lady's Book* also frequently mentioned the importance of the sideboard to a proper dining room, explaining that "every dining-room should have its large and well arranged china cupboard." "Our Dwellings," *Godey's Lady's Book and Magazine* 69 (October 1864): 352. See also Clark, "Vision of the Dining Room," 146–53.

36. Henry Ward Beecher, *Eyes and Ears* (Boston: Ticknor and Fields, 1863), 359–60. See also "House Furnishings," *Godey's Lady's Book* 50 (March 1855): 285; "The Linen Closet," *Godey's Lady's Book* 51 (July 1855): 94; "Our Dwellings," *Godey's Lady's Book* 69 (October 1864): 352.

37. Manufacturers began to mass-produce silver-plated items in the 1840s, for example, after English inventors perfected an electrolytic process of transferring silver onto base metals. The price of silver plate declined further after the Comstock silver lode was discovered in Nevada in 1859. While silver service was unaffordable to most Americans, silver-plated dishes fell within the means of many middle-class families by the 1860s. See Dorothy Rainwater, "Victorian Dining Silver," in Grover, *Dining in America*, 173–77; Marina Moskowitz, *Standard of Living: The Measure of the Middle Class in Modern America* (Baltimore: Johns Hopkins University Press, 2008), 30–32, 38.

38. The number of specialized utensils burgeoned in the 1870s. Historian Marina Moskowitz catalogued the listings from an 1870s Reed and Barton's catalogue as follows: "salt spoons, mustard spoons, teaspoons, desk spoons, tablespoons, bar spoons, coffee spoons, berry spoons, preserve spoons, rice spoons, mustache spoons, sherbet spoons, child's spoons, egg spoons, table forks, medium forks, dessert forks, child's forks, fish forks, lined fish forks, oyster forks, pickle forks, long pickle spears, short pickle spears, twisted pickle spears, oyster spears, butter knives, cake knives, cake servers, cheese knives, child's knives, crumb knives, fish knives, fruit knives, pie knives, desk knives, bon bon tongs, sugar tongs, sugar shells, sugar shovels, medium ladles, oyster ladles, soup ladles, gravy ladles, cream ladles, nut picks, julep strainer, and cheese scoops." Moskowitz, *Standard of Living*, 35–37.

39. Wall, *Archaeology of Gender*, 132–34; Susan Williams, *Savory Suppers and Fashionable Feasts: Dining in Victorian America* (New York: Pantheon Books, 1985), 37, 67, 78–90; Lorena Walsh, "Consumer Behavior, Diet, and the Standard of Living in Late Colonial and Early Antebellum America, 1770–1840," in *American Economic Growth and the Standard of Living before the Civil War*, ed. Robert E. Gallman and John Joseph Wallis (Chicago: University of Chicago Press, 1992), 228–29.

40. Catharine Beecher, *Miss Beecher's Domestic Receipt Book: Designed as a Supplement to Her Treatise on Domestic Economy*, 3rd ed. (New York: Harper and Brothers, 1850), 237.

41. Beecher, *Treatise*, 307; Leslie, *House Book*, 254–56.

42. Mrs. E. F. Haskell, *The Housekeeper's Encyclopedia of Useful Information for the Housekeeper in All Branches of Cooking and Domestic Economy* (New York: D. Appleton, 1861), 411–12. See also Mrs. J. C. Croly, *Jennie June's American Cookery Book* (New York: American News Company, 1866), 6.

43. According to historian Cary Carson, "inventories routinely record piles of napkins and motley assortments of wood, pewter, tin, and pottery hollow wares." Cary Carson, "The Consumer Revolution in Colonial America: Why Demand?," in *Of Consuming Interests: The Style of Life in the Eighteenth Century*, ed. Cary Carson, Ronald Hoffman, and Peter J. Albert (Charlottesville: University Press of Virginia, 1994), 598.

44. Pintard, *Letters*, 4:8; 2:381, 380.

45. "To Cookstove Inventors," *Cultivator* 5, no. 2 (February 1848): 63. One of these homes belonged to the next-door neighbor of New York lawyer George Templeton Strong. In January 1840, Strong reported, "the kitchen range recently erected at No. 106" Greenwich Street, next door to Strong's family's home, was improperly installed and burned a hole through the wall between the houses and set Strong's house on fire. Allan Nevins, ed., *The Diary of George Templeton Strong*, 4 vols. (New York: Macmillan Company, 1952), 1:124.

46. "Dining-Room Stove," *Plough, the Loom and the Anvil* 7, no. 12 (June 1855): 745; Dustan diary, January 11, 1856; April 11, 1856; June 25, 1857. See also entries for June 23, 24, 27, 1857; May 24, June 6, 1858; Sloan, *City and Suburban Architecture*, 57. See also 65. An excellent study of the cookstove is Priscilla Brewer, *From Fireplace to Cookstove: Technology and the Domestic Ideal in America* (Syracuse, NY: Syracuse University Press, 2000).

47. For advertisements that mention stoves and cooking ranges, see *New-York Tribune*, June 18, 1846; *Loom*, May 29, 1846; *New-York Tribune*, May 2, 1846; *New-York Times*, April 2, 1853, 6; *Water-Cure Journal*, June 1857; *New York Observer and Chronicle*, June 9, 1859; December 30, 1869; April 1, 1875.

48. Mrs. Cornelius, *The Young Housekeeper's Friend: Or, A Guide to Domestic Economy and Comfort*, 12th ed. (Boston: Tappan and Whittemore, 1853) 19; Mrs. Cornelius, *The Young Housekeeper's Friend. Revised and Enlarged* (Boston: Thompson, Brown, 1875), 21; Haskell, *Housekeeper's Encyclopedia*, 2; see also 32, 406. For other references in cookbooks to maintaining cookstoves, see Mrs. H. W. Beecher, *All around the House, or, How to Make Homes Happy* (New York: D. Appleton, 1881), 97, 279; Mrs. J. Chadwick, *Home Cookery: A Collection of Tried Receipts, Both Foreign and Domestic* (Boston: Crosby, Nichols, 1851), 146; *The American Housewife: Containing the Most Valuable and Original Receipts in all the Various Branches of Cookery; and Written in a Minute and Methodical Manner. Together with a Collection of Miscellaneous Receipts, and Directions Relative to Housewifery. By an Experienced Lady*, 8th ed. (New York: Newman Ivison, 1853), 131; Croly, *Jennie June's Cookery Book*, 8, 18–19.

49. *The American Home Cook Book, with Several Hundred Excellent Recipes, Selected and Tried with Great Care, and with a View to Be Used by Those Who Regard Economy, and Containing Important Information on the Arrangement and Well Ordering of the Kitchen. The Whole Based on Many Years of Experience.* By an American Lady (New York: Dick and Fitzgerald, 1854), 12; Croly, *Jennie June's Cookery Book,* 9, 16; "The Household," *New York Evangelist* 54, no. 10 (March 8, 1883): 7; "Sayings and Doings," *Harper's Bazaar* 8, no. 40 (October 2, 1875): 639. See also Thomas Jefferson Murrey, *Valuable Cooking Receipts* (New York: White, Stokes, and Allen, 1885), 9, 56.

50. "The Household," *New York Evangelist* 53, no. 43 (October 26, 1882): 7.

51. Brewer, *Fireplace to Cookstove,* 151; Ruth Schwartz Cowan, *More Work for Mother: The Ironies of Household Technology from the Open Hearth to the Microwave* (New York: Basic Books, 1985), 53–62.

52. Haskell, *Housekeeper's Encyclopedia,* 31; Cornelius, *Young Housekeeper's Friend,* 1853, 88.

53. Lea, *Domestic Cookery,* 58. See also 12, 16. Beecher, *All around the House,* 95.

54. White quoted in Brewer, *Fireplace to Cookstove,* 141; Mrs. A. M. P. Annan, "Mr. Chancy's Cooking Stove," *Godey's Lady's Book and Ladies' American Magazine* 24 (February 1842): 99–107; K. H., "Keeping House," *Godey's Lady's Book and Magazine* 88, no. 528 (June 1874): 525.

55. Beecher, *Eyes and Ears,* 360–61.

56. Ibid., 361–63.

57. Croly, *Jennie June's Cookery Book,* 9, 16; Brewer, *Fireplace to Cookstove,* 146–47. For instructions for blacking the stove in cookbooks, see Chadwick, *Home,* 146; Lea, *Domestic Cookery,* 213; Haskell, *Housekeeper's Encyclopedia,* 406.

58. Sarah Josepha Hale, *The Ladies' New Book of Cookery: A Practical System For Private Families in Town and Country; With Directions for Carving, and Arranging the Table for Parties, etc. Also Preparations of Food for Invalids and for Children* (New York: H. Long and Brothers, 1852), 66; Cornelius, *Young Housekeeper's Friend,* 1853, 12.

59. For information on the growth of books and publishing, see Robert Gross and Mary Kelley, eds., *The History of the Book in America,* vol. 2, *An Extensive Republic: Print, Culture, and Society in the New Nation* (Chapel Hill: University of North Carolina Press, 2010), especially 75–144; Scott E. Casper et al., eds., *A History of the Book in America,* vol. 3, *The Industrial Book, 1840–1880* (Chapel Hill: University of North Carolina Press, 2007), especially 1–40; John Kasson, *Rudeness and Civility: Manners in Nineteenth-Century Urban America* (New York: Hill and Wang, 1990), 34–47.

60. E. R. Fordyce, "Cookbooks of the 1800s," in *Dining in America, 1850–1900,* ed. Kathryn Grover (Amherst: University of Massachusetts Press, 1987), 85–113. On the history of cookbooks see Carol Fisher, *American Cookbooks: A History* (Jefferson, NC: McFarland, 2006); Jessamyn Neuhaus, *Manly Meals and Mom's Home Cooking: Cookbooks and Gender in Modern History* (Baltimore: Johns Hopkins University Press, 2003), 7–27; Janet Theophano, *Eat My Words: Reading Women's Lives through the Cookbooks They Wrote* (New York: Palgrave MacMillan, 2003); Anne Bower, *Recipes for Reading: Community Cookbooks, Stories, Histories* (Amherst: University of Massachusetts Press, 1997).

61. Carol Berkin, *First Generations: Women in Colonial America* (New York: Hill and Wang, 1997): 79–103; Jeanne Boydston, *Home and Work: Housework, Wages, and the Ideology of Labor in the Early Republic* (New York: Oxford University Press, 1994).

62. "The Kitchen," *Ladies' Repository,* 33.

63. Haskell, *Housekeeper's Encyclopedia*, 7–8. See also "How to Economize and Conduct a Home," *Godey's*, 231; "Advice to Housekeepers," *Godey's*, 392.

64. *Home Journal* 36, no. 532 (September 6, 1856): 3; "What It Costs for Housekeeping Articles," *New-York Daily Times*, April 24, 1852, 3.

65. *New York Observer and Chronicle*, May 16, 1867, 160.

66. "Hints for Housekeepers," *Ladies' Home Magazine* 9 (June 1857): 360.

67. See, for example, "A Word More of Draperies," *Godey's Lady's Book*, December 1851, 368; "A Chat upon Window Curtains," *Godey's Lady's Book* 54 (March 1852): 227; *Godey's Lady's Book* 52, no. 90 (January 1856): 90; "Curtain for a Bay Window," *Godey's Lady's Book and Magazine* 58 (June 1859): 354; and the "New York Fashions" column in *Harper's Bazaar* 12, no. 20 (May 17, 1879): 311; 14, no. 23 (June 4, 1881): 354; 16, no. 22 (January 2, 1883): 338; 17, no. 20 (May 17, 1884): 306.

68. Grier, *Culture and Comfort*, 16, 22–53, quotation on 32.

69. Andrew Sandoval-Strausz, *Hotel: An American History* (New Haven, CT: Yale University Press, 2008), 65.

70. "Ceiling and Wall Covering Decoration," *Art Amateur: A Monthly Journal Devoted to Art in the Household* 7 no. 5 (October 1882): 104.

71. Foster Coates, "How Delmonico Sets a Table," *Ladies' Home Journal* 8, no. 12 (November 1891): 10.

72. Charles Ranhofer, *The Epicurean* (New York: Charles Ranhofer, 1894).

73. Murrey, *Valuable Cooking Receipts*, 1885, quotation on 3.

74. Ibid., 7, 61, 74.

75. Beecher, *All around the House*, 72–74.

76. Reed & Barton executive, quoted in Moskowitz, *Standard of Living*, 20.

77. Moskowitz, *Standard of Living*, 53–58.

78. "How Shall We Dine?," *New-York Tribune*, March 24, 1874.

79. "Household Column," *New-York Times*, June 18, 1876 and October 8, 1876, both p. 9. See also "Household Column," April 16, 1876; October 29, 1876; November 26, 1876; December 5, 1876; December 17, 1876; March 19, 1876; April 1, 1877; June 24, 1877; July 8, 1877; October 7, 1877; October 14, 1877; October 28, 1877; March 17, 1878, all p. 9.

80. Williams, *Savory Suppers*, 168; Anne-Marie E. Cantwell and Diana DiZerega Wall, *Unearthing Gotham: The Archaeology of New York City* (New Haven, CT: Yale University Press, 2001), 218–19. A 1990s archaeological study of the Five Points turned up one privy that "included matching dishes and serving pieces, as many as six tea sets, including three imported from Staffordshire, one of bone china, and one of Chinese porcelain, and extensive glassware including an unusual lacy pressed square bowl manufactured in New England, and numerous cut decanters." Likewise, a nearby cesspool turned up patterned dishes, gilded ceramics, and imported glassware dating to the 1850s. Wall, *Archaeology of Gender*, 147–49;

81. "The Household," *New-York Times*, August 13, 1876, 9; "The Magazines and Reviews," *Methodist Review* 3, no. 6 (November 1887): 938.

82. Catharine E. Beecher, *Letters to Persons Who Are Engaged in Domestic Service* (New York: Leavitt and Trow, 1842), 89.

83. "House Servants," *Harper's Weekly*, May 9, 1857, 20. On the formalization of servitude in the nineteenth century see Dudden, *Serving Women*, 44–52.

84. Dudden, *Serving Women*, 37.

85. Clark, "Vision of the Dining Room," 153–54. See also Kaye, *There's a Bed in the Piano*; Lockwood, *Bricks and Brownstones*; Richard Bushman, *Refinement of America*;

Williams, *Savory Suppers*; Kenneth Ames, *Death in the Dining Room and Other Tales of Victorian Culture* (Philadelphia: Temple University Press, 1992); Schwartz, *More Work for Mother*.

86. Catharine Sedgwick, *Home* (New York: George Dearborn, 1837), 28. See also Beecher, *Treatise*, 144–45.

87. From the 1830s to the 1860s, an average of three new etiquette manuals were published annually in the United States, many published into the thirtieth edition. As the center of American publishing, New York City disseminated this information to homes within its vicinity and far beyond. Arthur M. Schlesinger, *Learning How to Behave: A Historical Study of American Etiquette Books* (New York: Macmillan, 1946).

88. Kasson, *Rudeness and Civility*, 57–69.

89. Veblen, *Leisure Class*, 49.

90. Sedgwick, *Home*, 48.

CHAPTER SIX

1. G. T. Ferris, "How a Great City Is Fed," *Harper's Weekly*, March 22, 1890, 229–32; James Fenimore Cooper, *Notions of the Americans as Picked up by a Travelling Bachelor* (1825; reprint, New York: Frederick Ungar Publishing Company, 1963), 136–41.

2. Moses King, *King's Handbook of New York City: An Outline History and Description of the American Metropolis* (Boston: Moses King, 1892), 48.

3. Robert Rydell, *All the World's a Fair: Visions of Empire at American International Expositions, 1876–1918* (Chicago: University of Chicago Press, 1987), 2, 4.

4. On imperialism and American consumerism and popular culture in the late nineteenth century, see ibid.; Kristin Hoganson, *A Consumer's Imperium: The Global Production of American Domesticity, 1865–1920* (Chapel Hill: University of North Carolina Press, 2007); Catherine Cocks, *Doing the Town: The Rise of Urban Tourism in the United States, 1850–1915* (Berkeley: University of California Press, 2003), especially 174–203; Gail Bederman, *Manliness and Civilization: A Cultural History of Gender and Race in the United States* (Chicago: University of Chicago Press, 1996), 1–44; John Kasson, *Amusing the Million: Coney Island at the Turn of the Century* (New York: Hill and Wang, 1978).

5. Historian Andrew Haley discusses the colonization of ethnic cuisines in his study of American restaurants in the Gilded Age and Progressive Era. Haley argues that cosmopolitan dining "was as much a celebration of middle-class consumer power as it was an embrace of ethnic diversity, and middle-class urbanites championed and supported those ethnic restaurants that best catered to their preferences." *Turning the Tables: Restaurants and the Rise of the American Middle Class, 1880–1920* (Chapel Hill: University of North Carolina Press, 2011), 109.

6. King, *King's Handbook*, 837; Ferris, "How a Great City Is Fed," 229–32.

7. Donna Gabaccia, *We Are What We Eat: Ethnic Food and the Making of Americans* (Cambridge, MA: Harvard University Press, 2000), 55–56.

8. Department of the Interior, *Report on Manufacturing Industries in the United States at the Eleventh Census, 1890*, part 2, *Statistics of Cities* (Washington, DC: Government Printing Office, 1895), xxxv, 93, 137, 401; part 1, *Totals for States and Industries* (Washington, DC: Government Printing Office, 1896), 77.

9. King, *King's Handbook*, 70.

10. For descriptions, see ibid., 838–40.

11. D. Appleton and Co., *Appleton's Dictionary of New York and Its Vicinity*, 6th ed. (New York: D. Appleton, 1880), 236; Ferris, "How a Great City Is Fed," *Harper's*, 229–32; King, *King's Handbook*, 70.

12. Frank Marshall White, "The Orange, Lemon, and Grape Trade," *Harper's Weekly*, January 26, 1889, 64–66; Ferris, "How a Great City Is Fed," *Harper's*, 229–32.

13. White, "Orange, Lemon, and Grape Trade," *Harper's*, 64–66.

14. Ferris, "How a Great City Is Fed," *Harper's*, 229–32.

15. Ibid.

16. Ibid.; A. F. Matthews, "New York's Fish Market in Lent," *Harper's Weekly* 3, no. 17 (March 17, 1894): 254.

17. Matthews, "Fish Market in Lent," *Harper's*, 254–55; Ferris, "How a Great City Is Fed," *Harper's*, 229–32.

18. Ferris, "How a Great City Is Fed," *Harper's*, 229–32; Department of the Interior, *Report of Manufacturing*, part 1, *Totals for States and Industries*, 730.

19. *Appleton's Dictionary*, 236; King, *King's Handbook*, 837.

20. King, *King's Handbook*, 877–908, quotation on 878.

21. Joy Santlofer, "'Hard as the Hubs of Hell': Crackers in War," *Food, Culture & Society* 10, no. 2 (Summer 2007): 200–203; Harvey Levenstein, *Revolution at the Table: The Transformation of the American Diet* (New York: Oxford University Press, 1988), 35–36; King, *King's Handbook*, 878.

22. Levenstein, *Revolution at the Table*, 32.

23. New York's oyster industry extended back to the 1750s, when New York merchants earned up to 20,000 pounds sterling annually from selling the preserved shellfish to Europe and the West Indies. After an initial process of industrialization, including the mass transplantation and cultivation of Chesapeake Bay oysters on the shores of Manhattan, Staten Island, Long Island, and New Jersey, oystering became one of New York City's most lucrative and important industries by the 1840s. William Smith, *The History of the Province of N.Y. from the First Discovery to the Year MDCCXXXII* (London, 1757), 676; Adolph B. Benson, ed., *Peter Kalm's Travels in North America / the English version of 1770, revised from the original Swedish* (New York : Wilson-Erickson, 1937), 237; *The Independent Reflector* (New York: James Parker, 1752–53); Mark Kurlansky, *The Big Oyster: History on the Half-Shell* (New York: Ballantine Books, 2006), 62; *New York Herald*, October 30, 1854.

24. "City Intelligence," *New York Herald*, December 2, 1848, 2; "Shell Fish, &c., from the North," *Daily Picayune*, October 28, 1854, 7; "New York Provision Markets," *New York Herald*, January 18, 1853, 3; "Fulton Market," *New York Herald*, February 5, 1853; "Catherine Market," *New York Herald*, March 3, 1853, 2; *New York Herald*, October 30, 1854.

25. "City Intelligence," *Herald*, 2; "Shell Fish &c.," *Daily Picayune*, 7; *New York Herald*, February 5, 1853; "The City's Oyster Market," *New-York Times*, September 10, 1883, 2; Kurlansky, *Big Oyster*, 172–75, 178; "New York Harbor Traffic," *Harper's Weekly*, September 1, 1894, 832; "How the City Is Fed," *Christian Union* 42, no. 14 (October 2, 1890): 428; Ferris, "How a Great City Is Fed," *Harper's*, 229–32; "Oyster Culture," *Lippincott's Magazine of Popular Literature and Science* 1 (May 1881): 481; "Oysters Now in Season," *New-York Times*, September 1, 1883, 8.

26. Gabaccia, *We Are What We Eat*, 68, 70; Robert Ernst, *Immigrant Life in New York City, 1825–1863* (1949; reprint, Port Washington, NY: Ira J. Friedman, 1965), 88.

27. Gabaccia, *We Are What We Eat*, 64; Jane Ziegelman, *97 Orchard: An Edible History of Five Immigrant Families in One Tenement* (New York: Harper, 2011), 25.

28. Gabaccia, *We Are What We Eat*, 112; Ziegelman, *97 Orchard*, 28–29; Ernst, *Immigrant Life*, 87, 88, 73, including a translation from the German newspaper *Staats Zeitung* about German predominance in various food trades. See also Stanley Nadel, *Little*

*Germany: Ethnicity, Religion, and Class in New York City* (Urbana: University of Illinois Press, 1990), 63.

29. James A. Baldwin, New York State Census of 1855, quoted in Ernst, *Immigrant Life,* 70; Ernst, *Immigrant Life,* 87; Nadel, *Little Germany,* 82. On German market gardeners' petitions in the mid-1850s, see "Washington Market—Meeting of the Gardeners of New York," *New York Herald,* June 14, 1858, 8; "The Market Gardeners before the Mayor," *New-York Daily Times,* May 29, 1855, 4. See also "The Market and the Market Gardeners," *New-York Daily Times,* May 31, 1855, 4; "Marketmen and Middlemen," *New-York Daily Times,* June 14, 1855, 4.

30. "The Foreign Movement on the Sunday Question," *Harper's Weekly,* September 24, 1859, 610. See also "Our Germanic Contemporaries," *New-York Times,* June 3, 1859, 4.

31. Tyler Anbinder, *Five Points: The Nineteenth-Century New York Neighborhood That Invented Tap Dance, Stole Elections, and Became the World's Most Notorious Slum* (New York: Free Press, 2001), 400–404.

32. "The Chinese in New-York," *New-York Tribune,* June 21, 1885, 9.

33. Wong Chin Foo, "The Chinese in New York," *Cosmopolitan* 5, no. 4 (June 1888): 300–303.

34. "A Sicilian Café in New York," *Harper's Weekly,* November 2, 1889, 875.

35. "Chinese in New-York," *Tribune,* 9.

36. *The Sun's Guide to New York: Replies to Questions Asked Every Day by the Guests and Citizens of the American Metropolis* (New York: R. Wayne Wilson, 1892), 198. See also Suzanne Wasserman, "Hawkers and Gawkers: Peddlers and Markets in New York City," in *Gastropolis: Food and New York City,* ed. Annie Hauck-Lawson and Jonathan Deutsch (New York: Columbia University Press, 2009), 155.

37. *Sun's Guide to New York,* 198; E. Lyelle Earle, "Character Studies in New York's Foreign Quarters," *Catholic World* 73, no. 408 (March 1, 1899): 784.

38. Jacob A. Riis, *How the Other Half Lives: Studies among the Tenements of New York* (1890; reprint, New York: Charles Scribner's Sons, 1914), 115–16.

39. Gabaccia, *We Are What We Eat,* 74. In *How the Other Half Lives* (115).

40. Luc Sante, *Low Life: Lures and Snares of Old New York* (New York: Vintage Books, 1991), 105.

41. Madelon Powers, *Faces along the Bar* (Chicago: University of Chicago Press, 1998), 15–17; Perry R. Duis, *The Saloon: Public Drinking in Chicago and Boston 1880–1920* (Urbana: University of Illinois Press, 1983), 16–46.

42. Sante, *Low Life,* 104–20.

43. "The Story of a Sweatshop Girl: Sadie Frowne," *Independent* 54 (September 25, 1902): 2279–82.

44. As one account explained: "Former Chief McCullah made several ineffectual attempts to break up this horde of street venders. But the Hebrew peddler would march off patiently to the police court, pay his fine, and be on hand at the same spot to greet the policeman on his return." Earle, "Character Studies in New York's Foreign Quarters," 783. See also *Sun's Guide,* 198; Riis, *How the Other Half Lives,* 57–60, 115–16.

45. King, *King's Handbook,* 213, 214–15. First quotation on 213. Emphasis mine; "Our Restaurants," *New-York Tribune,* July 6, 1868, 3; second quotation from "The Restaurant System: Choice Cuisine at a Reasonable Price, *New-York Times,* May 24, 1885, 3; "A Japanese Restaurant in New York," *Harper's Weekly,* August 31, 1889, 707.

46. "Middle-Age Cookery," *New-York Times,* October 25, 1872, 4; King, *King's Handbook,* 214–15.

47. *Leslie's Illustrated Newspaper* 2, no. 29 (June 28, 1856): 35.

48. "Lager Bier," *Frank Leslie's Illustrated Newspaper*, October 4, 1856, 278.

49. Edward Winslow Martin, *The Secrets of the Great City: A Work Descriptive of the Virtues and the Vices, the Mysteries, Miseries and Crimes of New York City.* (Philadelphia: Jones Brothers, 1868), 50; *Leslie's*, June 28, 1856, 35; *Appleton's Dictionary*, 220.

50. *Redfield's Traveler's Guide to the City of New York* (New York: J. S. Redfield, 1871), 23.

51. "German Restaurants," *New-York Times*, January 19, 1873, 5.

52. Ziegelman, *97 Orchard*, 167–68.

53. "German Restaurants," *Times*, 5; "Cheap Restaurants," *New-York Times*, August 6, 1871, 5.

54. Gabaccia, *We Are What We Eat*, 97–121.

55. "A New Cuisine," *New-York Times*, January 21, 1872.

56. John S. Billings, M.D., *Vital Statistics of New York City and Brooklyn, Covering a Period of Six Years Ending May 31, 1890* (Washington, DC: Government Printing Office, 1894), 22; Foo, "Chinese in New York," 304.

57. Edwin H. Trafton, "A Chinese Dinner in New York," *American Magazine* 17 (February 1884): 183.

58. Ibid., 186, 183.

59. Ibid., 186, 187.

60. "Two Chinese Institutions," *Harper's Weekly* 8, no. 25 (1888): 635.

61. Hoganson, *Consumer's Imperium*, 8–12, 43–56.

62. Vance, "NY Restaurant Life," *Frank Leslie's Popular Monthly*, January 1893, 102. Andrew Haley makes a similar argument about cosmopolitanism and restaurants on the national level at the turn of the twentieth century. Haley, *Turning the Tables*, 7–9, 92–117.

63. Haley, *Turning the Tables*, 116.

64. Ferris, "How a Great City Is Fed," *Harper's*, 229–32.

65. Haley, *Turning the Tables*, 106–7; "Restaurant System," *Times*, 3.

66. "Restaurant System," *Times*, 3.

67. *Appleton's Dictionary*, 181. On Moretti's, see "A Modern Boniface," *New-York Tribune*, January 4, 1880, 5.

68. *Appleton's Dictionary*, 181; "Restaurant System," *Times*, 3.

69. "Cheap Restaurants," *New-York Times*, August 6 , 1871, 5.

70. As early as 1854, an article in *Home Journal* described the foreign tables d'hôte as places that offered a more "quiet dinner" than the "tumultuous, loud, and indigestive" American eating houses. "Dining Down Town," *Home Journal* 2, no. 413 (January 7, 1854): 2. "Men Who Live Downtown," *New-York Times*, December 4, 1881, 3. This article also explains: "If there is anything in the world calculated to make the human stomach rise in its might and declare that it will never do another day's work it is the average 'American' restaurant."

71. "Household Column," *New-York Times*, November 19, 1876; December 3, 1876; April 8, 1876; May 21, 1876, all p. 9.

72. On the growing exclusivity of first-class restaurants in the Gilded Age, see Haley, *Turning the Tables*, 19–42.

73. "Restaurant System," *Times*, 3.

74. Ralph M. Hower, *History of Macy's of New York, 1858–1919* (Cambridge, MA: Harvard University Press, 1943), 160; King, *King's Handbook*, 214; Quotation from *Sun's Guide to New York*, 190, 318.

75. *Sun's Guide*, 214;

76. "Dining for Fifteen Cents," *New-York Tribune*, February 20, 1881, 2; *Appleton's Dictionary*, p. 181; "The Astor Next to Go?," *News and Courier*, June 3, 1908, 9.
77. "Fair Women at Lunch," *New-York Times*, December 20, 1884, 4.
78. Ibid.
79. On saloons and the free lunch, see Madelon Powers, *Faces along the Bar*, 207–26; On women and the free lunch see Kathy Peiss, *Cheap Amusements: Working-Class Women and Leisure in Turn-of-the-Century New York* (Philadelphia: Temple University Press, 1986), 28.
80. "Notice to the Public: The Gosling Restaurant," n.d., Library of Congress, Printed Ephemera Collection; Portfolio 209, Folder 1; "Literary Intelligence," *Literary World*, December 4, 1852, 364. See also *Louisville Daily Journal*, November 30, 1865; *Boston Herald* notice reprinted in *New York Herald*, November 20, 1842.
81. *Daily Picayune*, March 22, 1865. See also "Gossip with Readers and Correspondents," *Knickerbocker, or New York Monthly Magazine*, 37, no. 5 (May 1851): 476; "Intermingled Leaves of Gossip and Travel," *Knickerbocker* 46, no. 3 (September 1855): 330; "Personalities," *Independent* 42. no. 2171 (July 10, 1890): 13; Edwin H. Trafton, "Some Dinners I Have Eaten," *Frank Leslie's Popular Monthly* 20, no. 2 (August 1885): 139, where he describes a meal he ate at a Chicago restaurant following the Great Fire and notes that it was a "gastronomic triumph," though "the dinner was not a 'swell' one, in the Delmonico, or Hotel Brunswick, or Pinard, sense."
82. *Current Literature* 1, no. 1 (July–December 1888): 38.
83. On the inferiority of American foodways, see, for example, Albert Rhodes, "What Shall We Eat?," *Galaxy* 22, no. 5 (November 1876): 665–75. On p. 667, Rhodes mentions a "member of a royal family" who visiting the United States proclaimed "that we were the worst fed of all civilized peoples"; "Concerning Restaurants," *Harper's New Monthly Magazine*, April 1866, 592–93.

CONCLUSION

1. Terese Leob Kreuzer, "Market Opens amidst Its Uncertain Future," *Downtown Express* 20, no. 51 (May 4–11, 2011), http://www.downtownexpress.com/de_419/market-opens.html; New Amsterdam Market website, accessed April 19, 2012, http://www.newamsterdammarket.org/about.html.
2. Gabrielle Langholtz, "The Mast Brothers Live Up to Their Name," *Edible Brooklyn*, Fall 2011; Andrew Grossman, "Cocoa Arrives by Sail," *Wall Street Journal*, June 15, 2011.
3. Fleisher's Grass-Fed and Organic Meats, http://www.fleishers.com/about-our-meat/is-it-affordable, accessed April 19, 2012.
4. Terese Loeb Kreuzer, "Howard Hughes Pitches Pier Plans," *Downtown Express*, http://www.downtownexpress.com/?p=5553; New Amsterdam Market website, http://www.newamsterdammarket.org/about.html, accessed April 19, 2012.
5. "The Swill Milk Poison," *Leslie's*, 6, no. 133 (June 19, 1858): 34.
6. Andrew Haley, *Turning the Tables: Restaurants and the Rise of the American Middle Class, 1880–1920* (Chapel Hill: University of North Carolina Press, 2011), especially 7–9, 222–36.
7. Lisa Miller, "Divided We Eat: What Food Says about Class in America and How to Bridge the Gap," *Newsweek*, November 22, 2010.
8. Monica Bhide, "As Cash Flows In, India Goes Out to Eat," *New-York Times*, April 20, 2005, F1.

9.  Michael Pollan, *The Omnivore's Dilemma: A Natural History of Four Meals* (New York: Penguin, 2007) and *In Defense of Food: An Eater's Manifesto* (New York: Penguin, 2009).

10. *Food, Inc,* DVD, directed by Robert Kenner (New York: Magnolia Home Entertainment, 2009).

11. James McWilliams, both a food historian and food reformer, makes a similar argument in *Just Food: Where Locavores Get It Wrong and How We Can Truly Eat Responsibly* (New York: Back Bay Books, 2009), 6–10.

# INDEX